"A delightful, well-informed, i ›
the fraught generational dynam

—SAMUEL BAUER, PHD; SVP of Brand and Communications,
BairesDev (Texas)

"Genius! This is a must-read for anyone wanting to expand their understanding of Gen Z and use this knowledge to improve their business
practices in order to adapt to the ever-changing vista that is this generation. I have seen Steve's knowledge applied in training staff from across the
world. Do yourself a favor and learn from the best in the business!"

—REBECCA OSBORNE; Kovacevic Lawyers (Australia)

"This is a groundbreaking must-read if you have any intention of understanding Gen Z and influencing future outcomes, whether it be in business,
education, or relationships. Good luck staying relevant if you are not armed
with Steve's insights!"

—HARLAN M. SANDS, JD, MBA;
former President of Cleveland State University (Ohio)

"*Aliens Among Us: Ten Surprising Truths about Gen Z* should be required
reading for anyone who plans to still be in business in 5 years. Understanding this generation may be the only surefire way to future-proof your
business. Steve's stories and insights bring the material to life. Plus, he
shares examples from real life! Steve brings a unique vantage point in combining his research with over 25 years of first-hand experience. With all its
practical takeaways, this book will not stay on the shelf; you will reference
it again and again as you lead this generation."

—SARAH OHANESIAN; Keynote Speaker & Productivity Consultant,
former Chief Marketing Officer (Pennsylvania)

"If you have ever even subconsciously thought, 'Oh, that's a fad the kids
are into these days,' then you MUST read this book! As challenging as it is
insightful and witty, Steve uses stories to bring Gen Z insights to life—and
data to bring these truths home. What's more, the research that he has done

is fully grounded in the realities of running a business and being a father, so it is pragmatic and useful. I highly recommend Aliens Among Us for any business leader, parent, or person wanting to thoughtfully engage the next generation."

—Dr. James Waters, MSc, PhD;
Entrepreneur & Research Consultant (United Kingdom)

"Acting as a 'generational interpreter,' Steve Robertson navigates the reader through the complex and paradoxical, yet wonderful world of Gen Z in a clear and systematic way. Through means of numerous concrete examples and practical advice, he reinterprets problems of generational disconnect as opportunities for connection. *Aliens Among Us* is a testament to Robertson's passion to equip coming generations for a world constantly in the making—a must-read for parents and employers alike."

—Dr. Jaco Smit, MA, MSc, PhD (Netherlands)

"Infused with years of wisdom, Steve Robertson takes us on a brilliant exploration of human behavior in Aliens Among Us. It is an invitation to understand newer generations: their complexities and differences through an incredibly thoughtful and unique insight on Gen Z."

—Ruben Muñoz Ramirez; Psychologist & Programmer (Mexico)

"It was a real pleasure to read *Aliens Among Us*, an interesting book full of insights for my work as a parent and educator. It changed my views, challenged my certainties, and I now feel closer and more attracted to this generation of aliens."

—Cristina Brichetti; The Camp Experts & Teen Summers (Italy)

"Steve Robertson understands younger generations in such a unique way. Seeing his body of work in both real life and in writing is wonderful, and I encourage readers to use this book as a practical guide to connect with Gen Z."

—Teran Tadal; Director of Equity & Inclusion,
Wharton Undergraduate Division at the University of Pennsylvania
(Pennsylvania)

"Steve Robertson approaches *Aliens Among Us* with incredible empathy, both for Gen Z and for those seeking to interact with them well. He dives into the fascinating historical landscape of the societal structures that have shaped this generation, while providing action insights into how you can connect with them."

—ANJALI BHATIA; CEO, Collegewise (New York)

"Utterly-thought provoking! As a Millennial, I often found myself frustrated at Boomers and, at the same time, perplexed by Gen Z. I work with both generations daily, and after reading just a few pages of this masterpiece, I found myself reflecting on my own life experiences with these generations. You will find wisdom on every page. Each generation thus far has seen tremendous change, and this will certainly continue. Thankfully we have Steve and his expertise in this field to help us navigate our way across the inter-generational dimensions!"

—SEAN MCKEND; Funded Trader & Educator, Ministry of Education (Dubai, UAE)

"Steve explores and explains Gen Z in such a clear, deep, and broad way, challenging us to rethink how we work, parent, teach, and ultimately, build something together with the younger generations. As we move along the chapters, ideas start to spark as he encourages us to embrace this journey called life with the "aliens"—whereas we, the older and "wiser" generations, may be the actual aliens in this extremely technological and digital world! After reading this book, I am 100% convinced that I need to change many small and big things in the way I do business in order to connect with Gen Z."

—MARCOS ASSAKURA; Finance Chairman of the Board, Dot Lib Information Group (Portugal)

"*Aliens Among Us* is as fascinating as it is relevant; as poignant as it is prescient. As a mother (and Millennial), I am grateful for the new perspective afforded to me, particularly about my own (status-quo-challenging) Gen Z middle schooler. I appreciate the values that Robertson urges readers to consider, advocating for dialectical thinking, openness to change, and genuine, meaningful connection. All readers will benefit from the empathy and information on every page. I look forward to gifting this book to the parents and educators I know."

—Rebecca Fox Starr; Author, Educator,
Maternal Mental Health Expert (Pennsylvania)

"In his eye-opening, debut book, Steve sets out to give you a new lens through which to look at Gen Z. *Aliens Among Us* provides valuable insights and strategies to engage them more effectively. From a business standpoint, understanding and leveraging the strengths of Gen Z, who are the future consumers and talent of the economy, is vital for survival. This book acts as a 'survival guide' of sorts for business leaders who are looking to overcome the challenges of an intergenerational workforce and build a sustainable business that stands the test of time."

—Tina Wells; Entrepreneur, Business Strategist, Author,
Founder of RLVNT Media (New Jersey)

"After a skeptical start to this book, it has become evidently clear that I will need to read it more than once to extract and benefit from all the wisdom I now recognize. Steve has numerous anecdotes and relevant stories as he clearly communicates a message that is applicable to both parents and business leaders. This is an insightful, high-impact read, and everyone reading it will extract massive benefit."

—John Thöle; CEO, Social Entrepreneur, Educator,
founding member of Edunova (South Africa)

"Combining his vast experience in managing thousands of Gen Z's over the years through summer camps with his genuine commitment to empower them and those who lead them, Steve's fascinating insights widen the lens and build a bridge to understanding a generation that is both 'alien' and truly awesome. This is essential reading for those who are sincere about engaged leadership and want to harness the 'awesome' for trailblazing a new generation of teams."

—Kee-Leen Irvine; Executive Producer, Shark Tank South Africa,
Family Feud SA, Bachelor SA, Dancing with the Stars SA, South Africa's
Got Talent, The X-Factor South Africa, et al. (South Africa)

"We can all remember a point in time when that generational "shift" happened in the blink of an eye. Steve, who has been around young minds for over twenty years, takes the opportunity to capture this shift and give us a deep look into Gen Z by opening up an elegant discourse into what has unfolded right in front of us. Be ready to be surprised and feed your curiosity into the world of Gen Z."

—LORENZO ERRICO; former Digital Marketing Manager
for Linkin Park and Head of Marketing Operations
for Universal Music Group: Germany (Germany)

"If you interact with Gen Z at any level, this book is a must read! Steve nailed it, giving me language and vocabulary to things I have pondered for years regarding this generation: how they are wired, how they process, how they implement, and how they execute. Furthermore, I have a newfound respect for a people group who have been misunderstood and mislabeled for far too long. Steve Robertson has become a leader among leaders in the space of cross-generational understanding, giving him authority on multiple levels to speak accordingly."

—TRACY FOX; Chief Revenue Officer at Botdoc (Colorado)

"Aliens Among Us is a well-grounded, insightful dive into Generation Z. Specifically, the challenges and opportunities they face and how it will impact their values, interactions, economic choices, and personal growth. This book will provoke business leaders, educators, and community leaders to reflect on their own mindsets and embrace the constant process of evolving that is required for cross-generational success."

—DAVID CAMBRIDGE, PhD; Owner of Bridge Educational
Services and Solutions (Pennsylvania)

"Steve Robertson consistently offers valuable and actionable insight. He has informed so much of how I've successfully connected with Gen Z in various contexts. The wisdom you'll gain from *Aliens Among Us* can tremendously improve your relationships with the Gen Z individuals in your life, as it has mine!"

—DR. TROY PODELL; Supervisor of Secondary ELA and Humanities,
Downingtown Area School District (Pennsylvania)

"In *Aliens Among Us*, Steve brings decades of experience to provide an enlightened perspective in this practical guide to understanding and appreciating Gen Z. This book provides a clear process and tactics to connect, engage, and empower the next generation. As an educator and a parent immersed in the Generation Z culture, learning about this historical progression that shaped this generation brought clarity and direction to creating more meaningful interactions and effective learning environments. This is a must-read!"

—LORI PETERS, MA, MS; Professor at George Washington University (Washington, D.C.)

"It doesn't matter where you live, what you do for work, or how you interact with others in your community—you are being influenced by Gen Z on a daily basis, whether you realize it or not! In *Aliens Among Us*, Steve paints a picture of our coworkers, colleagues, and friends that will make you think twice and will, ultimately, give you a level of understanding you did not have previously. I have spent many hours discussing how technology can reduce our reliance on under-performing staff (when they actually show up), but I now have a better understanding that Gen Z is not only our future workforce, but our future customers and the future of our business! This book has given us a new lens to drive economic success in this new world."

—JOSH EPSTEIN; Senior Director of Event Operations & Security, Washington Commanders (Washington, D.C.)

"The world we are living in is moving forward at a rate unlike anything we have seen before. The importance of connection has never been more evident, and there is a generation among us who needs it. Steve is able to put to words what we are all thinking, and not only that, he provides actionable insights into how we can serve Generation Z. Through a legacy mindset, *Aliens Among Us* equips you, challenges you, and calls you to action!"

—LUKE SHEPHERD; Team Lead, Recruiting at HubSpot (Australia)

"I have had the pleasure of personally knowing Steve Robertson for several years. Our conversations are like a fine bottle of intellectual wine that matures the more time you spend with it. They are food for thought that has helped me understand more about Gen Z and how to approach them properly. He is amongst the few people capable of coming up with tangible insights, through his research and interaction with thousands of kids in summer camps, that can help us understand how to interact with the 'aliens among us."

—LEO SOULAS; Data Scientist & Entrepreneur (Greece)

"When thinking of Gen Z, too often, older generations (of which I am one), get it wrong. We look with fixed eyes at shifting norms, a changing demographic, and a generation who are growing up in a rapidly shrinking world. In *Aliens Among Us*, Steve Robertson asks us to think again about how we see this rising generation of young people and to consider the many ways they will impact the planet. As we better understand how the Fourth Industrial Revolution has shaped Gen Z, we will need to consider more fully what the ramifications will be for business and industry, for education, and for every facet of life."

—TIMOTHY P. WIENS, ED.D.;
Head of PK-12 Private School (Georgia, U.S.)

"Steve has peered ten years into the future and is sounding an alarm that few others are ringing. In this book, Steve gives you the ability to see what's coming and equips you with the tools needed to prepare your life, family, and business for 2025 and beyond. If there was ever a time to abandon ship and build a new boat with the younger generation, that time is now!"

—ADAM BOWER, M.DIV. (Pennsylvania)

"Having known Steve Robertson for a decade, I have learned that he is interested in learning about the future of the world, as well as learning from the generations who will one day lead our world. Steve is at the forefront to observe and write about the Gen Z population as an expert in his field. If you want to understand Gen Z, open this book and absorb from Steve's learned experiences."

—DR. CALEB MEZZY; Digital Marketer,
Assistant Professor at Neumann University (Pennsylvania)

"Steve is the OG. I can't think of another human being on this planet who has worked with as many 'aliens' as he has after many years of running one of the most premier summer camp programs on the East Coast. As a former camper turned staff member, he made an impact on my own life and supported me in my crazy endeavors. Two decades later, I'm in my thirties and the founder of a creative marketing agency, building brands and managing social media for some of the world's largest organizations, where we often target Gen Z with products and entertainment. As I read this book now, Steve's experiences hit close to home. I've seen it first-hand in our messaging to this generation, as well as in our own hiring and office culture. Gen Z is mighty, their purchasing power is rising, and us adapting is essential."

—Jason Schutzbank; Entrepreneur, Web Architect,
Founder of Brand Knew (California)

"Having known Steve as a colleague and friend for over 20 years, he has always shown great insight and expertise in innovative ways to mentor and manage the workforce. As the owner and director of a sleep away camp, I have turned to Steve for guidance as I train and guide my staff and campers. I am excited to share this book with my leadership team, knowing the strategies Steve illustrates in this book will help us give our staff and campers a more rewarding summer experience."

—Steven Bernstein; Director of Camp North Star (Maine)

ALIENS AMONG US

ALIENS AMONG US

Z

Ten Surprising
Truths about
Gen Z

STEVEN ROBERTSON

BATTLE GROUND
creative

Aliens Among Us: Ten Surprising Truths about Gen Z

Copyright ©2022 by Steven J. Robertson
All rights reserved.

Published in Houston, Texas, by Battle Ground Creative
First Edition

ISBN: 978-1-947554-05-4 (softcover)
ISBN: 978-1-947554-06-1 (ebook)
SOCIAL SCIENCE / Sociology / General

Battle Ground Creative is a publishing company with an emphasis on helping first-time authors find their voice. Named after an obscure city in Washington State, we currently operate offices in Houston, Texas and Philadelphia, Pennsylvania. For a complete title list and bulk order information, please visit www.battlegroundcreative.com.

The websites and references contained within this book are intended to serve as a resource with no guarantee expressed or implied as to the accuracy of their content.

Copyedited by Jared Stump
Edited by Lisa Thompson
Cover design by Steven Smith
Interior graphics by Corinne Karl
Interior design and typeset by Katherine Lloyd

Printed in the United States of America

This work is dedicated to four pillars in my life:
My mom and dad (Elsie and Neil)
and my wife's parents (Will and Elaine).

You have each shared such wisdom from your life experiences
and invested so much in me over the course of my life.
The legacies you leave continue to inspire me.

Contents

Z

ALIENS
AMONG US

I love the movie *District 9* (2009) and not just because it takes place in South Africa. It contains the perfect analogy for describing Gen Z. Interestingly enough, it was released in 2009, around the same time the oldest members of this generation became teenagers. If you haven't seen the movie, this is a bit of a spoiler alert. The main premise is an alien invasion. While there are lots of movies like this, *District 9* is a bit different because the aliens aren't coming to attack or declare war on humanity; they are actually refugees seeking a new home on Earth because their home planet is dying.

In the film, an alien mothership arrives and hovers over the city of Johannesburg—of all places. Over one million malnourished aliens are found on board the ship and confined to a camp called District 9. Nearly twenty years later, the mothership is still hovering over the city, but all is not well below. Tensions are high between the humans and the aliens, with one resident saying something like, "This was supposed to be temporary, but it soon became clear that these aliens are not going home."[1]

We see a montage of signs around the city that communicate sentiments like "For use by humans only" and "No aliens allowed" while local residents voice their disgust with the aliens that they have been dealing with for two decades. The locals say such things as, "They must go. I don't know where. They just must go!" and "If they were from another country we might understand, but they aren't even from this planet!" A news

1

reporter explains that the people are so disgusted with the aliens because they don't think like humans. They see certain actions as recreational that humans obviously view as destructive, such as setting fire to a truck or derailing a train.[2]

The alien invasion has caused the people of Johannesburg to reach their breaking point, and they demand action. So the government hires a private company to evict the now 1.8 million aliens (they've grown!) from District 9 and relocate them to a new camp far away from human inhabitants. The rest of the movie follows these efforts.

I believe this film parallels the way other generations—even some Millennials—have responded to Gen Z. At first, they might have sympathy for this generation. They might believe, "These poor kids. They've grown up in a crazy time—all this economic unrest and global turmoil. No one had any money because there was this big recession, and now they can't even go outside and pursue normal activities without possibly being a victim of some kind of crime." Other generations demonstrate an initial compassion, but that quickly wears off when the older generations begin to realize just how different this new generation is, when they begin to see that this new generation has no intention of assimilating to their ways of doing things and fitting in to the world they have created. Perhaps the older generations are even rightly concerned with behaviors that Gen Z views as no big deal, in a similar manner to the aliens, who find it fun to set objects on fire.

Early in *District 9*, the lead character talks about how the relocation of the aliens will cause the humans of Johannesburg to live safely and happily because the aliens will be "far, far away." He's hyping himself up for this eviction operation that's about to take place, summoning the courage to declare, "This is our land, and they need to go."[3]

Whether we are talking about District 9 aliens or the human Generation Z, these may seem like reasonable sentiments. We think, *We were here first. There's more of us than them. We're doing them a favor by allowing them to live on this planet with us.* If we're honest, this is how many of us think about Gen Z, and we're waiting for them to grow up and get their act together because this is how the world works, and if they're going to be successful, they've got to figure out how they fit into what *we've* been doing for the past several decades.

The problem with this way of thinking is it ignores the reality that the world is changing—and changing rapidly at that. If the world continues moving in this way (which it will), Gen Z is not going to be the odd one out; the older generations will be. What amazes me is that this phenomenon actually plays out in the film. The main character goes to District 9 to evict the aliens, but he ends up being infected with something that begins to turn him into an alien himself. The film shows this progression, and at one point, the transition is so pronounced that the man has one human eye and one alien eye. He's becoming the very thing he's trying to avoid, the thing he's trying to push to the side so he doesn't have to deal with it.

We see this same phenomenon in our world today. We've tried to label and categorize this new generation. We likely don't call them Gen Z, but we lump everyone under the age of thirty together. We may refer to all of them as "Millennials" or "kids these days," but what we call them is irrelevant. What is relevant is we have this group of people we don't understand, and we aren't sure what to do with them. The easy approach is to dismiss them, to rope them off in a corner, and to ignore them because they are just so different from us and those differences make us uncomfortable. This may work for a time, but sooner or later, we will be faced with the reality that they *are* the future. And we, like the lead in District 9, are becoming the aliens in our world. It's inevitable: A time will come when the world looks less like our world and more like *their* world, and we will be the strangers seeking refuge in it.

Perhaps that moment is already here.

A NEW LENS

For the past three decades, I have helped lead summer camps and enrichment programs for children and teens ages five to eighteen. We've had well over one hundred thousand students attend from nearly every state and a hundred different countries. Many of these programs are held at prestigious college campuses and private schools around the United States each summer, giving students the opportunity to experience life on a college campus, meet new friends from across the globe, and develop skills—from sports and science to business and medicine—that they will use for the rest of their lives. Many of these students go on to become staff workers for these summer programs. I have helped recruit, hire, train, and manage tens of thousands of seasonal workers. In the summer of 2022, we expect to hire at least two thousand summer staffers. I'm also the father to two Millennials (those born between 1981 and 1996). Over the years, I've noticed many distinct differences between Millennials and Gen Z, both at home and in our summer programs.

When I first noticed that Gen Z behaved, engaged, and reacted differently than their Millennial predecessors based on their environment, situations, and how I communicated with them, I thought it was just teenagers going through a phase, but this was more than that. The differences seemed relatively minor at first. However, as I spent more time around them, I noticed fundamental differences between Gen Z and Millennials. That's not necessarily groundbreaking, as each generation has been a bit different than the previous generation. But this generation seemed to be wired differently, and their actions were impacting everyone else as well.

While driving in New Jersey recently, I paused for a funeral procession to pass by. Turning my hazard lights on, I pulled over to the left at an intersection. I wanted to turn left anyway, so I planned to sit there until the procession passed by. Midway through, the light turned red, but the procession continued through the red light. I wasn't shocked by this, as it is customary for a funeral procession to continue through a red light rather than separating the line of vehicles. However, the Gen Z driver on the side street, who now had a green light, was totally shocked that a line of cars was proceeding through the red light in front of him—even though they were driving rather slowly with their hazards on and little flags that said funeral on top of each vehicle. I couldn't help but notice how dumbfounded the young man was. After each car, he attempted to go, only to slam on the brakes as another vehicle entered the intersection in front of him.

This went on for some time until a standoff ensued. The young driver was in the middle of the intersection, and a car in the funeral procession had slammed on the brakes to avoid hitting him. The inexperienced driver had his window down at this point and was yelling at the older driver, who appeared to be a Gen Xer. "What the hell are you doing? I have a green light!"

He threw up one hand in disgust as he barreled through the intersection. The car behind him, who still had a green light, politely stopped and allowed the procession to continue. The Gen Xer driver rolled his eyes and shook his head.

This exchange was a perfect picture of the disconnect that often exists between Gen Z and other generations. You see, the Gen Xer was shocked that this young man was not respecting the established tradition of stopping for a funeral procession, but the young driver was not intentionally disrespecting anyone. He was unaware of the tradition and was baffled as to why multiple cars would all run a red light, one after the other. Neither party understood the other, and both thought they were right and the other was clearly in the wrong.

After discussing this incident with a friend, I decided to look up the laws regarding funeral processions. I was surprised to learn that there is no law that permits vehicles that are part of a procession to proceed through red lights and stop signs. In fact, very few states allow this unless an officer is present to direct traffic. It is more of a customary action, an unwritten rule. It's simply "the way things are done."

However, a new generation is emerging that is challenging the status quo in nearly every arena. Often, this is intentional. Other times, as was the case with this inexperienced driver in Jersey, they do it without even trying.

I've recently begun fly fishing in my free time, which has taken me to some incredible places. I've fished the Madison, Yellowstone, Gallatin and Missouri rivers in Montana as well as the Sacramento River in California. Before long, I realized I needed a pair of polarized sunglasses to make me a better fisherman. In short, these glasses allow you to see beneath the surface of the river so you can see the fish.

I went to the store and was looking at a granite block next to the display of sunglasses. I could see the outline of an etching on the block, but I couldn't make out enough details to know what it was. However, after putting on a pair of polarized glasses, I looked at the block again, and it looked totally different. With the glasses off, it was a simple block with something going on that I couldn't quite make out, but with the glasses on, it was a full-color landscape.

I am writing this book because leaders from all walks of life have practically demanded it. I have spoken to parents, educators, and business leaders around the world, sharing insights I have learned about this new generation. Whether I am speaking with a business leader, school administrator, or a total stranger who overheard me talking about Gen Z with someone else, the reaction is nearly always the same: Tell me more.

For many organizations, Gen Z is not only the fastest-growing customer group but also the group that can make the greatest impact on a team. At the same time, they are also one of the toughest generations to decode.

The primary purpose of this book is to give you a new lens through which you will look at Gen Z. Just as my new set of lenses for fly fishing allowed me to see beneath the waterline, we need to look at this generation through a new lens. When we do this, what was previously a rough outline will become a detailed landscape, and we'll be able to understand and relate to this generation.

A change in perspective always precedes a change in behavior or attitude. When you change the way you think about Gen Z, it will change the way you interact with them, the way you speak into their lives, the way you parent them (if you are a parent), and the way you lead them in the workspace.

All these changes will be for the better although this journey will require us to let go of some old mindsets and lenses that we have previously viewed Gen Z through. Some of us are aware we have been looking through these lenses and some of us are unaware, but most of us see Gen Z through our own type of lens and, as a result, we do not see them clearly, we do not understand what makes them unique, and we do not know how to interact with them in a way that is beneficial for everyone.

> A change in perspective always precedes a change in behavior or attitude.

I recognize that not everyone may appreciate the differences that Gen Z brings to the table the way I do. One of the primary reasons why we Gen Xers and Boomers want the younger generations to be more like us is because we don't want to change the way we have done things for decades, especially since our methods have worked in many cases and aren't necessarily broken. However, I would argue that everything needs to be updated and refreshed from time to time.

We must realize that just because something is new doesn't mean it's bad. Just because something has never been done before doesn't mean it shouldn't be done. And just because things are changing doesn't mean the old way was bad; it just means we have found a new and perhaps better way of doing things that is more appropriate for today's world. At the same time, we can easily become territorial and defensive. We may say we are open to change, but our actions often tell a different story even if we think we are being open-minded.

We've seen this every time Apple unveils a new major change for the iPhone. Here are some common reactions: Okay, the headphone jack is going away, so there's just one jack for the headphones and the charger.

What's going on here? Are they just trying to make more money? I paid thirty dollars for these headphones—and thirty dollars for the second and third pairs for when I lose them. Now I've got to do this all over again because the old ones don't work with this year's model. Oh, and now the headphones are called AirPods; they're well over a hundred dollars, and they're wireless. What on earth? It was bad enough when they changed them the first time. Why couldn't they just leave them alone?

The problem with this way of thinking is it causes us to miss out on all the benefits this change can bring. I know one person who was quite resistant to AirPods at first—in fact, he had stopped upgrading his iPhone when the headphone jack was changed so he didn't have to get new ones. He didn't like feeling forced to do things a new way, and he certainly didn't like spending money to do so.

Over time, his phone got slower and slower until it just didn't work anymore. He finally upgraded; he got the new headphones and realized it wasn't as bad as he thought. He could handle this change. A short time later, he tried the AirPods and never looked back. The way the headphones plugged in was a small change that seemed to serve no other purpose than to annoy the user. But this new change, this was revolutionary. He no longer had to worry about the cord tangling when he put the phone in his pocket—or untangling it when he took it out of his briefcase. He could even be on a call and leave his phone on the desk while he paced back and forth. As it turned out, the AirPods weren't just for him to hear; a built-in microphone allowed the person on the other end of the line to hear him. It was a better user interface; it looked more professional; it was simply better in every way. He wondered why it had taken him so long to adapt to this new way. Even the cost to upgrade no longer mattered to him because the new way was so much better.

> Just because something is new doesn't mean it's bad. Just because something has never been done before doesn't mean it shouldn't be done.

While this story is humorous, it's how many of us live. We just want to cruise through life and avoid as many disruptions or inconveniences as possible, but in doing so, we miss out on many things. For many of us, this is the story of our relationship with technology, but it's also likely the story of our relationship with our children and with the younger generations at work. We may not pay a literal cost with connecting in a different way with a new generation, but it does require an investment of our time and a willingness to shift our perspectives. We may not see much of an ROI at first glance until we actually make this shift.

—— —— ——

Many years ago, I learned an important lesson that continues to impact my leadership today. As a tennis professional in South Africa, I was fortunate to work alongside a number of the top coaches in the world. As a coach, I spent a great deal of time observing my players and telling them what they were doing wrong. I became quite good at identifying the smallest of errors made by an athlete I was working with. Finding fault came very easily to me.

One day, I was with another coach, watching—and yes, judging—a young athlete in action. The routine he was going through was stretching him as a player, which made it very easy for me to see all his flaws. After watching this young man for twenty minutes, I leaned over to his coach and asked, "So, what do you think?"

She replied with a simple yet deep sentiment that lives with me to this day.

"There is a lot about that forehand that is amazing," she said. "If we made this little tweak, I know it would be even better."

This statement may not seem like much to you, but for me—an expert in finding fault—it made me realize that I was magnifying every fault and making it bigger than it really was. I had built my professional success on being able to zoom in and identify what was wrong to the point where I would often discount or overlook all that was *right*. Often, what was wrong was only 10 percent of the equation, while 90 percent of the athlete's performance was spot on. They may not have minded this much since I was their coach, but could you imagine having me behave this way as a leader, especially in today's world?

I see so many leaders today who are highly skilled at quickly identifying problems. I believe this skill is essential for leaders at all levels, but what I learned that day is 90 percent of what is taking place is usually amazing and what needs addressing is only 10 percent of the equation. As a leader, it's important for me to interact with my team so that they realize I know this rather than in a way that comes across like 90 percent of what they are doing is wrong and only 10 percent is amazing. This can quickly lead to the employee feeling as if their contribution isn't valued, which could cause them to begin looking to take their skills elsewhere. This is especially true when it comes to Gen Z, where 72 percent of high school students desire to start their own business.[1] They all have access to the gig economy where quite literally they can quit a job one day and have an endless stream of freelance work the next via one (or multiple) apps.

> Ninety percent of what is taking place is usually amazing and what needs addressing is only 10 percent of the equation. As a leader, it's important for me to interact with my team so that they realize I know this.

We have identified two common ways that we Gen Xers and Boomers respond to Millennials and Gen Zers: We either refuse to embrace them and their world and become passive bystanders, or we are active and hands-on but come on far too strong with our primary focus being to find fault. Whether we are too passive or overly aggressive in our approach, the end result is the same: We don't connect with the next generation on the level that is possible, and our potential impact is limited.

If you look at virtually anything in your life, even what you love, you are bound to find something you don't like. This is true with nearly everything. Because we tend to focus on what we don't like more than on what we do like, what we don't like can often seem much bigger than it really is. When we focus on the 10 percent of something that we don't like, we miss out on the 90 percent that we love.

I'm sure you see the parallel I am drawing to Gen Z. By no means do I think this generation is perfect, and they certainly don't claim to be; they are figuring out life one day at a time like the rest of us. I would change some things about them if I could. However, rather than focusing on what I don't like or understand about them, I want to focus on the 90 percent about them that I do like. Otherwise, I might miss out on all the wonderful things this generation has to offer.

We must shift our mindsets and tell ourselves, "Gen Z will say and do things that seem radically different from my way of thinking. However, I will set that aside and focus on what we agree on. Not only that, I will allow them to challenge me to discover new and better ways of thinking, being, and doing. I may actually really like a lot of these changes once I get past the ten percent that I don't like."

I have found that the 10 percent rule has very little to do with what is right and what is wrong, what needs to be adjusted and what needs to be approached differently. Instead, it has taught me that communication is the underlying key as uncommunicated expectations are rarely met.

We once had an employee who a few members of our team were struggling to connect with. As time went on, these team members grew more and more unhappy with this person's performance. One day, one of them began sharing their frustrations in a meeting. I listened for a moment, then began sharing with them what I have learned from the 10 percent rule.

"Do each of us have spouses, significant others, parents, or other loved ones who love us completely?" I asked.

They all agreed that each of us did.

"At the same time, would every one of these people in our lives like to tweak or change one or two things about us?"

Again, a resounding yes was given around the room, and one member of our team said their spouse would change not one or two, but five or six things about them. We all shared a laugh, and I continued unpacking this principle.

"So when we consider this employee, if we are honest, ninety percent of what they do is amazing. They are raising the bar in many ways, and it's undeniably good for our business. Yet here we are having this conversation, focusing on the ten percent that we want to see changed. This doesn't mean we have to ignore these things and just be happy with what we have. Let's look closely at what makes up this ten percent and put a plan in place with this employee to reduce it bit by bit so we can all get along and be productive in the workspace. And don't forget, *ninety percent of what we have seen from them is amazing.* Don't allow your frustrations over the ten percent to cause you to lose sight of that."

In the end, the employee in this story spent many great years with us before deciding to move on to something new, but we parted ways on excellent terms, and the obstacles we encountered early on were removed by our utilization of the ten percent rule, which helped us clarify and be specific about what needed to be addressed. This positioned our leaders to have more measured, constructive conversations and to not become so focused on flaws that we lost sight of why we hired the person in the first place. After all, 90 percent of what they brought to the table was amazing. We just needed to see them through a new lens.

One of the most fundamental shifts we need to make in the way we see Gen Z is to recognize that they are a distinct and unique generation. Many of us Boomers and Gen Xers tend to lump everyone under thirty into one homogenous group, which we commonly label "Millennials." I've seen this happen for some time, but it became quite pronounced in March 2020 when the COVID-19 pandemic was first ravaging the northeastern United States, and we were beginning to shut everything down for two weeks. Right in the middle of this, many young people decided to travel to Florida for their previously planned spring break trips. This was national news, but what was interesting was how many people kept referring to them as "Millennials." One congressman tweeted: "Time for Millennials on spring break to grow up. Stop swarming beaches and bars and spreading Coronavirus. Forget your selfishness. Show some responsibility like previous generations who made America the greatest nation on earth."[2]

It wasn't long before Millennials (and those belonging to other generations) set the record straight. This tweet had 251 replies. Some of the top replies included these sentiments:

"Just because someone is younger than you does not make them a Millennial."[3]

"I think you mean Gen Z, Boomer."[4]

"They're Gen Z … but otherwise I agree."[5]

"Millennials are mostly near 30 and super unlikely to be on Spring

Break. Millennials are a certain generation, not a catch-all for anybody younger than you."[6]

"Seriously, I'm technically a Millennial and haven't had a spring break in fifteen years."[7]

For several days, the following sentiment was shared on various social platforms: "These aren't Millennials on the beach. This is Gen Z. Millennials are working from home, watching Netflix, and yelling at their Boomer parents not to go outside!"[8]

News outlets began to pick up on this, publishing articles with titles like, "It's Gen Z you want": Millennials are defending themselves from accusations that they're out partying and ignoring warnings amid the coronavirus pandemic"[9] and "Millennials want to make it clear that they're not the ones on Spring Break."[10]

At this moment, many people realized—some for the first time—that the young people around them belong to two distinct generations that, while they have some similarities, are also very different. One of these key differences is Gen Z grew up in a world where the sky was always falling, a world where mass shootings, global terrorism, and social upheaval were par for the course. So for some of them, when they heard warnings of a deadly virus, it was just "another thing" that could get them, and it wasn't going to mess up their spring break trips, long ago booked and saved up for. It didn't mean Gen Z wasn't concerned; they were just used to the threat of imminent death—both real danger and hyperbole—and they had learned to adapt and live their lives in this world. Other generations have had very different experiences, so they respond in different ways. When you look at Gen Z's actions through this lens, it helps you to see where they are coming from, regardless of whether you agree with their decisions.

In fact, I saw one member of Gen Z who was interviewed who said just that. In essence: "We've been planning this trip for a long time, and we worked hard to save up for it. We aren't really concerned about the virus; we're just out here enjoying ourselves and having a good time."

Some of these young people would express regret for their actions later, but that is not the point. The point is, back in March 2020, when nearly every other generation was responding one way (back before polarizing opinions began to develop), Gen Z responded in a totally different way, and I'm willing to bet if we look at a myriad of other situations and circumstances, we would find that this is a consistent pattern.

I'm not trying to make any sort of political statements here but want to drive one point home: Gen Z is not just "the new Millennials." They are a unique generation that has grown up in a very different world than Millennials (and the rest of us). As a result, we have produced a type of human that has never existed before—almost as though they are from a different planet.

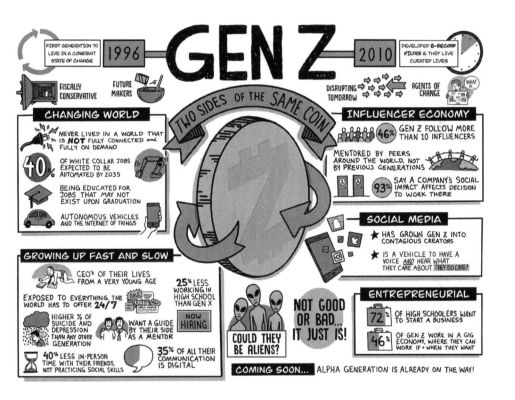

Z

TRUTH #1
Gen Z Has Been Transformed by a Perfect Storm

We live in a truly unique time in history where numerous forces have come together to alter the way humans do—well, almost everything. We don't just live in a world where technology has advanced, though it has, but we live in a world that has fundamentally reshaped the way we think and live. These changes affect all of us but most profoundly, Gen Z, the first generation to grow up in this sort of "new world" brought about by what I call *the perfect storm*.

This perfect storm is a culmination of various factors at play in our world today, which have created a generation that is wired very differently than any previous generation. This is why we jokingly refer to them as "aliens." The graphic below will illustrate four of the primary components that have created this perfect storm of epic proportions:

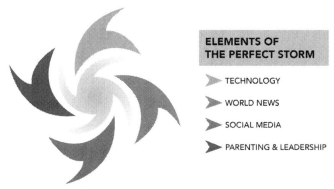

ELEMENTS OF THE PERFECT STORM

- TECHNOLOGY
- WORLD NEWS
- SOCIAL MEDIA
- PARENTING & LEADERSHIP

The Fourth Industrial Revolution has created the capacity for new technologies that arrive at a much faster rate than ever before. There are no longer generation gaps between new technologies. When Millennials were born, the mobile phone was in a large briefcase that one carried around like they were a world leader on the brink of nuclear war and few had them. By the time they learned how to drive, the mobile phone had evolved into something nearly everyone had, but the camera wasn't that great, the web access was expensive, and texting took much longer. Now, as they have become adults, the smartphone is in nearly everyone's pockets—offering a full keyboard for texting, texts that type themselves as the user dictates them while driving or performing another task, a camera better than the professional cameras photographers used ten years ago, and instant access to all the knowledge of the internet. It's at the point where cell phones are commonplace even in developing countries, and nearly everyone has access to the internet.

Technology has given us these devices that nearly all of us have, and these devices have given us always-on access to a constant onslaught of world news. Every celebration, heartbreaking tragedy, untimely celebrity death, and caught-on-tape moment is delivered to us in real-time, wherever we are.

It didn't used to be this way. Not long ago, news came through our television sets at the end of the workday, as we were transitioning from the office to home, right before we ate dinner—or, if we missed that broadcast, right before we went to sleep. For some, the news did not arrive until the next morning in the form of a rolled-up newspaper tossed on our driveway (an ancient way of life younger generations have not experienced).

Then came cable news networks, which transitioned the news from appearing on the driveway each morning or during a regulated time slot in the evening to being always on, 24/7. Still, news was confined to a box in our living rooms. We could get away from it. It didn't follow us around, unless we happened to catch a soundbite in the break room or the waiting room of the doctor's office.

In the early 2000s, headlines began to regularly appear in our email inboxes, giving us much quicker access to the news while working at our desks or while communicating at home with our aunt in Cleveland.

Within the decade, everything began to change at an accelerated pace. Now, the smartphone brings us news alerts through push notifications that you swipe away, only to open a social network and see everyone discussing the same thing.

The number of news outlets also began to increase while the standard for what was newsworthy began to decrease. As smartphones began to appear in nearly everyone's pockets, a new kind of news outlet that only exists online was born, and these news outlets are even more "always on" than cable news because they contain multiple channels that can cover various topics at the same time, which spread far more quickly through social media. And the content that is being spread has shifted rapidly. It's no longer just about world leaders or celebrities or even local events but caught-on-tape moments of Karen in Minnesota or Steve in Florida, and a sort of outrage comes with these stories, an "oh my gosh—how could they?" Our friends are sharing these posts on social media or texting them to us (or perhaps both), and we seem to feel this pressure to have an opinion on what someone you've never met did in another state in the normal course of their life—all while you are trying to go about your own life.

Social media has certainly accelerated the spread of news, changed what qualifies as news, and created a new form of peer pressure that leads to actual medical diagnoses for many. It has effectively rewired our brains, creating new anxieties and fears.

> Social media has effectively rewired our brains, creating new anxieties and fears.

Just writing this is bringing up a combination of anxiety and exhaustion, as it is reminding me of certain subjects I have seen and heard in the last few hours. I'm sure the same is true for you. Even if you live off the grid somewhere, it's hard to escape. This constant onslaught of information that is shared so quickly through screens has a way of working itself into everything. At some places, you can't even pump gas anymore without a screen flipping on and someone trying to sell you something or share some sort of urgent message. It's everywhere.

I'm a Gen Xer and have witnessed these changes take place over time—shorter periods of time, of course—but still, I remember what the world was like before all this. The same is true with Millennials, even those born in the 1990s. They saw these changes take place during their teenage and early adult years. But Gen Z is different. Perhaps the older members of this population recall some of the overlap, but most know no other world—and Gen Alpha was born right in the thick of it.

All these changes in our world—the technology, the always-on news, social media—have their place in society, and certainly, they have many positive aspects. However, it would be a disservice to dismiss the numerous side effects we have all developed as we attempt to adapt and cope with this new world. In the midst of this radical change that we are either experiencing or were born into, we are also seeing an alarming vacuum of parenting in the home and leadership in the workplace. All these forces have come together to create a perfect storm and a new kind of human. There is no way Gen Z and the generations that follow can become anything close to the generations that came before them. This is why I call them the *alien generation* because they are so foreign compared to anything we've experienced before.

The Rapid Advancement of Technology

History class taught us that the first Industrial Revolution occurred in the 1700s with the invention of the steam engine. Over the next two hundred years, manufacturing continued to be revolutionized with the inception of electricity, oil, combustion engines, and cheap steel. This was the second Industrial Revolution. The third Industrial Revolution was perhaps the most striking as factory jobs were eliminated or moved overseas, and most Americans became office workers. The Millennials were widely talked about as the generation that came of age at the height of this revolution, but many people are unaware that a fourth revolution is underway and leaving its mark on a new generation. You see, unlike Millennials, who remember painfully slow dial-up internet, most members of Gen Z do not remember a world without smartphones and lightning-fast speeds, and members of Gen Alpha were likely handed a smartphone or tablet before they learned how to walk.

INDUSTRIAL REVOLUTIONS

1700 –1800s	Late 1800s – Early 1900s	1980 –1990s	2000s – Present Day
The Steam Engine	**Steel Production, Electricity, Oil, Combustion Engines**	**Personal Computers & the Internet**	**Increased Speeds, Smartphones, Cloud Data, Artificial Intelligence**

The fourth Industrial Revolution has created new technologies that advance at an unprecedented rate, which is the reason we now have "aliens among us" and why our younger generations are so different from any generation that came before them. This is the first component of the perfect storm.

Unlike the first three industrial revolutions, what is most unique about this era is it doesn't merely change *what* we are doing. Rather, it changes *us*. We haven't simply found better ways to do things, such as steam power or electricity. We don't just have computers in the living room or at the office; this new technology goes with us—from the laptop in our briefcase to the smartphone in our pockets and even to phones on our wrists in the form of a watch. This technology is built into the very fabric of our homes and cars. We can turn on the lights or adjust the temperature of the room with the touch of a button and use voice commands to order food and have it delivered. When someone comes to the door, you don't have to get off the couch or stop doing laundry to see who is at the door because the doorbell now has a camera in it.

We rarely vacuum our house anymore because I purchased a Roomba that quietly does the cleaning for us. Even this technology has advanced—it doesn't just meander through my house aimlessly because it's equipped with a AI (artificial intelligence) that creates a blueprint of my house as it cleans. It knows the kitchen from the living room, and within each room, it knows where the couch and TV are, and it learns not to bump into those objects. I have an app to view which room Roomba is in; I can tell Roomba to clean here or there from my office. I can also block out areas I don't want cleaned, such as that pesky chair where Roomba always seems to get stuck or my daughter's room if too much stuff happens to be on the floor. She has actually learned to work with our robotic vacuum and will make sure her floor is clean if she knows Roomba is coming through during the day while she's gone. My entire family is learning to work with this AI that becomes smarter and smarter each day as it learns our home. At the same time, the Roomba technology is so much more advanced than previous models that it needs us less and less. Once it is done cleaning, Roomba returns to its "CleanBase," where it docks and empties itself. A second powerful vacuum sucks the dirt out of Roomba and stores it in a larger bag that only needs to be emptied by a human at most once a month. Perhaps one day, a new device will take the dirt Roomba collects from the CleanBase to the curb on garbage day. This may seem crazy, but everything I just described also seemed crazy ten years ago.

> What is most unique about this era is it doesn't merely change *what* we are doing. Rather, it changes *us*.

Let's take a look at the way we access movies and music to see another rapid change today. The way we listen to music has undergone many changes in my lifetime: records, eight-tracks, cassettes, CDs, and most recently, digital downloads. Before VHS tapes were invented in the mid-1970s, we had to rent a projector to watch movies at home. The movies were on big reels that had to be changed midway through, making the VHS tape revolutionary. DVDs then came on the scene in the late 1990s and early 2000s, and of course, then there was Blu-Ray, which was a much less radical transition from VHS to DVD and one that never fully took hold. That's because both music and movies have taken a radical shift in recent years.

Digital downloads were radical because they shifted consumers away from owning a physical product. Sure, it existed in a certain space because you would download the content to your computer and perhaps transfer it to your iPod, but you no longer owned a physical copy that you had full control over. One way this manifested was with copyright. Many of these files, while you paid to own them, were encoded so they could only be played on a certain device. Users could authorize their devices to play their downloaded content, but each account could only authorize so many devices. This simply did not make sense for large families with multiple screens who would need to pay twice for everyone to access one movie as opposed to purchasing a DVD that could be passed around. What digital downloads did, however, was provide the opportunity for the content to exist in more than one space at a time, while a physical DVD could only be in one place at a time. You had to physically remove it from one device in order to access it on another.

This was a huge evolution, a radical shift, but it wasn't long before another shift would take place and digital downloads would evolve into streaming. It wasn't enough for the content to be available digitally; more options were needed. Streaming opened up the world of content in a dramatic way. The content is available instantly; it doesn't need to be downloaded first (all that is needed is internet access). This, however, is only a small tweak compared to the overhaul streaming brought to the content space. The major shift was the reality that *all* content was now available with one fixed monthly fee. As Apple Music advertises, "Stream 60 million songs ad-free."[1]

This was revolutionary. If you don't like the movie you're watching after the first half-hour (or if you're a member of Gen Z, the first five minutes), you can simply return to the menu and select another movie. You can even rate the movie you didn't like, so the recommendation engine knows you didn't like it. In fact, the AI working behind the scenes likely already detected you didn't like this movie when you gave up after a few minutes and began watching something else. No doubt it observed and noted that you only watched a small portion of one movie but then watched another movie all the way through. This was not the case ten years ago. If you didn't like the movie, you would probably stick it out anyway because there was nothing else to watch and you had already paid for it. If you switched movies, you would have to pay twice, and what if your movie came from Redbox? It's not like you would leave your house and drive back to get another one. Perhaps you would get lucky and find something else on TV, but most of the time, you would stick with one thing even if you didn't like it—or turn off the TV entirely and do something else.

Streaming marked the first time that users were introduced to truly endless options. This was especially true when Spotify changed the music space. It was revolutionary that iTunes gave us the capacity to preview, purchase, and download only the songs we loved for ninety-nine cents each, rather than paying ten or eleven dollars for an entire album when we may only like a song or two. However, it was even more revolutionary to be able to pay ten dollars *a month* and listen to *as much music* as one wanted. Spotify was very fortunate in catching on quickly with virtually every artist and label signing up in a short period of time. There were certainly some holdouts—the most notable being Taylor Swift—but even she finally relinquished to the way of the future after three years of not allowing her music to be streamed.

Three years may not seem like a long time to not have access to something, but for Taylor Swift's younger fans, it seemed like an eternity. Many had already switched from buying physical CDs to digital downloads through iTunes, and in those three years, the music space evolved rapidly. For most Gen Z users (and other generations as well), this was enough time to shift from owning digital downloads to streaming music through Spotify. After just one year, Apple launched their own streaming service—Apple Music—and all sorts of options now exist for streaming music. I am simply using Spotify as the primary example because I believe they were the first to make streaming music popular.

The most valuable aspect about streaming (whether it's music or movies) that most of us overlook is the *way* it functions. For example, one of the most valuable things about Netflix is not the streaming service itself. All streaming services do essentially the same things: provide on-demand content for users to consume. That's pretty simple. But with so many options—not just what to stream but where to stream from—how do companies like Netflix, Hulu, Amazon, YouTube, and others keep users engaged?

The most valuable thing about Netflix is not the ability to stream content, but the recommendation engine algorithm. This AI analyzes what I've watched and predicts what I want to watch next. This invisible feature is always working behind the scenes, long before it becomes visible in the "recommended for you" section of my homepage. It's not only looking at what I watch but what I stop watching before reaching the end. I'm sure it also gathers data on how long it takes me to watch a show or movie. Do I watch all the way through with minimal interruptions? Or does it take me several days to make it through an hour-long program, watching a little here and there? This could be a lack of interest, or it could just be the way I consume content. The AI knows. It notices if I do this with everything I watch or if it's out-of-the-ordinary behavior for me. This data is highly useful in predicting my future behavior. Most of us are creatures of habit, and whatever streaming service we use takes advantage of this to keep us engaged.

Think about how valuable this data must be. Not only that, but Spotify knows what I'm listening to, how many times I played through a single song, how far I made it through an album, what genres I spend the most time listening to, and how many hours total I listen to music each week. Amazon has even more data on my life because they don't just have my streaming habits from Prime Video; they know what I've searched for, what I've purchased, and how many different brands of any one item I considered before making my ultimate selection. They actually have data that can tell you what brand of toothpaste people who watch *CSI: Miami* and *Law & Order* are most likely to purchase, and they can tell you whether these people prefer owning physical DVDs or streaming episodes of these shows. As one of my friends who works in this space as an app developer put it, "Amazon is really just a data collection company."

I wouldn't be surprised if all this data collected by AI is used to target ads to fit my preferences, only showing me what I want to see and not wasting my time with what I don't want to see. We know this happens online through "tracking cookies" that know what websites we've visited. It's why you see an ad for shoes on Facebook right after looking at shoes on a website. Some even say that our devices are constantly listening to us (they probably are), taking in our offline conversations, and using this to sell us ads. Though this may or may not be widespread, the technology does exist. Perhaps one day, it may no longer be seen as an invasion of privacy but a helpful tool, like our own robotic personal assistant that can anticipate our needs before we even ask for them based on our viewing, listening, and purchasing history coupled with our browsing history and offline conversations.

Who knows what will become normal in the future? Fifty years ago, we certainly wouldn't have believed some of the things we are already doing now without thinking twice. Whether you are for or against this new technology, you are immersed in it every day. Most of us realize this has changed the way we do things, but you likely haven't realized how much it is changing *you*, or how rapidly this change is taking place. You may not be conscious of it on a day-to-day basis, but when you step back, you can see how quickly things are moving and how technology is expanding to impact every area of our lives.

> Most of us realize things are changing, but we often don't realize how much these changes are changing *us*.

When the Roomba was first introduced, it didn't truly clean for you as mine does today. You had to push buttons to tell it what size a room was, you had to empty it yourself, and you had to make sure you plugged it in every night. The user still played a significant role in the cleaning process. Now, Roomba has sensors and AI that detect the size of a room and any obstacles, the device empties itself, and when it's done for the day it returns "home" to its base where it charges itself until the next cleaning.

If you reflect for a moment, you will recognize that virtually all of our technology works this way. It's getting faster, smarter, and more affordable, and it needs us less and less. This brings into focus the fourth Industrial Revolution, which has done more to change our world in two decades' time than any other invention in history, perhaps because it's not just *one* thing that has been introduced—it's everything, It's not just, "Hey, we have these things called lightbulbs now, so you can use them instead of your oil lamp," but, "Here are these hundreds of new technologies, and by the time you get a grasp on any one of them there's likely going to be something different that takes its place."

This is why the older generations struggle so much with tech; they're used to changes taking *decades*. Back in the day, a car or a TV would last for several years—but now we only use them for a few years before our model is so out-of-date that we must upgrade to the new one. There's never any sense of arriving or that something is finished. There is always more out there to achieve and grab hold of—no wonder our young people are so unsettled. In fact, we're *all* a bit unsettled because we have not yet adapted to this new world. Now, it's not just the TV itself that is evolving; the content *on* the TV is evolving at lightning speed. Most TVs (and the channels) used to be the same, but now our TVs have apps that open up an endless world of possibilities.

Will we reach the point where we ditch our cable boxes, satellite dishes, and DVD players and not even miss them? It seems a bit crazy when you think about it: not long ago, these *were* the cutting edges of entertainment, and DVDs were the new thing that was arguably better than VHS. But now, with streaming, we can get rid of all of this clunky equipment and the physical products cluttering our shelves because everything is in the cloud. I personally made this switch to streaming in 2018 and never looked back. Not everyone loves this change, but it truly is remarkable when you consider how much has changed in such a short period of time.

— — —

Professor Klaus Schwab, the founder and executive chairman of the World Economic Forum, has witnessed these trends for more than forty years and is convinced that "we are at the beginning of a revolution that is fundamentally changing the way we live, work, and relate to one another."[2]

As Schwab explores in his book *The Fourth Industrial Revolution*,

> Previous industrial revolutions liberated humankind from animal power, made mass production possible and brought digital capabilities to billions of people. This Fourth Industrial Revolution is, however, fundamentally different. It is characterized by a range of new technologies that are fusing the physical, digital and biological worlds, impacting all disciplines, economies and industries, and even challenging ideas about what it means to be human. The resulting shifts and disruptions mean that we live in a time of great promise and great peril. The world has the potential to connect billions more people to digital networks and dramatically improve the efficiency of organizations ...[3]

Technologies are in the works that we don't even know about yet, but they have massive implications for the way we live. They have them in the defense, in medical spaces, and in high-level, top-secret areas. They aren't in mass production for the general public, but they are there.

For example, a few years ago, Google revealed a massive breakthrough by claiming their 54-qubit Sycamore processor had completed a calculation in just over three minutes that would have taken the world's previous most powerful supercomputer ten thousand years to complete.[4]

> "It is characterized by a range of new technologies that are fusing the physical, digital, and biological worlds, impacting all disciplines, economies, and industries, and even challenging ideas about what it means to be human."

IBM, the manufacturer of this supercomputer that Google allegedly beat, said it would have taken their machine just two-and-a-half days (not ten thousand years) to perform the calculation, but Google still has them beat by being able to perform the same calculation in mere minutes.[5]

The New York Times quoted scientists comparing Google's feat with the Wright brother's first flight in 1903.[6] Like the quantum computer, it would be years before the airplane became mainstream and accessible, but the initial flight proved it possible, and Google did the same thing in 2019.

"The original Wright flyer was not a useful airplane," said University of Texas at Austin computer scientist Scott Aaronson in an interview with *The Times*. "But it was designed to prove a point. And it proved the point."[7]

Aaronson went on to say he believed IBM was right and Google's initial calculation of ten thousand years was a bit off, but it was still a major scientific breakthrough,[8] and this is proof that technology is expanding rapidly at speeds ordinary people cannot keep up with.

So why don't we have access to these technologies? Let's look at an example of electric versus gasoline-powered cars.

Most of us would objectively agree that electric cars are better. Of course, as soon as I say that, some of you will probably disagree, and you might be rattling off a list of reasons why an electric car is *not* better than the one you have now.

- They're too expensive.
- The range isn't broad enough.
- How will I plug it in if it dies on the way home from work?
- I'll probably end up paying the same in electricity as I do for gas anyway.
- Is the process of making all these batteries even "green" when it's all said and done?

All these arguments represent only about 10 percent of the equation. I believe most of us would objectively agree that electric cars are better for the environment with less emissions and less noise pollution. If we were starting a new country today—building it from scratch—we would quite possibly only allow these cars within its borders. However, we don't do this in *this* country because we have billions, probably trillions, invested in our current infrastructure. We've already got all the gas stations and oil refineries, all the miles of pipelines, and so forth. This change, if it is to come, will take a very long time. You can't just take away the old and replace it with the new. You can't just swap one for the other; they must both exist alongside each other for a period of time with an overlap. This could take decades, even hundreds of years. At least, that's how it's been historically. Except now, with our rapid advances in technology, these changes can happen instantaneously. You upload one thing, and in minutes, it replaces what was there before. Tesla even offers you the capability to do this to your car: you connect the vehicle to Wi-Fi, download an upgrade, and it can suddenly do something it couldn't before.[9] With all this innovation, it's no surprise that Tesla is now worth one trillion dollars[10] after Hertz announced they would purchase one hundred thousand Teslas by the end of 2022 at a cost of more than four billion dollars.[11]

This announcement should not come as a surprise as, nine months prior, General Motors announced they would phase out all new gas and diesel-powered vehicles by 2035,[12] and Ford was close on their heels with a similar announcement that they will be all electric in Europe by 2030.[13] As

The New York Times so eloquently put it, "The age of electric cars is dawning ahead of schedule."[14] This ripple effect is now unstoppable, but we still find ourselves in a transition space—and we will still be in this transition space after 2035 as electric and gas-powered vehicles share the road until we fully transition to a new era.

How a Tesla upgrades itself is similar to how we embrace change in our own lives at times. Perhaps we download the new operating system for our iMac, and it completely replaces what was there before. The differences are often subtle, and at times, they are more drastic. But what we did was completely remove one thing and replace it with another. The old has gone, and the new has come in a moment, and there's no going back to what we had before. Other times, there's an overlap, but it doesn't always take decades like it does with cars. There are smaller overlaps. For example, the majority of our population transitioned from flip phones to smartphones in a much shorter period of time. Historically, the phone evolved at a substantially slower pace, but now the process has accelerated.

When the iPhone was first introduced, it was revolutionary. Do you see what this thing can do? But now, with each update, it's really not that much more exciting. Certainly, a 2019 iPhone is better than its 2007 prototype. But has that much really changed in twelve years? Did it really need to take that long for us to get a better camera and a bigger screen? That's not revolutionary; it's simply improving what already existed. It took three years for the thing to get a front camera. Okay, now you can unlock the phone with your fingerprint … oh, wait, we're going to take the home button away, but don't worry; you can unlock the new phone with your face. Just look at it, and you're good to go! No more headphone jack—we'll use wireless earphones with no cord that just kind of sit in your ears and arguably make you look a bit like an alien.

I'm sure you see the point. None of this is revolutionary. It's not really twelve years of innovation; it's perhaps a few years' worth of innovation stretched out over a twelve-year time period. Perhaps the iPhone 20 will have the ability to read our minds. Now that would truly be revolutionary.

- - -

The most important thing you need to see here is this expedited advancement of technology is primarily doing two things: making rapid change happen even more quickly and creating endless options.

These two changes have changed our expectations and not just what we expect from technology. What we expect from the world, our friends, employees, bosses, and co-workers is all shifting quickly because we live in an increasingly instant society where everything is available right when we need it.

> Our expectations are rapidly shifting because we live in an increasingly instant society.

We've become so used to this that we're thrown for a loop when we encounter things (or people) that simply don't work that way.

A Pervasive Onslaught of News and Messages

The expedited advancement of technology has created a world where information and messages are constantly coming at us. From text messages to emails, news to advertising—not to mention social media and the internet in our pockets to look up anything at any time—we are inundated with a constant stream of information from across the globe. This new world assaults our attention. No longer do we have to wait for entertainment until we get home from work and plop down in front of the television; no longer does our news come to us in the form of a newspaper read over breakfast or an evening broadcast at a specific hour. Everything is instantly available, right in the palm of our hands. We can't drive down the road without seeing ads or even shop for groceries without our attention being diverted by the advertisement on the handle of our shopping cart. There are video screens in taxis, and gas station TV keeps us entertained so that pumping gas is no longer a moment of respite. We see ads at tollbooths, on restaurant menus, on the sides of downtown buildings, and on screens in the elevators of those buildings. Blank spaces are becoming endangered as "advertisers seem determined to fill every last one of them," *The New York Times* reported.

"Supermarket eggs have been stamped with the names of CBS television shows. Subway turnstiles bear messages from Geico auto insurance. Chinese food cartons promote Continental Airlines. US Airways is selling ads on motion sickness bags. And the trays used in airport security lines have been hawking Rolexes."[15]

It's *invasive*—but this is just the beginning. One trend in advertising included releasing *artificial aromas*, leading to several complaints after "Got Milk?" billboards at bus stops in San Francisco began emitting the smell of chocolate chip cookies. It's not just enough to see an ad for a product anymore; we are literally being forced to *smell* it. The crazy part is this ad campaign took place in 2007—not 2017—more than a decade ago. In the end, the city asked the California Milk Processing Board to turn off the smell.[16] Imagine being in that conversation. "Your bus stop ads smell like cookies, and people don't like it. We're going to need you to turn off the smell."

In 2012, Dunkin Donuts took it up a notch in South Korea by equipping buses with "Flavor Radio." This technology released the smell of Dunkin's coffee into the air when the company's ads played over the bus speakers, forcing the smell of coffee into the nostrils of 350,000 daily commuters, which resulted in a 29 percent increase in coffee sales, including a 16 percent spike in customers at stores located by bus stops.[17]

A market research firm estimated that an individual living in a city in 1977 saw up to two thousand ads each day. By 2007, that number had grown to five thousand, and 50 percent of individuals surveyed said they thought advertising was out of control.[18] This was well over a decade ago.

The justification for this rampant increase in advertising was expressed in *The New York Times* article aptly titled "Anywhere the Eye Can See, It's Likely to See an Ad": "Marketers used to try their hardest to reach people at home, when they were watching TV or reading newspapers or magazines. But consumers' viewing and reading habits are so scattershot now that many advertisers say the best way to reach time-pressed consumers is to try to catch their eye at literally every turn."[19]

"We never know where the consumer is going to be at any point in time, so we have to find a way to be everywhere," said Linda Kaplan Thaler, an executive at a New York ad agency.[20]

"What all marketers are dealing with is an absolute sensory overload," another marketing executive stated.[21] It should be noted that in her mind, the advertising agencies—not those who are dealing with sensory overload—are portrayed as the victims.

What is the result of all this sensory overload? While there are many side effects, one of the most notable is people today are much more easily bored than those who lived in years past. We don't know what to do with dead space. When we've driving down the road, we need music playing. Many states need laws and the threat of a fine to get us to put down our phones and just drive. We're all guilty of these things.

Could this be a contributing factor to why nearly twice as many teens are being diagnosed with ADHD today compared with twenty years ago?[22] It's not so much that humans are more easily distracted these days; we just have *more* things to distract us.

Add to these outside forces the reality that cell phones and texting have made most of us constantly available. Anyone can text you at any point throughout the day (or night). It's becoming perfectly normal to fire off quick messages asking people to do something for you *while they're at work*.

If we are always moving through life at breakneck speed, bouncing from one thing to the next, we will have no space for margin in our lives, no space for our brains to reset. We move from one thought to the next, and it becomes more and more difficult to focus. It can sometimes take longer to accomplish rather simple tasks because we have so much on our minds. It's not just what happened to us throughout the day but what happened in the lives of others that we learned about through the news or social media. We were not designed to bear such a weight, and this is especially true of Gen Zers, who are consistently exposed to the heartache of the world from a young age, which can eventually lead to empathy fatigue.

We need to go back a bit further in time now, because these changes started before the perfect storm began.

In the summer of 1980, a man by the name of Ted Turner launched the Cable News Network. better known as CNN, it was the first channel to offer 24/7 news coverage. Before this point, most news was confined to time slots of less than half an hour, once around dinner time and again before bed. But

Ted had an audacious idea, and people told him it would never work, that there would never be enough news to fill so many time slots.

What happened next was no surprise. Stories were stretched or repeated to fill the time slots; the talking heads began to make news out of incidents that previously wouldn't have been news—or would have only been mentioned in passing in the 70s.

Today, cable and satellite televisions packages offer several round-the-clock news options, including CNN's archrival, Fox News, which was launched in 1996. This radically altered the way news was brought into our lives, long before the internet and social media became commonplace.

No one had malicious intent per se or even intended to do this at all, yet a sort of monster was inadvertently created that the average person would now have a difficult time escaping without going off the grid.

News and the numerous opinion derivatives practically stalk us. News isn't just rolled up and tossed on your driveway before dawn or something that comes on in the evening while you're fixing dinner. It is constant. It begins the moment you wake up in the morning, follows you throughout the day, and is waiting before your head hits the pillow. It spills over into offline life as well. People ask, "Did you hear about this? What do you think of that? I can't believe this happened."

It often feels as if we can't escape it. Just like the invasive advertisements, news follows us constantly, and our desire to stay well-informed has a way of edging out our desire to remain sane. You can't avoid it if you try. You have all these messages coming at you constantly, making it difficult to focus on the task at hand—whether it's a project at work or something you love or simply spending time with your family after a long day at work. These messages are often presented in such a compelling way that ordinary, every day, real life has trouble competing. We must remember that Gen Z does not remember the simpler times many of us grew up in. They don't even have a grid for that kind of life because they have grown up in a world that has not existed before.

— — —

The second half of this element of the perfect storm is mean-world syndrome. The news and media we are exposed to doesn't just cause information overload; it affects us on a much deeper level and can increase anxiety and cynicism to an unhealthy degree.

Mean-world syndrome is a hypothesis coined by Dr. George Gerbner in the 1970s[23] after pioneering a groundbreaking analysis on how television influenced one's attitude and the way they viewed the world. In essence, mean-world syndrome is a cognitive bias that causes people to perceive the world as more dangerous than it actually is.

We can see this in thinking that if we set foot in a certain part of town, we will be the victim of a crime. However, data may actually show this area of town is improving, and we are actually more at risk in places we already frequent that feel safer because they are familiar. It can also be seen after a major crisis, like a shooting at a movie theater in Colorado that causes our anxiety to rise the next time we go to a movie in New Jersey. We think because it happened there, it will happen here as well, and although it was an isolated incident, the media coverage can lead us to believe it is commonplace and could happen anytime, anywhere. There is a level of truth to this, but statistics show that while mass shootings are increasing, they really aren't that common. We put ourselves much more at risk through everyday actions, such as driving, yet these things do not feel as threatening.

Mean-world syndrome may affect us in more subtle ways as well. We may not feel a rise of anxiety as we walk into the movie theater, but we may look around the room and take note of where all the exits are, a behavior we didn't exhibit before being exposed to the violent and tragic event on the news. At one time, we could choose to just not watch the news; it was relatively easy to tune out. Now it's in the palm of our hands, and we can log on to Facebook and read what everyone thinks about it. We may see someone we respect panicking, which could cause us to panic ourselves, even if data suggests the panic is unwarranted.

Gerbner's Cultural Indicators Project created a database of over three thousand television programs and thirty-five thousand television characters while documenting trends in the types of content that was being produced for viewers and how this content affected the way they viewed the world.[24] This data would then be used to evaluate Gerbner's cultivation theory, which claimed that prolonged exposure to certain types of media cultivates one's perception of reality through both images and ideological methods viewed on television. In essence, the more time people spend engaging in the world created by television, the more likely they are to believe that social reality aligns with that which they have seen portrayed. This also changes the way one reacts to world events, proposed laws, and so much more. Our picture of reality changes when we look through more than one lens (not just our own), and this can be positive or negative, depending on the context.

In essence, world news and technology, which makes it more readily available, sets the stage for *all* of us to live in irrational fear. You may think, *This isn't me. I don't buy into this stuff,* but I would argue that media has created at least one, if not multiple, irrational fears in every single one of us. One of the biggest impacts of news is the fear it creates and that it stays in your subconscious all day, regardless of what you are doing. This is the second part of the perfect storm.

Prior to the pandemic, we were living in one of the safest, healthiest, and wealthiest times in recorded history. Yet I would say that we have never been more fearful.

In 1800, the global child mortality rate was over 40 percent, meaning nearly half of children died before reaching the age of five. By 1960, that number had fallen by more than half to 18.5 percent, and by 2015, it was just over 4 percent. This is taking into account the *entire* world population; surely, the rate is significantly lower in developed countries.

GLOBAL CHILD MORTALITY RATE

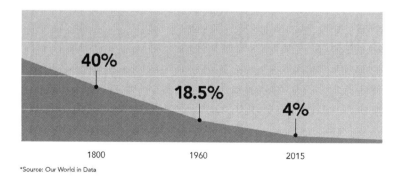

40%

18.5%

4%

1800   1960   2015

*Source: Our World in Data

In 1800, the average global life expectancy rate was less than 29 years. If you lived to the age of thirty, you had beat the odds. The United States fared slightly better with a life expectancy of thirty-five years. By 1950, the life expectancy in the United States had reached sixty-eight years, and the global life expectancy was an average of just forty-six years. By 2015, this disparity had all but vanished, with a US life expectancy of seventy-nine years and an average global life expectancy of seventy-one years. Not only are children more likely to survive into adulthood, they are living significantly longer than they did in times past.

GLOBAL LIFE EXPECTANCY

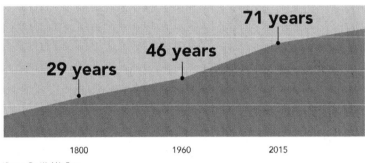

*Source: Our World in Data

Of course, quality of life must also be factored into the equation when considering whether or not we are living in the best time in history. The same researchers who compiled data on child mortality and life expectancy also took a look at the percentage of the world population living in extreme poverty. For this study, "extreme poverty" was defined as living on less than $1.90 per day. This international dollar rate was adjusted for price differences between different countries as well as inflation.

In 1820, a whopping 89.15 percent of the world's population was living in extreme poverty with just 10.85 percent of the world living above the poverty line. By 1910, conditions had improved slightly, with 74 percent of the world living in extreme poverty, which is still the vast majority. Imagine a world where three out of every four people experience extreme poverty. Quite frankly, it's a bit depressing to think about.

In 1950, 63.35 percent of the world was still living in extreme poverty. Conditions had been improving continually over the last 130 years, but after this point, global poverty would begin to be eradicated at an accelerated rate. Finally, in 1970, a tipping point was reached with 52.15 percent of the world above the poverty line. By the year 2015, a significant impact had been made with 90.02 percent of the world above the poverty line and just 9.98 percent of the world living in extreme poverty. We still have much ground to gain here, as one in every ten people living in extreme poverty is still significant; however, the data not only tells us that we are living at the best time in human history but that conditions have improved the most in our modern, digital age as technology advances at an exponential rate. Once again, these numbers are an average of the entire world, and developed countries are faring far better.

GLOBAL POPULATION LIVING IN EXTREME POVERTY

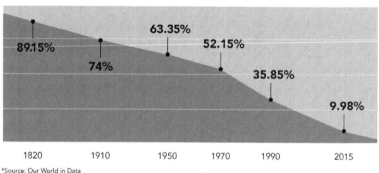

*Source: Our World in Data

Now, let's look at the next metric: literacy. In 1800, just over 12 percent of the world's population was literate. One hundred years later, things had not improved much. In 1900, just 21.4 percent of the world was literate, and 78.6 percent was illiterate. A tipping point was reached sometime between 1940 and 1950 in spite of a world war taking place. By 1950, 56 percent of the world's population was literate. In 1980, 70 percent of the world was literate, and by 2015, more than 86 percent of the world population had achieved literacy.

LITERACY OF GLOBAL POPULATION

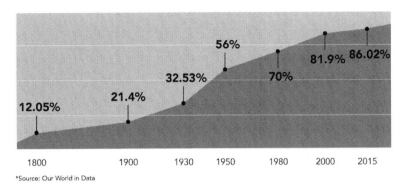

*Source: Our World in Data

Finally, we will take a look at basic education. In 1820, 83 percent had not attained any level of education. This metric progressively improved over the next two hundred years with the most exponential changes occurring from 1960 to 2000. By 2019, the statistic had been essentially inverted: 86 percent of the world's population have a basic education, and just 14 percent have no education at all.

BASIC EDUCATION

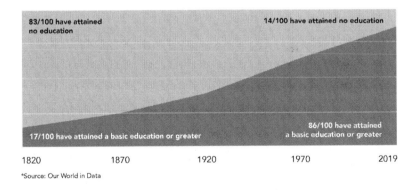

*Source: Our World in Data

Looking at these metrics tells me that the world has gradually been getting better over the last two hundred years, and these changes have accelerated dramatically in the last one hundred and even fifty years. While turning on the news or scrolling through social media could lead us to believe that things are awful (the worst they've ever been), the data suggests otherwise, and this data gives us a new lens to see where we are currently in the course of human history.

The same researcher who compiled this data (a Millennial from Germany named Max Roser) also conducted a survey that revealed the vast majority of people do not recognize the world is changing; they have not yet been given this new lens. This 2015 study found more than 9 out of 10 people do not think the world is getting better in time,[25] but this narrative does not fit with empirical evidence.

Roser stated, "The media does not tell us how the world is changing, it tells us what in the world goes wrong. One reason why the media focuses on things that go wrong is that the media focuses on single events and single events are often bad. Look at the news: plane crashes, terrorism attacks, natural disasters."[26]

Because our newsfeeds are often filled with these negative events, we might think things are worse than they are, leading us to develop irrational fears. The perfect storm has instilled these irrational fears in all of us, even those who "don't watch the news." It's inevitable, no matter how intentional we are to mitigate it. To continue Roser's quote: "Positive developments, on the other hand, often happen very slowly, and never make the headlines."[27]

If we do nothing, we will continue to think the world is worse than it is because negative events happen quickly and without warning and receive widespread coverage—even though these events are happening in a world that is progressively improving year after year. This is why we need a new lens. Only when we change our lens can we see our fears in proper perspective. It's not that we ignore them but that we bring balance and perspective. We don't have to stick our fingers in our ears and pretend nothing bad ever happens, but we should recognize not only the negative headlines but the positive developments—even when the change we desire is slow and gradual.

> You won't be able to change your behavior until you have a new perspective.

Seeing through a new lens is an ongoing process. It's not "one and done" but something we must continually do if we want to see clearly and reverse the effects the perfect storm has had on all of us. Gaining a new perspective is crucial because you won't be able to change your behavior until you have a new perspective.

But there's even more! We now not only live in a world where media has a significant amount of access into our lives; we choose to put ourselves out there through social media, which opens the door even wider to an onslaught of news and messages that are changing the way we think and live.

The Rewiring of our Brains through Social Media

Emojis are the perfect example of the cultural revolution brought on by smart phones and social media. While there is some debate about the nuanced emotions certain emojis seek to convey, they are generally universally understood. You may not be able to speak someone's language, but you can communicate in emojis that have the same meanings regardless of linguistic differences.

Now, Facebook and Apple have made it easier than ever to respond to messages and texts. You can simply "like" or "love" texts and get your point across without typing a single word. Whether this is good or bad, it is the way of the future and is changing the way we communicate. However, this facet of the perfect storm is not about the shortening of "I'm laughing at your comment" to "lol" to the "haha" reaction one can use while texting on an iPhone. That is just the tip of the iceberg on how our brains have been rewired through social media.

In the last section, we talked about how we are constantly bombarded with advertisements on various messaging channels. However, I think news is often worse than advertisements. It is relatively easy to tune out an ad if we are not interested, and we can even engage with the ad without being moved to action. The advertisers, of course, want us to take action and purchase their products, and a memorable ad does have a way of getting in our heads, but I could watch a really witty or moving Jeep commercial, talk about it with my friends, and never actually drive a Jeep. I enjoyed it, but it didn't alter the way I lived.

The news, however, delivered by social media, is much more subtle. Since social media is always on—even more than the cable networks of the 1980s and 1990s—it has accelerated the spread of news and lowered the bar as to what qualifies as news. This isn't necessarily bad in itself, but so much of it has become about picking a side, and a newfound peer pressure can pit friends, neighbors, and even family members against each other. A typical conversation might go like this: "What's your opinion on this? Oh, really, that's what you believe? Well, that's different from my opinion, and I believe that people who hold your opinion are heartless and don't care about (fill in the blank), and so I can't be friends with you."

I've watched family members cut off other family members because they voted differently or held a different viewpoint on a certain subject. And I'm not trying to say these topics don't matter but that we've created a new kind of social pressure where, at times, not choosing a side (perhaps genuinely because you can't support any of them) is just as bad as choosing the wrong side. I'm not just talking about politics; it goes so much deeper than that, and it has rewired our brains, created new anxieties and fears, and even led to actual medical diagnoses for many.

Perhaps you saw someone you care about post their strongly worded and deeply rooted opinion on a certain topic. You realize they hold a very different viewpoint than you do, which can cause you to walk on eggshells around them because you are afraid of how they will respond when they find out you see the issue differently than they do. This fear can move offline and cause us to avoid people who would otherwise be very close friends we would share everything with. Twenty years ago, these conversations probably wouldn't be as emotionally charged because they would happen in person. We wouldn't casually see someone's deeply held beliefs while scrolling through an app; we wouldn't have all the time alone to think about what they believe and have conversations with them in our heads and work ourselves up about it to the point where our anxiety levels may be so high when we actually speak to the person that we feel the need to defend our viewpoint, and the conversation becomes heated much more quickly. It's no longer, "Oh, you have a different opinion than me. I didn't realize that. Let's discuss this more." We've already seen the opinion projected online in a one-way manner without much room for dialogue, and we've had time to assign meaning to their opinion. Based on this, we decide what type of person they are. Even if we have a lot of history with them, this newfound revelation can quickly shift if it is not followed with real, face-to-face dialogue. It's much more difficult to get mad at someone who is sitting across from you than it is to get mad at a screen.

Let's rewind a few decades to a world before social media. We had the internet, but it was still young. High-speed internet was not commonplace, and not as much information was available online as there is today. Back then, sales teams were more likely to go door-to-door. Now, they would probably use tracking cookies to follow us around the internet and show us ads for items we were just looking at, even after we've moved on to something else. Our primary sources of news were through the TV, newspaper, or at the water cooler. Even breaking news did not break nearly as quickly. If the president said or did something that people didn't like, coworkers might discuss it the next day, not within the hour because someone received an alert or saw a headline on social media.

Beyond this, news was largely confined to the immediate community. If you lived in, say, Cleveland, your news mostly consisted of events that had taken place in northeast Ohio. Sure, you heard about national and global events, but if someone said or did the wrong thing in San Diego, you probably would not hear about it. But that's changed: now you hear about these events almost instantaneously. When someone said or did some outrageous, shocking thing, it's caught on tape.

This, of course, started with 24/7 news coverage, perhaps even before that. It's certainly been true about celebrities or politicians for as long as anyone can remember. But now, ordinary people face the same scrutiny. I've seen videos of ordinary people who did something wrong or upset someone. A person pulled out their phone and began filming them to let the world know what they had done, and word quickly spread. Often, the person is identified by name, and other details about them come to light—such as where they live or work—in a practice known as "doxing."

I don't want to get into the weeds here and discuss the ethics of this practice; it's just important to understand that this happens in the world we live in, and some people do not think twice about it. They share the footage they've captured, which sometimes results in unintended consequences.

They may not necessarily be trying to maliciously ruin someone's life (though this could inadvertently happen); they may have just gotten caught up in the moment when someone wronged them and used the device in their pocket to fight back.

Here's the point: When these situations spread like wildfire across the internet, when they are discussed in online forums and on social media, we might face a bit of social pressure to have an opinion, whereas not long ago, the local community—not the entire world—would have judged these situations.

> Some things are not good or bad— it just is. We must adapt and learn to deal with these new realities.

Clearly, there are both downsides and merit to this. The pressure of the world watching can be positive if it brings about change and if poor behavior stops. However, we also see a negative side effect. It may seem crazy, but I would say it is not a stretch to say we are now all expected to play the role of judges and juries— watching video clips or reading articles and rendering a verdict whether on social media or within our social circle on who was right and who was wrong. We're on jury duty every day of our lives. Again, I am not saying this is totally wrong—as I like to say about so many scenarios we find ourselves in today: "It's not good or bad—it just is!" But we must recognize that it is happening so we can determine what we will do to adapt to this new world and determine how we will respond. Another downside is that our circles of concern have radically enlarged in recent times, which can lead to anxiety and empathy fatigue.

So much was going on in each of our lives *before* the perfect storm hit us. Regardless of the phase of life or our careers, we all have multiple things vying for our attention at any given moment, and we are all trying to find the balance between our work, home, and social lives. Now we add to this how the expedited advancement of technology has made us more connected and easier to reach (which is both good and bad), opening us up to a constant onslaught of news and messages. On top of that, social media has rewired our brains and changed our expectations to desire answers now, and a lack of parents and leaders who are equipped to meet this moment has created a perfect storm of epic proportions.

It would be one thing if those who have gone before us—or even our peers—had walked this path before and had answers for us, but all this is so new and happening so fast that most of us are unaware that it's even happening. We're just hit with the resulting negative emotions (such as empathy fatigue), and we don't know what to do with them. Yes, Gen Z has figured out ways to cope with this world, but much of this is in their subconscious. It's not an intentional engagement to combat the issues of our day as many of us haven't even been able to define what these issues are until very recently.

A few years ago, after a mass shooting at a high school, a friend responded to it. There have been so many of these lately that I don't recall which one it was, but his words stuck with me. "I don't care," he told me. "And what I mean by that is I don't have the capacity to care. I *should* care. I *want to* care. The last few times that [a school shooting] happened, I stopped working. I cried. I thought of the families, the kids, the first responders, running in to save the day. But this time, the only thought in my mind was, 'Oh, another one,' and I went right back to what I was doing. My reaction surprised me, and I feel bad that I don't feel bad."

My friend shared his thoughts on Facebook and was both surprised and relieved to find that many others felt the same way he did. To be clear, it's not that no one cared about a tragedy. It's just that the tragedy was not the first of its kind. Other similar tragedies had happened in a rather short window of time, all involving people they didn't know personally in a place they had not previously heard of.

My friend and his friends were struggling with empathy fatigue. It's not that they didn't care; they didn't have the *capacity* to care because their minds were burdened by so many other things. Of course, these events matter and are serious, but because our minds are filled with so many messages and inconsequential details we tend to think are more important than they actually are (the "he said this; can you believe it? What's your opinion?" phenomenon), we often have no capacity to think about and care about what actually matters because our circles of concern have become too big. We must figure out how to pare them down into what matters most to us and focus on that. This doesn't mean we are indifferent or heartless when disaster strikes but that we now have space to actually process—and to ultimately let go of it if it is not within our circle of concern.

Social media also creates a new kind of comparison that can be quite toxic. In the past, you might have been jealous if your neighbor got a new car or a boat, but now we have a glimpse into what *everyone* is doing, what they just purchased, where they're going on vacation, the college their kids got into, and the list goes on and on. You don't have to wait until your ten-year high school reunion to find out how your nemesis turned out because you've probably been following their life online for the last ten years, seeing everything great that has happened to them in real time. After all, people rarely post their bad days or worst flaws for the world to see.

Seeing the highlight reels of our friends is where the toxic thoughts can come in, the thought that our life is somehow not as exciting as theirs or we don't measure up to others. This is especially since we usually scroll through social media when we're bored, and we see how much fun everyone else is having. Of course, we forget that they probably waited for a moment when they were bored to post photos. This can compound our negative feelings—not only is someone else enjoying life we aren't experiencing, but we are wasting our time while everyone else is out having fun. What is even worse is seeing someone in your friend group post a photo with your other friend(s). We think, *Why are they hanging out without me?* We wonder why we weren't invited and often jump to extreme conclusions like, *They must not like me.* Perhaps we weren't included for a specific reason, but rationale is often lost here as our minds fast track to the worst possible scenario. Speaking of worst-case scenarios, social media also opens the door to cyber bullying 24/7. We even see mild forms of this when it comes to Facebook debates on hot-button issues—and even if you don't post about controversial topics, you still might feel anxious about not saying the right thing when it comes to sensitive issues or worry that your silence will be construed as an opinion in itself.

We often find ourselves paralyzed by fear of missing out (FOMO)—not just missing out on invitations to hang out with our friends but missing out on experiences. We've seen so many people post about visiting a particular place, and we want to visit there as well, but we're busy with work or perhaps don't have the finances to travel. We think, *When will I get to go?* We see another person went, which only makes it worse. It's the fear of being left out and of not having enough time to do what you love or want to do all rolled into one.

There is no margin in our lives. We don't know how to be bored anymore. When we have a moment of downtime, we pick up our phones and start scrolling. We don't know how to just be. Our patience has worn thin. When something isn't ready the moment we need it, we are shocked. Waiting five minutes feels like eternity. Even though we have a phone to entertain us, it's also changing our expectations and teaching us to be more anxious and easily frustrated when situations don't turn out like we expect them to.

I will also admit that not all of this is bad. Social media includes many positive aspects, and technology has helped us create new life hacks that make our lives or jobs easier.

The main point to recognize here is that social media has become the primary form of communication for the next generations. Some of it is good; some of it is bad, but that is not the point: it doesn't matter whether it's good or bad—it just is. It's the way of the future when it comes to communication, and so rather than trying to keep young people off it, we need to teach them to be aware of these pitfalls and use social media well as the powerful tool that it is.

A Lack of Parenting and Leadership for this Moment

The final component of the perfect storm is perhaps the simplest yet the most profound. In a world where technology is rapidly advancing, where we are constantly assaulted by news and messages, and where our brains have been rewired by social media, we need people who will come alongside us and help us navigate this new world. We need parents who will guide their children and leaders and who will help develop those under them to become the best versions of themselves, not just cogs in a machine that solely exist to perform a certain task.

Unfortunately, I have seen a vacuum of both parenting and leadership— what Bruce Tulgan calls "an epidemic of under-management"[28]—as we face a critical moment in history. Previous generations were over-managed, and many of them have swung the pendulum in the other direction when it comes to their own kids. There is no management, and the kids are left alone (in their bedrooms, not necessarily at home) as the perfect storm rages all around them, and they are not immune. Perhaps parents are not aware that a perfect storm is afoot as they are caught up in the hectic pace of the modern world as well. This doesn't inherently mean they are negligent parents, as many factors are at play. Some parents are still trying to sort life out for themselves and are not equipped to help their children do this. Others are caught up in their careers or otherwise absent. Some feel they are doing the right thing because their kids are safe at home in their bedrooms, often on screens, but they don't recognize that the screens have, in many ways, taken over their role rather than supplementing it. Because their kids are in their rooms and not out and about, parents might perceive they are safe and pay less attention to what they are doing.

> I have seen a vacuum of both parenting and leadership—what Bruce Tulgan calls "an epidemic of under-management"—as we face a critical moment in history.

Then, others overparent and, despite their attempts, have actually become irrelevant to their children, who have filtered out Mom and Dad and instead prefer to be mentored by their peers. Some would say this has always been the case, that peer-pressure is not new, but we are now seeing it at a whole new level— coupled with the rejection of previous generations. We don't have many parents today who understand how to enter their children's worlds in a way that isn't overbearing or micromanaging, in a way that actually works— which, again, is one of the reasons I am writing this book.

In the workspace, many managers do not manage. This is not due to technology, though, interestingly enough, technology has apparently made some managers lazy. They fail to set goals with their team and follow up, and many do not even think about what they need to do to lead their teams well. Others see that everyone is in the office and that they seem productive. Much like the kids in their rooms, managers can easily overlook younger workers who perhaps need more coaching. When leaders do step up and lead, the last few decades have produced more "sage on stage" type of leaders rather than what Gen Z really needs: a guide by their side who will help them cope with this new world that is creating a different kind of human. Once again, they will not lead in an overbearing or micromanaging sort of way but in a way that allows them to offer value to the next generation in a manner that is well received.

> The perfect storm has left Gen Z particularly underdeveloped in communication, problem-solving, perseverance, and gratitude.

Managers and leaders must recognize that Gen Z is coming into the workplace as a product of this storm that has shaped them in new ways, and one of the glaring differences between them and previous generations is a serious deficit of soft skills among Gen Z. This is not merely an outside criticism but a reality that many of them are painfully aware of. They are particularly in short supply and practice when it comes to communication, problem-solving, perseverance, and gratitude. What a marvelous opportunity to help Gen Z progress in these areas, especially if they see the need but aren't necessarily aware of the storm that has created it.

Our world today needs parents and leaders who will neither overparent nor underparent but who are willing to learn new skills and sharpen old ones in order to fine-tune their approach to deliberately connect with Gen Z and the generations that will follow them. When we find this sweet spot, we can help them reconcile with the perfect storm and navigate their way through it.

A friend of mine serves as a great example. I recently convinced him to learn how to play a computer game that a number of kids—including his—were playing. He accepted the challenge and dove in. He practiced the game, read blogs, and soon played with his son and a group of his son's friends. Afterward, he asked his son for feedback on a specific move, and they spent an hour practicing together as his son coached him.

The next time they played, the son's friends noticed his dad's progress and commented on it.

"Yeah," the son nonchalantly replied, "I've taken him under my wing and am coaching him."

This "reverse mentoring" changed their relationship as father and son—for the better. When my friend needed to talk with his son about changing a behavior or attitude, he used gaming analogies to frame the conversation, taking the elements of teamwork that his son was familiar with from gaming with his friends and applying them to other scenarios. He soon found numerous crossovers, and he could address almost any negative behavior or attitude he saw in his son by using gaming as a framework.

The results were spectacular, and this is a terrific example of someone who took the time to figure out how to speak alien—how to learn the language of a generation and connect with them in a new way. This dad is now a sort of local hero among his son's friends, and he has more influence in their lives than he ever imagined was possible—all because he made the choice to enter their world rather than insisting they adapt to his.

Takeaway

The perfect storm, as I call it, is the foundation for this book. You do not need to do an in-depth study of the fourth Industrial Revolution or how technology, messaging, and social media are changing our worlds. We are already immersed in this every day, and we have experienced how a range of new technologies have fused the physical, digital, and biological worlds, impacting all disciplines, economies, and industries, and even challenging ideas about what it means to be human.

What you must understand to grasp my thesis is *how* all these changes affect the way Gen Z lives and interacts with one another, with other generations, and with the world around them.

Whether it's a smartphone or some sort of wearable technology, new tools have changed the way we engage and interact with one another and with the world we live in. As a result, young people are growing up differently today than at any other point in history; it is not too much of a stretch to say we are growing aliens.

There are all sorts of external pressures in today's world that you and I did not grow up with, but Gen Z has never lived without these pressures. This has wired them differently, and when we understand this, we will have a new lens that becomes the foundation to understanding them and seeing them differently—and dare I say, seeing them correctly. This will be pivotal in determining how we think about business, leadership, talent acquisition, employee development and retention, marketing, and even how we parent our own children.

TRUTH #2
Gen Z Is Growing Up in a World that Has Never Existed Before

As early as 1894, a newspaper in California used the term "the tipping point."[1] However, it wasn't until the late 1950s that University of Chicago professor Morton Grodzins coined the term in relation to human behavior, long before Malcolm Gladwell made the theory widespread with his 2000 book.

A tipping point occurs when a group of people, or a vast majority of a group's members, dramatically changes its behavior and adopts a new practice that was previously foreign to the group. Scientists have found that when a mere 10 percent of a group adapts a core belief, this belief will ultimately be adopted by the vast majority of the group.[2] This is a significant difference from Gladwell's theory, dubbed "the Law of the Few," which stated 20 percent of a group needed to adopt a core belief before the tipping point would tip.[3] I believe Gladwell was correct when he said that although you only need one fifth of a group to buy in before you reach the critical tipping point, certain *types* of people must buy in. This is what he means by the Law of the Few. It's not just any few people but a certain type of people who are connected in all the right ways to the rest of the populace. Or as we would call them today, *influencers*.

Until the tipping point tips, we find ourselves in this transition space. Whether it's 10 percent or 20 percent is really irrelevant; what is relevant is that a tipping point is coming. It's inevitable, and once we reach that point, there will be no turning back. Quite literally, a point will come for some organizations where the options will be "adapt or die." Personally, I prefer to adapt now, to be an early adopter, because I take great joy in engaging in the process rather than resisting it. This, I believe, is the law of future-proofing.

--- --- ---

Imagine you are living back in the 1800s, and electricity has just been invented. Sure, it's not perfect, but it's objectively better than what you had before. It would seem a bit ridiculous, wouldn't it, for you to say, "You know, this electricity is great for some people, but I prefer to sit in the dark." (Of course, you wouldn't really be sitting in the dark; you would have a kerosene or gas lantern.) This would actually work for you for a while. The early adopters, early majority, and late majority would get their electric lights, but there would still be places for laggards like yourself to buy your kerosene lights and whatever you need to operate them. I mean, even today, in 2020, kerosene is still available to purchase. However, while this is technically still an option, you don't really see anyone using it to light their home. A few might be out there; perhaps five, ten, or a hundred people still use kerosene lamps as their primary source of light, but these individuals are extremely few and far between.

The fact of the matter is, even those who were most resistant to change eventually embraced the electric light. We don't even think about it now—whether a light is electric or kerosene—they are all virtually electric, and we don't know the difference.

This is what is taking place today as well as with many things. We are in the process of transitioning from one way of doing things to another, and while some say, "I'll never do things that way!" they, too, will find themselves using electricity in short order, so we might as well all embrace it and experience the benefits of it right now, rather than constantly lagging behind and having to play catch up. Certainly this is true of anyone who works in a modern workspace where Gen Z is beginning to establish themselves and bringing change with them.

One of the ways we see these changes at work is in the transportation space with the cars we drive. Our vehicles used to contain cassette players, then CD players (and there was an overlap where some cars contained both), then AUX cables that connected to your phone and could access all of its music. Today, however, cars are becoming more and more integrated with our phones, connecting to them wirelessly through Bluetooth.

I recently rented a vehicle and was surprised to find no built-in GPS or CD player. Well, to be honest, I really wasn't surprised. I can't remember the last time I used my car's CD player and didn't miss it. And what is the point of putting a costly GPS that will become obsolete in a few years into a vehicle when you have the latest GPS technology via your phone? Actually, nothing was built into the vehicle to play music other than the radio. Instead, you plugged your phone into the car via USB. Forget banning cell phones while operating cars—just make the phones work with the cars. When I plugged my phone into my rental, not only did I have instant access to all my music but when I used the maps app on my phone, it showed up on the vehicle's built-in touchscreen, and I could control it by using buttons on the steering wheel. If I needed to make a call or send a text while driving, I could safely do so through voice commands. I've had this technology in my vehicle for some time, but I have only recently been able to plug my phone into *any* vehicle, and everything automatically syncs to make it my vehicle in seconds.

New technology in cars in and of itself is not revolutionary. The feeling of novelty I experienced with my rental car isn't any different than when cassette players first appeared in cars that previously only had radios. In fact, I would even say that was more revolutionary because it took us from having to listen to whatever happened to be playing on the radio station to being able to choose our own music. (You could change the station but had no control over what was being played.) We've simply added more options over the past decade. First, we connected our phones to our cars with AUX cords and could listen to all the music on our phone. Now, our phones connect to the car wirelessly, and we can stream any song ever created without first curating it onto our phone by paying to download the song. We now have instant access to everything—as long as we have an internet signal on our phones, which is the default for most of us unless we are in the mountains or some other remote location. And we are already moving toward cars that drive themselves.

That might have stopped you in your tracks. *Wait a minute, Steve— you're taking us from cars that sync with our phones to cars that drive themselves?*

Absolutely, because this is the next evolution. It's not just Tesla; it's the way of the future. The next big change isn't about what is in the car but about the way the car works. This technology has already been created; it's already here. We already have elements of autonomous cars in the cars we are driving right now with features like lane assist, blind spot monitors, backup cameras, and cars that can parallel park themselves.

This technology is not more widespread with more autonomous cars because it has been intentionally slowed down. Some of this is because the general public is afraid of change. They think self-driving cars aren't safe and might ask, "Didn't you hear the story about the person who got killed by one?" Or they simply don't want to let go of what they have now and think, *It's not broke. It works for us. Why change it?* The interesting thing about this fear is that it ignores the fact that humans cause thousands of accidents every day. How many accidents have there been with self-driving cars?

I was curious, so I did some research and found that between 2014 and 2017, self-driving cars were involved in a total of thirty-four accidents in California, where thirty-six companies had permits to test these vehicles, typically with a human driver behind the wheel.[4] What is even more interesting about this data is the vast majority of these accidents are the result of people rear-ending the self-driving car because it refuses to run a red light.[5]

As one article reported, "The self-driving cars were at fault in only four incidents, and in autonomous mode in only one of those four. In six out of the ten incidents in which the cars were in manual mode (with human drivers in control) at the time of the collision, the cars were previously in autonomous mode until drivers took over for safety reasons."[6]

There you have it: Self-driving cars were involved in thirty-four accidents in California over a three-year period, but they were only at fault in four of these incidents and only being powered by a computer at the time of the crash on a lone occasion. That's the number of self-driving car accidents: one.

Compare that to the number of overall car accidents in the United States: more than six million,[7] which claim the lives of roughly forty thousand drivers, passengers, and pedestrians each year.[8] What's worse is the number of accidents seems to increase year after year. In 2011, there were only 5.338 million car accidents in the United States, which is still awful, but the number increased every single year through 2016, when it reached a peak of 7.277 million.[9] This number fell to 6.5 million car accidents in 2017[10] but began increasing again each year in 2018 and 2019.[11] While I'm sure the number of accidents did decline in 2020 with so many people working from home instead of commuting, we've seen a sharp uptick in car accidents over the last decade.

Many factors are at play in these accidents with distraction (likely from the increased use of smartphones) and alcohol among the top contenders. However, I can tell you what is *not* a factor in these accidents: automation. Self-driving technology is not to blame for any of these accidents, but it is to blame for a few isolated incidents here and there, which unfortunately led to many people calling for the whole concept to be shut down.

> Many factors are at play in these accidents ... but the one thing that is *not* a factor is automation.

Our attempts to slow down self-driving cars will work. It will slow down the advancement of this new technology, and already has. However, the change that will ultimately come is inevitable. You can resist it, but a time will come when you go from being in the majority resisting the new to the lone holdout who is seen as archaic and out-of-touch, just as we would think someone is crazy if they rode a horse because they "don't like cars" even though this was the primary mode of transportation for most people at one point.

So why are we so resistant to new technology that, while imperfect, clearly makes us objectively safer?

I'm not talking about the nuances of how self-driving cars would work if everyone suddenly had one, but our overall attitude to the concept. Some of us think, *Wow, that's so cool. I want to drive one.* But the rest of us would rather drive our own cars. We're content with this arrangement, and it's not just that we don't care about this new technology or it doesn't interest us. No, something much deeper is at play; our baffling aversion to the new in the face of data tells us much more is at stake here. We like our cars because they make us *feel* safer, even if we actually aren't. We are scared of that which we can't control. We may not be conscious of this. Very few of us look in the mirror, and say, *You know, I just realized I'm afraid of things I can't control.* This, how-ever, doesn't make it any less true. People have been afraid of what they can't control for some time.

> The more we embrace new technology and new generations, the less "alien" they will seem.

We see this manifest in nearly every arena as our world transitions into a new era. In July 2014, Taylor Swift wrote a now-infamous essay for *The Wall Street Journal* on the future of the music industry, wherein she said, "Music is art, and art is important and rare. Important, rare things are valuable. Valuable things should be paid for. It's my opinion that music should not be free, and my prediction is that individual artists and their labels will someday decide what an album's price point is."[12]

As one commentator pointed out, in our modern world, music is not rare, and album sales were already plummeting.[13]

A few months later, when Swift's new album *1989* released, it was nota-bly missing from Spotify's music catalog. A month later, the rest of her albums were pulled from the streaming service as well, much to the dismay of her fans. She quickly justified her decision and referred to streaming as an "experiment" saying, "All I can say is that music is changing so quickly, and the landscape of the music industry itself is changing so quickly, that every-thing new, like Spotify, all feels to me a bit like a grand experiment. And I'm not willing to contribute my life's work to an experiment that I don't feel fairly compensates the writers, producers, artists, and creators of this music. And I just don't agree with perpetuating the perception that music has no value and should be free … I thought, 'I will try this; I'll see how it feels.' It didn't feel right to me."[14]

What is most interesting about this statement is the reality that most young listeners were *already* listening to her music for free. They were much more likely to listen to her songs on YouTube and "pay" by watching ads than they were to pay money to download her entire album, let alone buy a physical copy.[15] These are the ones who took the legal route. Countless others were illegally downloading her music—and other artists—for free online. Even if it paid artists less for their music than iTunes, Spotify would prove to essentially shut down the illegal download market once and for all.

It took a few years, but I think Taylor Swift finally allowed her music on Spotify because she realized this was not just an experiment; it was the future of the music industry. The way consumers listen to music was inevitable, which is why the rest of the big players were quick to offer their own streaming services. There were certainly some negative aspects to this new reality, but both the performer and the listener also reaped a lot of positive benefits. Regardless of her personal feelings, Swift realized streaming wasn't either negative or positive; it was just the future the music world was moving toward, and she needed to embrace it or get left behind to some extent. Of course, she had the benefit of being a wildly successful musician. Others had to give in to streaming much sooner if they had any hopes of continuing their careers in the music space. For lesser-known artists, not putting their songs on Spotify would be a similar career death sentence as an author not putting their book on Amazon. Sure, they lose 40 percent of their profits right out of the gate, but in today's world, if a book isn't on Amazon, it doesn't exist in the minds of most consumers and will quickly be filtered out.

What Swift eventually learned is what many companies have already learned or are in the process of learning. Sometimes, it's better to give your customers something for free in order to gain access to their lives. Once you're in, you can figure out how to monetize the relationship. This is especially true with Gen Z; they want you to build a relationship and connect with them before you try to sell them stuff. (*Anyone* can do that, but it requires more skill to build relationships with your customers when selling stuff, though important, is not the end game or at least not the *only* end game).

Aside from the concerns Swift raised when she initially resisted allowing her music to be streamed on Spotify, there is much less fear overall regarding copyright and royalties with streaming than there was with digital downloads. With streaming, the user doesn't actually own anything; they are simply paying to access it. If you paid to download a song or movie from iTunes, you can still access it ten years from now, and you don't need to maintain a subscription.

> You have to build a relationship and connect with Gen Z before you try to sell them stuff. What can you give your customers for free in order to gain access to their lives?

Interestingly enough, most users don't seem to mind the biggest consumer downside to streaming: You always have to pay. For some reason, we seem okay with this. We will keep paying indefinitely to access something as long as it holds our interest. We like streaming (access) over ownership because it satisfies our desire to have things on-demand. Many of us—not just Gen Z—have been rewired to expect this immediate access. We also like having more choices. It's all right there at our fingertips. Immediately. Even two-day shipping feels like an eternity at this point. If we get tired of one thing, we can cancel our subscription and go elsewhere. You can always have the newest new thing and let go of the older things. Your eggs aren't all in one basket. It doesn't matter if they stop making DVDs because you haven't invested hundreds or thousands of dollars in a technology that will one day become obsolete. What you subscribe to will change as times change, or you'll stop using it. Finally, you will have less physical clutter in your space, which is a big win as many seek simplified living spaces as one way to combat the constant noise of life after the fourth Industrial Revolution. Our digital space may be constantly cluttered with a barrage of messages, ads, and updates, but this doesn't mean our physical spaces have to be. For some, it's the only escape, as it's just not practical to go off the grid if you want to stay relevant to your employer.

The new era is here, and it's coming, but we must understand it is not a utopia. Researchers have noted that Gen Z is the first generation to have a lower quality of life than the generation before them[16], primarily due to rising costs of college tuition, rent, healthcare, and other essentials while salaries aren't increasing as quickly. I don't want anyone to think I am imply-ing that what we are transitioning to is perfect or that any of us (myself included) have this new world figured out. Rather, I am trying to commu-nicate that the voices that are shouting that "these kids" need to learn "how the real world works" will soon be completely irrelevant. They are actually wrong about this generation. While they are certainly not perfect, this gen-eration has many wonderful things to offer, and we can benefit greatly from their contributions.

In many ways, the changing era we live in today is similar to the Wild West. Gen Z and all of this new technology are creating a Model T, but many of us are still riding horses. We aren't really sure what is being built or what it will look like. We aren't even painting by numbers and have no idea what the picture will look like or how it will turn out. Nearly two-thirds (65 percent) of children entering junior high school in 2021 will end up working in jobs that do not currently exist.[17] We are in a confusing time of overlap, of transi-tion—what I have been calling a perfect storm—where some of the old rules that have governed our worlds and our workplaces for decades still apply. At the same time, new rules have also been introduced. There are new players in the game, and we are all still figuring out how all of this works.

Perhaps one of the best examples of this applies to phones and cars. We've had cars and phones for quite some time; neither one is new. But what has changed over the last twenty years is the *way* our phones operate. Not only that, another fundamental change is that our phones aren't attached to the wall now; they go with us. They aren't just for talking; we can send text messages on them. Forty years ago, phones and cars didn't really overlap much. You were either in a car, or you were on the phone—you certainly weren't operating both at the same time. But now we have this problem of people using phones to talk and text and see how much money is in the bank and move money from one account to another and trade stocks and check the weather and see where the best Mexican restaurant is located. This overlap has created a new problem. We definitely

> Nearly two-thirds (65 percent) of children entering junior high school in 2021 will end up working in jobs that do not currently exist.

face a danger here, and the knee-jerk reaction may be, "You know, we didn't have any problems before these darn phones. Why don't we just get rid of them?" (as though there were never any accidents before phones).

A new era is coming—and is already here in many ways—we can sidestep impulsive reactions, pausing instead to ask ourselves, *Okay, so how do we manage this? How do we make these two things work together?* We've already made a lot of progress in this space. We've passed laws that crack down on using our phones while driving, but at the same time, we've incorporated features into our cars that make them work more seamlessly with our phones with minimal distractions—such as hands-free calling and voice-to-text. We have our texts read to us through the speakers in our car that used to only be for music or perhaps listening to talk radio, and we dictate texts back that the car safely sends while we're driving down Main Street. We're in transition, and we will probably stay in transition for the foreseeable future. The two—the old and the new—are colliding but rather than retreating to the old and rejecting everything new (as if banning phones in cars outright will work), we are leaning into the awkwardness of the transition and saying, "Let's find a way to make this work, because there's something here that will enhance all our lives if we just stick with it."

We may eventually reach the point where the car helps manage the phone. So the car might steer you over to the shoulder and cut power to your engine if you insist on texting while driving. If self-driving cars are possible, this hybrid variation is certainly possible as well. Of course, this is all hypothetical, but who knows? What we do know is we have entered a new era, and this change is unstoppable.

However, those around us may not embrace this new era as quickly as we do, and we are all still collectively in transition. The greatest problem with being in transition is we often do not have the data to perform an analysis that gives us a full picture of where we are; we just know that seemingly two groups of people—those who are embracing the way of the future and those who are resisting it—are somewhat in conflict.

Incremental changes bring us from one change to another within the transition space, but not everyone recognizes these changes. Many people act as though Gen Zers are like the aliens in *District 9*—they weren't there, and then, all of a sudden, one day a whole bunch of them are flooding the streets of the city, and we have to figure out what to do with them. No! The truth is, this generation has been growing up in our homes and attending our schools for over twenty years. But some of us didn't begin to realize this was a different generation until they began to disrupt our workplaces. Still, many of us consider them to simply be Millennials, as if everyone under thirty is a Millennial, even though most Millennials are well into their thirties.

It's the same way with generations as it is with everything else. We may not notice regular, incremental changes, but we do notice the major shifts that result from the incremental changes to the point where we walk into work one day and feel as if we are surrounded by aliens—or that we ourselves are the alien.

When we update the iOS on our iPhones (my apologies to Android users, but I'm sure you'll be able to follow the analogy), we likely don't notice the hundreds or perhaps thousands of behind-the-scenes and subtle changes. We may not even notice the addition of an app or feature. The small changes can go unnoticed because they are so minor, so trivial. If we do notice them, we likely don't think about them much. However, each of these changes moves us closer and closer to a tipping point, to the iOS that is dramatically different than the one before. At first, we think, *No way; this is different! I'm not sure how I feel about this.* But then, after a while, we get used to it. The major shift becomes the new way of doing things, and it feels perfectly normal; it's only uncomfortable at first because we aren't used to it.

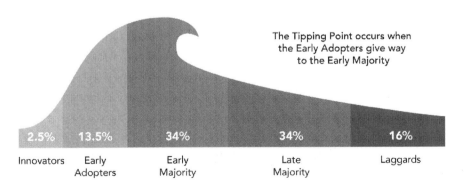

INNOVATION ADOPTION CURVE

The Tipping Point occurs when the Early Adopters give way to the Early Majority

2.5%	13.5%	34%	34%	16%
Innovators	Early Adopters	Early Majority	Late Majority	Laggards

Those who update their iOS immediately because they love the new features are the innovators. In fact, they are likely beta testers for Apple who had the new iOS before anyone else.

The early adopters are those who update immediately because they realize this will soon be the new reality. They know they must adapt, and they are probably excited about the new features but not excited enough to give them much thought or become beta testers.

The early majority are the ones who see the Apple update when it releases on Monday but wait until the weekend to update because they want to back their phone up to the cloud first. They know they must adapt, but they likely feel indifferent, perhaps even a bit apprehensive, about it.

The late majority are the ones who adapt on the back end of the tipping point. They update their iOS a few months after it releases because their apps are updating, and their phone is starting to lag behind because the core software isn't meshing well with the apps that have been redesigned to function best on the most current iOS.

The laggards are those who are recovering from their resistance to new technology. They still have the iPhone 6 while everyone else has the iPhone 12. They refuse to update their iOS until their apps literally stop functioning. "I realized I had to adapt when I could no longer do online banking from my phone," one laggard told me. "Chase stopped supporting their app on my iOS due to security and technical reasons. Capital One and Santander soon followed suit, and I couldn't access any of my accounts. That was when I gave in and updated. It wasn't because I wanted to, but because I had to. But as I began to use this new technology, I found that my fears were unfounded. I actually liked the new iOS better and wondered why I had resisted it for so long."

This conversation reminded me of a famous quote, often attributed to Henry Ford, who ignored what his customers wanted when he created the Model T: "If I had asked my customers what they wanted, they would have asked for a faster horse."

Perhaps Henry Ford recognized that he was an early adopter, and the shift from horses pulling coaches to cars that the user drove themselves was inevitable. He didn't listen to the laggards because he knew what they wanted wouldn't matter in ten years. His work was disruptive—it challenged people and made them uncomfortable—but the new era he ushered in proved to be objectively better than what existed before, and even the laggards would eventually break down and trade their horses in for cars. This is why, today, riding horses is sport or entertainment and not a primary mode of transportation.

As I write this, I would say that we are somewhere between early adopters and the early majority in terms of our adaptation to Gen Z in the workplace. While there were significantly more laggards in terms of acceptance of Millennials, the generation who created the biggest workplace disruptions, most people have come to accept that these young people exist and actually want to work, so they know they must adapt to working with them.

Those who grab hold of this message quickly might perhaps have the chance to become early adopters. Certainly, they will make it into the early majority. Pioneering in this space may be a bit messy simply because of the lack of data available. Even some of the observations I will make lack proven scientific data and any research studies because I am essentially sharing with you in real time as I observe them. However, as I have now seen them show up time and time again in members of the Gen Z cohort—even members growing up on different continents—I am confident that now is the time to act on this information because if we wait until all our proverbial ducks are in a row, it will be too late. We'll still adapt, but as laggards, we will be swept away by the competition.

The nature of your work will also determine which group you fall into on the innovation adoption curve. So in some industries, the tipping point has already appeared to have tipped while in other industries, all seems well with business as usual. Surely those who are fascinated with different generations—the behavior researchers of society—find themselves in the early cohorts. The first early adopters were likely teachers and those like me and my team, who began hiring Gen Zers while they were still in high school. Granted, many companies initially hired Gen Zers in high school for entry-level, minimum-wage jobs. However, most of these businesses are just looking for warm bodies to fill a role that virtually anyone can do.

Imagine what could happen if we intentionally hired Gen Zers to help them develop the tools they need to break into the mainstream workforce with a competitive advantage. This is what we sought to do with the summer staff we hired to help run our camps. We had roles that needed to be filled, but we were also very intentional to invest in those who filled those roles. We knew that in doing this, we were not only investing in them, but we were investing in the future of our business as we built a reputation of being a great place to work.

— — —

Now that we understand that a tipping point is coming—and is, in fact, already underway—we must ask ourselves where we are headed and what we are "tipping" into. The tipping point, in terms of Gen Z, is leading us into a new era where our world will look radically different, and nearly every area of society will be affected.

This new era will bring about a unique set of challenges, but overall, we will be better off in this new space than where we were before or even than we are now. The sooner we embrace the new era, the sooner we can leverage what Gen Z has to bring to the table for the betterment of our society as a whole. In doing this, we will also future-proof our homes, our schools, and our workplaces.

Takeaway

INNOVATION ADOPTION CURVE

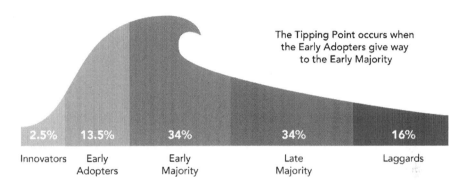

The Tipping Point occurs when the Early Adopters give way to the Early Majority

| 2.5% | 13.5% | 34% | 34% | 16% |

Innovators · Early Adopters · Early Majority · Late Majority · Laggards

Where are you when it comes to embracing the next generation? Or do you still just want a faster horse?

The tipping has already begun, but many of us have not yet shifted our mindsets and are therefore in danger of becoming irrelevant and losing our influence and ability to connect with the next generation. In the business world, this will greatly impact recruiting and retention as well as our ability to market to a new generation of consumers.

Z

TRUTH #3
Gen Z Is Energized by the Power of Technology but Suffers from Tech Fatigue

When you wake up in the morning, what is the first thing you do? If you're like me, you likely reach for your Apple iPhone. Then, you may roll out of your comfy bed, adorned with sheets and pillows from Bed Bath & Beyond. You step into the bathroom where you're greeted with tile from Home Depot and a rug you found on Wayfair. You reach for your Colgate toothpaste and place a drop on your fancy Phillips Sonicare toothbrush you bought on sale at Costco. You step into the shower where your Johnson & Johnson and Bath & Body Works products are waiting.

A few minutes later, you return to your bedroom and dress in your Express jeans, shirt from UNTUCKit, and shoes you bought online from Zappos. You head downstairs, pour a bowl of Kellogg's cereal, and reach for your iPhone again. You begin scrolling through Facebook, Instagram, Twitter, Snapchat, and any other social media sites your friends use. You may check your bank balance on your phone before heading out the door. With your phone, you adjust the thermostat, turn off the lights, lock the front door, and set your alarm system as you grab your Samsonite satchel that contains your Apple iPad and MacBook.

As you walk down the sidewalk, you take two small white objects called AirPods (also from Apple) out of your pocket and place them in your ears.

You connect wirelessly to your phone in your pocket, and listen to the latest songs Spotify curated for you while you were sleeping. As you get on the train to commute downtown, you switch over to your favorite podcast to find five new episodes. You're behind. Which do you listen to first? You make your selection and begin listening. An idea hits you, so you take your phone out of your pocket and begin taking notes in Evernote, which syncs across all your devices—your iPhone, iPad, MacBook, and the iMac desktop computer you have back at home that you didn't even interact with this morning.

On the train, you see someone reading a book, which reminds you of the book you were enjoying on your Kindle. You forgot your physical Kindle device today, but you have the Kindle app on your iPhone. You pull it out of your pocket and begin reading, but you're distracted by the full-color advertisements on the walls of the train car. The closest is eighteen inches from your face. As you exit the train, there are more ads—on buildings, buses, even the sidewalk as you're crossing the street. You pull out your phone to tune it all out, where you're met with still more ads, notifications, and a text from your significant other, who has sent you links to two different restaurants on Yelp and needs help deciding where the two of you will eat dinner. You haven't even decided where you will have lunch, but you begin looking at the options, until a notification appears at the top of the screen. It's a text from your mom, and the preview tells you it's urgent.

As you're typing a reply, a group text thread begins exploding. There's already a crisis at work, and you're still two blocks from the office. You begin walking faster, jumping back and forth between apps—deciding on dinner, working on the reply to your mom, and trying to keep up with the texts from work so you won't be behind when you walk in the door. You then realize you completely missed another text thread from the night before, which contains relevant information to the project that's due by noon. That text thread sends you to Basecamp, where you begin reviewing project files. You narrowly avoid being hit by a car as you cross the street, but you didn't even notice because you were looking at your phone. You look up to see you've almost walked past your office building. You take a hard right and open the door where a colleague immediately asks if you saw their text. *Which one?* you think. She wants an answer now. You fumble for words but manage to satisfy her with your answer. You step into the elevator and press the button for your floor, already feeling as if it's been an extremely long day. You look down at your Apple watch; it's only 8:56.

Most of you are probably not shocked by this glimpse into the first few hours of a modern American workday. In fact, you might be wondering, *Why wasn't he just reading his texts on his Apple watch instead of pulling out his phone?* Or if you're an Android user, you likely didn't make it through the paragraph above because of how many times Apple was mentioned.

We are all constantly bombarded by information that comes at us all day long from every direction. It's gotten to the point where Apple added a "do not disturb" feature to the iPhone so you can disconnect from the world for six or eight hours and actually sleep.

A few years ago, digital marketing experts estimated most Americans are exposed to anywhere from four thousand to ten thousand advertisements each day.[1] Certainly, this number has grown, but we have been exposed to high amounts of ads for some time now. This isn't unique to Gen Z, but what *is* unique to Gen Z is widespread tech fatigue—because it's not just advertisements now or an interaction with a brand. We are constantly connected to nearly all the information in existence, and this information demands our attention. It's relatively easy to ignore the ads for personal injury lawyers on bus benches (unless you need one), but it's much more difficult to ignore the ads that pop up on social media that are curated to our unique tastes and interests thanks to tracking cookies. This is why you can search for something online, close the window, open a new window, and immediately see ads for the item you were just searching for. Some would even say that third-party apps, such as Facebook and Instagram, are listening to our conversations through the microphones on our smartphones so they can curate ads based on our conversations.[2]

If this is true, it is a massive invasion of privacy, but it would not surprise me because it already happened in Europe in 2019 when more than ten million users downloaded the app for La Liga, Spain's premier professional soccer league. The purpose of the app was to provide game information and scores, but it also had a feature designed to help identify bars that were streaming the games without paying the licensing fee. The app would use

GPS to locate a user in a bar or venue that might be showing a soccer game. If it was, it would then activate the phone's microphone to listen for audio from the game. If the venue did not have the appropriate license to broadcast the game, La Liga would issue a fine. However, in the end, La Liga themselves was ordered to pay a fine for violating the privacy of their app users, and they agreed to remove the feature.[3]

We're only seeing the tip of the iceberg here—and perhaps this is part of the new era we are entering as well; so much is vying for our attention that we have shifted to scratching the surface of many subjects and going deep with only a few.

At this point, we have only discussed how advertising has changed to bombard us with many more messages today than a decade ago. It doesn't end there. Gen Z is the first generation in history to live in a constant state of change brought on by what I call "the perfect storm." Thanks to modern smartphones, we are connected to the entire world 24/7.

This shift has taken place right as this generation came of age. (Gen Z was born between 1996-2010, and the iPhone was released in late 2007 when the oldest members of this cohort were eleven.) This explains why they are the first generation affected by tech fatigue on a massive scale. All generations are subject to it, but most of us know at least one Boomer who refuses to carry a cell phone, and Gen Xers and Millennials find it easier to detach because they didn't grow up with a phone in their hands. It wasn't part of the very fabric of their lives from birth. Gen Z, on the other hand, is not just the first generation to grow up with technology in their hands from a young age, but they are the first generation to grow up with multiple screens, sometimes at the same time. It's not just a smartphone. Now, we have content being pushed at us via our phone, tablet, laptop, desktop, and watch. The list goes on and on. As a result, our world has been drastically sped up; we live at a much faster pace than previous generations. This is both good and bad, but we must not get hung up on analyzing if it is "more good" or "more bad" because it just is! It is the reality of the world we live in today.

Here's one example: Twenty years ago, if you wanted to get in touch with someone, you waited until the end of your workday and dialed them at home. If they didn't answer, you left a message, asking them to call you back.

If it was more urgent, you may have called them at work, but this was rare. The point is, it was perfectly normal to wait six to ten hours to hear back from someone. In today's world, we think the sky is falling if we don't receive a response to our text in six minutes. We think, *Oh no, what happened to Bob? I hope he's okay! He hasn't texted me back in an hour. Do you think he's doing something? What could he possibly be doing for an hour that he wouldn't check his phone?*

> Gen Xers and Millennials find it easier to detach from technology because they didn't grow up with a phone in their hands. Now, we have content being pushed at us via our phone, tablet, laptop, desktop, and watch.

This is just when our friends and family try to get a hold of us. It's often even worse at work, where many of us are expected to be available via text at all hours of the day, well outside nine to five. This has always been somewhat true for those in salaried roles, and it gets worse the higher you go in upper management. Certainly, CEOs were interrupted with phone calls at home in the 80s and 90s. The difference is this trend has now spread throughout the entire office to employees of all ranks. I've even seen the expectation that hourly workers respond to work-related texts and even calls when they are at home, with their family, and off the clock.

And not just physical people are trying to get in touch with us. Most of these devices have apps, and these apps want to send us notifications and drive our behavior. Then we have all the emails and podcasts and everything we genuinely want to keep up with. Most of us have probably even *tried* to keep up with the onslaught of messages coming at us, only to throw up our hands in frustration when we realize we can't keep up.

Then consider the devices themselves. When you replaced your film camera with your first digital camera, you probably didn't expect that device to become obsolete in a few years—and you certainly didn't expect that within a decade, your *phone* would take even better photos than that camera. Now, most of us don't have much of a need for cameras outside our phones, unless we work in the photography space. (And even then, it's not an absolute requirement like it used to be—we are at the point where entire *films* are being shot on phones.)

You may think, *This is great! I don't need a camera anymore. In fact, I don't need a lot of things. The phone does it all for me.*

While this is all true, how long have you had your current phone? If it's more than a few years old, it's probably functionally obsolete, even with all the updates. While it still *works* and you may even be content with it, you might have a nagging sense that you're behind the rest of the world. Especially when the shifts are more drastic. For years, Apple has been improving the iPhone camera, but now there's portrait mode. Within a year or two, you're the only one of your friends with the inferior iPhone, even though it's only two years old, and you just finished making the monthly payments. It's already time for a new one before the old one has run its course.

This is what Kevin Kelly calls a world of endless upgrades, which leads to a constant feeling that you never arrive.[4] As Kelly says, we're "always becoming," which, in so many ways, is a positive thing. At the same time, this leads to massive tech fatigue because we constantly feel as if we need to do or buy something to catch up, and we're painfully aware that we don't have the money or the time.

We all live in this world. The difference is, Gen Z has grown up in it. The rest of us remember a different world, so it's easier to unplug and go back to that world even if it's only for a few hours or perhaps a day here and there.

Gen Z is different. They are digital natives. They know no other world, and they are experiencing a great deal of tech fatigue because they are bombarded with the unrelenting demands of information, updates, and inquiries, and they have to respond. It's mentally exhausting to attempt to keep up. Every night you come home, asking yourself, *What did I even do today?* and your brain feels completely fried.

Again, all generations deal with this to some degree, but just as information is doubling at lightning-fast speeds (which we will discuss further in truth number five), so is the rise of tech fatigue among members of the Gen Z cohort. In response, Gen Z has been the first generation to develop a coping mechanism entirely out of their subconscious.

What is this coping mechanism? It's a highly sophisticated eight-second filter.

Takeaway

Digital marketing experts estimate most Americans are exposed to anywhere from four thousand to ten thousand advertisements each day. This is just advertisements and doesn't include one's personal or professional life. Content is being delivered at a relentless pace through multiple mediums, and our friends and colleagues can contact us through numerous channels. The end result is our pace of life has been drastically accelerated.

Fully unplugging is not practical. Balance is key, but how do we achieve it? The increased speeds have caused many of us to experience tech fatigue, which can lead to physical symptoms, such as anxiety and depression. We feel completely overwhelmed and guilty that we can't keep up.

The solution is to find ways to filter, to let go of what's outside your circle of concern or what doesn't add value to your life, and to take time to unplug and recharge every once in a while. This could mean using your phone less frequently one day a week and getting outside instead. It doesn't mean you have to put your phone on airplane mode for twenty-four hours; even three or four hours of unplugged time can be highly beneficial, especially if you use the time to do something restorative, such as spend time with a close friend or get out in nature.

What is less beneficial is trading one screen for another. So you might not use your phone at all during the workday, but you're sitting in front of your work computer with your email open all day. Or you might not use your phone all day, but you've been binge-watching Netflix.

While watching a show likely requires less bandwidth than scrolling for the same length of time (and taking in hundreds if not thousands of different messages), it is still healthy to unplug at times and filter other times. It's no different from having a budget that tells your money where to go every month instead of swiping your debit card and hoping for the best. You're managing your time and choosing what to give your attention to. At planned times, you're choosing to limit how many messages can come your way and how many different channels (email, text, social media, etc.) they can use to reach you.

On the home front, parents should understand that helping children unplug is key. At the same time, they should also understand that being plugged in is necessary because that's how the world works now. Some may disagree strongly with this idea, but I would seriously caution parents to teach their children how to use technology well and to take healthy breaks, rather than banning it outright or setting very strict limits, e.g., an hour a day. This will ultimately leave your children feeling left out when all their friends are using technology a lot more than they are.

The most effective way for parents to navigate this is for they themselves to become the most compelling content in the lives of their children. It's not about banning the screen but about being more interesting, engaging, and exciting than the screen.

This may seem like a tall order, but you can accomplish this in many simple ways. It will not come through rigid rules but through intentional relationship. Once this is established, you can speak into their lives and invisibly create balance and give them a greater perspective. *Invisibly* is the key word here. Like the invisible curriculum we will talk about later in "Truth #9: Gen Z Needs a GPS," they will probably not even be aware that you're doing it. Thus, they will respond far more positively than if you take the "I'm the parent, here are the rules, get off your screens" approach.

Z

TRUTH #4
Gen Z Uses an Eight-Second
Filter and Has Curated Streams

Older folks commonly say that the younger generations have very short attention spans. "They're always on their phones, never paying attention anymore. We can't seem to connect with them at all. They seem so disconnected. They're so plugged in that they've tuned everything else out."

In a world plagued by tech fatigue, this actually makes sense. We have much more to distract us than we did fifty years ago, and this was true about Millennials as well. However, I have noticed that what we call "distraction" isn't distraction at all when it comes to Gen Z. It's actually unfair to call them "the most distracted generation." Rather, they have a highly sophisticated eight-second filter as opposed to an eight-second attention span. Please hear the distinction because it's critical. An attention span is a characteristic while the filter is an intentional process they utilize.

They might not even necessarily be aware of this; it's more of a coping strategy they have developed as a result of the world we live in. So much is coming at them all the time, so much is demanding their attention—all these things are causing what we now call tech fatigue. So they have to do something to keep from losing their minds. It's impossible for them or anyone else to live like this. So this generation has collectively and subconsciously developed a way to process and make sense of everything they are taking in. I call this the eight-second filter.

Here's how it works: Within the first eight seconds of coming into contact with a new message, concept, or advertisement, Gen Z decides if it is worth giving any more of their attention to. If they're searching the internet for the best deal on a new pair of jeans (they are far more likely to do this than to go to a physical store to try on different pairs), they aren't going to spend more than eight seconds on an individual product. During that time, they'll quickly scan the photos, price, peer reviews, star rating, and all the basic info. The text description of the item is irrelevant at this point because it takes too long to digest. If a particular pair of jeans doesn't catch their eye, it's on to the next one to repeat the process. Only when something really grabs their attention will they begin to read the description, specs, and sizes to determine if it's what they are really looking for. At this point, the item has made it through the eight-second filter, but they may not decide to purchase this item. They will probably have three or four tabs open on their phone with different jeans that made it through the filter while hundreds—perhaps thousands—of others were quickly and efficiently filtered out.

The reason this filter exists is because of the excessive choices in our modern world. When Colleen and I were first married, buying jeans was much simpler. We had no internet to browse, so we had to go to a physical store with limited options as to what could fit under one roof. The stores in that time were not specialized like they are now with entire online, and even brick-and-mortar stores, devoted to only selling jeans. Back then, we would have gone to a general clothing store or a department store if we wanted more options. Out of all the space in that store, perhaps 10 percent was devoted to jeans. We could look at each pair, all twenty or thirty, in under an hour. But now, we have twenty or thirty *thousand* pairs of jeans to choose from, many of which can be delivered right to our door without ever stepping foot inside a physical store. If they don't fit, no big deal. The company will email me a return shipping label. Some of these companies don't even *have* physical stores. I can refine my online search to some extent, but there are still way too many options. I'm forced to filter.*

---

* This is true for everyone alive today, regardless of their generation. However, Gen Z is the first generation to utilize this filter on a large scale and as their default way of making decisions. Many in my generation are still looking for the physical store, which limits their options.

This is how the eight-second filter came to exist. It wasn't because this generation is somehow more advanced than others or has some sort of superhuman, jean-scanning ability; it's simply a survival mechanism. With so many options, it isn't possible for us to choose, and the world isn't narrowing our options for us, so we are forced to subconsciously filter the choices on our own. I find myself doing this as well nowadays, but Gen Z has grown up doing it their entire lives. The eight-second filter solves the problem of tech fatigue, empathy fatigue (by helping them discover which causes they are most passionate about), and any other type of fatigue the modern world has created.

The eight-second filter is highly sophisticated and versatile. It doesn't just apply to choosing a pair of jeans. Perhaps we are watching our favorite TV show and a commercial comes on. In less than eight seconds, we either play it through, mute it, or fast-forward it using our DVR. We used to think the ability to pause, fast-forward, and rewind live TV was quite the novelty, but now everything is streaming and on-demand, whenever you want it, any time of the day or night. Commercials aren't the effective avenue they once were. You may even use a streaming service with no commercials.

But have you ever scrolled through the endless options of movies and shows you can stream, not knowing which one to pick? This is where you begin to filter. There's no way you'll watch a two-minute trailer on each movie.** You'll be doing that all night. Instead, you scroll past quickly until one catches your eye. The streaming service itself helps you with your filtering. It knows what movies you liked, which ones you watched more than once, which ones you stopped watching after twenty minutes, and which ones took you a few days to get through (as opposed to watching all at once). A powerful recommendation engine pre-filters the massive library of content for you, so you're only shown the streaming options you're most likely to be interested in—or what other users find most popular.

Think about the advertising messages that come your way through your screens. Begin observing how you react to them. Most don't merit a second thought. Because there are so many, not all of them register in your mind.

---

* Netflix has recognized this. I have observed that most of their movie trailers are now under thirty seconds, which is, on average, 400 percent shorter than the traditional movie trailer.

The ones that do are likely filtered out in a second or two. Now think about the messages that actually capture your attention—in eight seconds, they've likely been replaced with something else: another message, your spouse walking into the room, an important email or work task you need to attend to. Or perhaps you simply drove, walked, or biked past the message. Even if you were stationary, perhaps waiting for a train, the message was still likely filtered in less than eight seconds. Most messages are filtered out, but a few resonate with you, and you pay attention for more than eight seconds. Even if you have shifted your focus to something else a minute later, this item, idea, advertisement—whatever it is—has made it through your filter.

The eight-second filter is primarily used to process new ideas and information. If you want to take a vacation to Florida, you may spend a few minutes researching information online, only to get on Instagram later that afternoon and find you are met with ads for a variety of destinations across the Sunshine State.

Do you want to go to Orlando, Tampa, Miami, Jacksonville, Tallahassee, Sarasota, St. Petersburg, Daytona Beach, Jupiter, Melbourne, Pensacola, West Palm Beach, Key West, Key Largo, or the Everglades?

If you've never been there, you may be a bit overwhelmed. You may know you want something on the coast, which may lead you to gravitate to something with "beach" in its name, or you may skip the decision process entirely and just go to Disney World since you're familiar with the brand and it's already made it through your filter. In a world with too many options, you will often revert to what you are most familiar with because it makes you more comfortable. Whether it's the best option is irrelevant. You might even like something else more. But the overwhelming choices cripple you. So you either go with what is most familiar, or you quickly filter out 90 percent of your choices so the options are more manageable when you compare them to each other.

> In a world with too many options, we often revert to what we are most familiar with.

If you trust a person or brand, their recommendation will often bypass your filter. Today, this person doesn't have to be a friend of twenty years; it could be a digital influencer you've been following on Instagram for six weeks. Social media allows you to feel as if they are a part of your life, even if you've never met them or know very little about them outside of what their carefully curated profile tells you.

If the influencer is eating lunch at a trendy restaurant in Key West, you may be more inclined to allow Key West through your filter even if you had previously filtered it out. You want to go there so you can go to the same restaurant you saw in the pictures, the restaurant you have established trust with because someone you trust endorses it.

Next, Tampa pops up on your feed. You quickly scroll through some photos provided by the local tourism bureau. Within eight seconds, you've decided Tampa isn't for you. Miami, on the other hand, holds your attention a bit longer. You scroll through a few photos, click a few links, begin browsing hotel rooms; you've now spent three minutes on Miami. It's made it through your filter, but that doesn't necessarily mean it will be your ultimate vacation destination. It simply means it's now in your curated stream (more on this shortly) as a potential option.

> Your business doesn't just need to be online; you need Gen Z influencers who will advocate for your brand so it can get past the filters of their peers.

This is completely different than a brand having a website. In this new era, your business doesn't just need to be online; you need Gen Z influencers who will advocate for your brand so it can get past the filters of their peers.

The reason why this matters so much is because it encompasses far more than buying a pair of jeans or choosing where to go on vacation. Gen Z uses the eight-second filter to decide where they will eat, what they will watch, what brands they will wear, what type of car they will drive, what school they will attend, who they will date (swipe right), where they will live, where they will work, who they will socialize with—the list goes on and on. The point is, they use it for absolutely everything. Everything in their lives runs through this filter, and they call the shots. It's as though they are the CEO of their own life; they aren't waiting around for someone else to make their decisions for them.

The marketing world understands this. Just because their product has a thirty-second television commercial doesn't mean they have thirty seconds to win over their Gen Z clientele. So now the last eight seconds of a commercial—what used to be the climax—isn't nearly as important as the first eight seconds. If you fail to grab and hold their interest in those crucial early seconds, the next twenty seconds are futile. They're likely on their phones, looking at something else, until your message ends and the next appears. It's not their fault they were distracted; it's your fault for failing to grab their attention. You didn't make it past their filter. This is not only true for marketing teams but for business leaders and parents alike.

— — —

The eight-second filter explains how Gen Z takes in information, but leaves us with this question: Where does all this information go once it makes it past the eight-second filter? Once the information has been filtered in, it must go somewhere. The filter is just the entry point, not the final destination.

> Because Gen Z is the first generation to live in this world of constant change, they have developed multiple curated streams.

We all have streams of information in our minds, and if you're like me, you probably have multiple thoughts running through your head at the same time. This is not new, but what is new is the state of constant change we find ourselves in due to the perfect storm. Because Gen Z is the first generation to live in this world of constant change where they are inundated with information and everything is accelerated, they have developed multiple curated streams.

Unlike previous generations with no need to filter because they had fewer options, Gen Z is in control of what is in their streams. If you had no filter and just one stream, you would have to mentally pick out what you want in there and what you don't want, and everything would be lumped together—the conversation you had with a friend last week, the new concept you just learned at a work convention, the tense meeting with your boss, the bills waiting for you at home, the phone call from your sister you have yet to return, the humanitarian crisis in Africa you read about in this morning's paper, not to mention your personal interests and goals that need attention.

It's a bit overwhelming to lump all these things together, but previous generations made it work because there were limits on the speed at which new information was received. Before texting or even email, you would wait until you saw someone in person to share information with them. That could be weeks or months away, so you might write them a letter instead, depending on the importance of the information. If it was important enough, you might even pick up the phone. Now, you can send and receive dozens or even hundreds of messages a day, and your attention is much more in-demand, often from the same people multiple times throughout the day. Even with the help of a virtual to-do list and calendar reminders, it's too much to keep up with.

This is why Gen Z has subconsciously developed advanced ways of filtering, so they are more in control of what makes it into their stream in the first place—and, as I mentioned, they have multiple streams: a relationship stream, work stream, friends stream, and an entertainment stream. They have streams for the brands they interact with, which is the only way to know which of the thousands of varieties of toothpaste they should use. There's a stream for the places they want to visit, for the TV shows and movies they watch, and for the types of cars they prefer.

Most of the major auto manufacturers are now on Instagram and even partner with Gen-Z digital influencers to market their vehicles to their peers. Long before they walk through the doors of the DMV to obtain their driver's license, Gen Z has already curated the brands they like and filtered out the ones they don't, often to the point that the algorithms easily learn which brands are in their stream and only show them social media ads for that particular type of vehicle.

Choosing a college isn't much different, except there are now significantly more options, and it's not uncommon to travel across the country—or the world—for school. The filter helps curate the schools they like into their stream. This doesn't mean they make a decision on a school in eight seconds but rather that they decide if they want to dive deeper in their research of that school in the first eight seconds of seeing an ad, picking up a flyer that came in the mail, or doing their own study online. With far too many options, this is necessary, and it would be impractical to travel the entire country to tour twenty or thirty schools. Instead, they use the stream to pair it down to four or five schools before beginning any in-person tours, which may still take them all over the country. (I once met a mother and daughter from Hawaii who were visiting a small liberal arts school in central Pennsylvania before heading to the next school in the Southeast.) The difference is you're only choosing between a handful of schools to study in-depth before making your decision. The eight-second filter helps maintain the quality of the stream so Gen Z can dive deep into what interests them and ignore what doesn't.

> The eight-second filter helps maintain the quality of the stream so Gen Z can dive deep into what interests them and ignore what doesn't.

Companies have caught on to this. All my favorite podcasts are now available on Spotify. I don't have to go to the iTunes store and subscribe to each one because they are right there, next to my music playlists. The idea is simple yet brilliant. At one time, I had separate apps for each podcast I listened to. Each podcast had its own app. Sure, the same podcasts were available in iTunes, but I liked having individual apps because they provided extra content. The DVD brought us this era—the era of bonus features—but it is soon coming to an end. Now, the big thing is consolidated, simplified, and ironically endless streams that curate our individual tastes as we listen. Why do I need an individual app for each podcast? Why do I need a separate app for podcasts in general? Why not just consolidate it all onto the same app where I already listen to my music—an app that knows what I like and suggests new songs I might want to add to my stream. We're all curating, and our devices are helping us.

The other day, I was browsing through stock photos on Shutterstock.com to send to my marketing team when I noticed the homepage is now tailored to those with an eight-second filter and curated stream. First, when I landed on the site, I was presented with "You might like these" based on images I had recently viewed. The site is tracking my behavior and attempting to recommend photos I might like in order to keep me engaged. I spend much of my time here, or I use the search bar to look for specific images because I don't have time to sort through the millions of images on their website to find the perfect fit. I need something more curated, and the website helps me do just that.

Whether it's stock photography, a movie streaming service, or a social media algorithm, these recommendation engines are now standard. Facebook used to actually show you everything your friends posted, in chronological order of most recent, but they abandoned that model years ago. It started slowly at first, with the option to view everything or view highlights, but now we have no options. We only see the highlights—but not the highlights of all our friends because Facebook understands the difference between our close friends whose posts we regularly like and the person we knew in high school but would rather not see again, and they even give us the option to unfollow that person entirely without unfriending them, just in case the algorithm doesn't filter them out for us.

Filtering and curation are certainly becoming entrenched in our everyday lives to the point of affecting the romantic lives of Gen Z. The way Gen Z finds their significant others is radically different than previous generations, even Millennials. They are less likely to find a mate in college simply by attending classes or being present on campus as the social life of our universities has changed dramatically in a short span of time. Students have coped with this Gen Z reality by changing the way they date. They're not looking to meet someone at a bar or coffee shop or even be set up by mutual friends. Instead, they use apps that are far more sophisticated than the dating websites of the early 2000s. The primary difference is these apps show users far more eligible singles in their area, in part because it's more popular to use dating apps in 2020 than it was to be on a dating website in 2005. Filtering and curation are also built-in to the app. Swipe right, swipe left. If the person doesn't capture their attention in a few seconds, they're filtered out. This certainly has some negative side effects, but it's not necessarily ill-intended. There are simply too many people to choose from, and social media has given rise to the fear of missing out, making it difficult for young people to decide on who they want to date and ultimately marry.

Another interesting point about Gen Z is when something isn't ideal, they are slower to abandon it than Millennials. Instead, they tweak and refine—they curate it further. For example, if one grows tired of the "swipe right, swipe left" approach to dating (where you go through two hundred profiles, meet five of them in person, and only two are remotely interesting and not creepy—but not dateable), they won't abandon dating apps all together. Instead, they simply move on to another app. An entire market now exists among Gen Z for dating apps focused on serious relationships instead of short flings. One of these apps, Hinge, has the stated goal that a user will delete their app because they have found a long-term relationship. Sometimes, the filter isn't just for the people on the app but for the app itself. If one is looking for a short fling or a casual date, they can choose from several apps. But if one is looking for a more committed relationship, they can choose from an entirely different stream of apps. Both have a place, depending on the user's goals—and some have actually found the love of their life on the more casual apps.

Like much of what we have discussed, this example of dating is just the tip of the iceberg that illustrates our key point that filtering is how Gen Z makes most of their decisions. Their lives are curated in nearly every aspect. If we want to get their attention for the sake of having a place of influence in their lives or even just to sell them our product or service, we must get past their filters and into their curated stream. For too long, we have fought for Gen Z's attention when we really need to ask ourselves what is important to them (or to the niche group or individual we desire to reach) and take the steps necessary to show how we can add value to their lives. No longer does the old marketing adage of "You need this product!" apply. Gen Z looks at this pitch, no matter how flashy it may be, and asks, "Why?"

When we answer the "why," that's when we will find our way into their stream.[*]

***

[*] Author and speaker Simon Sinek has done an incredible job of unpacking why companies need to start with "why" and not "what" to reach a new generation. If you wish to dive deeper into this topic, I recommend his book *Start With Why*. He also has a TED Talk of the same name that can be found on YouTube, along with other videos of him speaking on this topic. Although much of his language centers around reaching Millennials, the "why" question is still highly applicable to Gen Z.

—— —— ——

Colleen and I were recently in California visiting our friend Will and his family. His four-year-old son was playing with dinosaurs. When Colleen noticed this, she asked if he liked *The Land Before Time*, the animated film series produced by George Lucas and Steven Spielberg. First released in 1988, these films were most popular in the 90s and early 2000s, with the fourteenth and final film released as recently as 2016, so it's not as if Colleen were referencing something prehistoric—though to Will's son, she might as well have been.

"What's that?" he asked.

Before Colleen could *explain the series, he was already on his mom's iPhone, asking Siri to pull up The* Land Before Time. A video clip from one of the films came up, and he watched for a few seconds before shutting it off.

"I don't like it," he said, turning back to Colleen.

Amazed, I asked Will if he had noticed what just happened. His son had just demonstrated the eight-second filter. In this instance, *The Land Before Time* had failed to become a part of his curated stream.

Will's son is actually part of the Alpha generation, the generation that comes after Gen Z. While we know even less about this generation, which consists largely of children of Millennials born in the last few years, we know they carry many of the same traits as Gen Z. As our world becomes more and more advanced, we will see how this generation develops their own unique characteristics in response. Perhaps they will be similar to Gen Z, or perhaps they will end up more like their parents. Perhaps they will develop new traits we have not seen in a generation up to this point.

—— —— ——

Once a concept, product, company, career, or even a person has made it into the curated stream of Gen Z, what happens next?

The answer is simple: They *deep dive* and invest in it fully. The filter and the streams simply serve to limit what they give their attention to. They aren't easily distracted; rather, they understand the world we live in will make everyone distracted if they have no filters. So they decide what is most important to them, subconsciously establishing their streams, and then begin filtering out what doesn't fit. Everything that comes their way meets this sophisticated eight-second filter. If it interests them, if there is room for it in one of their streams, it gets included—even if only to save it for later.

The app *Pocket* mimics this mental process, allowing users to save articles, videos, and photos for on-demand viewing at the touch of a button. Gen Z has so many different streams that a new industry is devoted to helping them retain information and keep track of what is in their stream. This is Pinterest in a nutshell. You scroll or search, pin what you like, and skip over what you don't. Facebook is beginning to take note of this (though they are late to the game, in my opinion), with the recently added option for users to save videos to watch later. Facebook, which was built by and largely for Millennials (not Gen Z), doesn't really have a built-in method of curation, and thanks to the algorithm, if you run across something you like but switch to another app or pause to respond to an incoming text, you may find that your feed has refreshed itself and the item you were looking at is now gone.

I cannot tell you how many times this has happened to me. Often, I only had a vague recollection of the topic (just that it interested me—this is a symptom of tech fatigue) and was unable to remember the title of the article or the name of the person who posted it. This makes it a bit tedious to search for the article, and I'm probably going to give up after eight seconds.

If Facebook wanted to get ahead of the game, they would add a built-in feature to save noteworthy items as you scroll, quickly filtering them into a curated mini-stream of articles to read on-demand, whether half an hour later, when you're done scrolling and ready to dive into what you've found, or little by little over the course of several days—with more items being added to the stream as you find them. It could even happen weeks or months later. The point is, this deep dive takes place on-demand at your leisure or when you have the brain space to devote to the items you're interested in. For example, if you're scrolling during a moment of downtime at work and run across an interesting but long article, you may filter it into the "read later" stream simply because you know you don't have time to give it the attention it deserves.

Interestingly enough, Instagram, which is owned by Facebook, *does* have this feature: the ability to curate items as you scroll to deep dive into later. They are clearly targeting different generations here, as it's widely known that Facebook tends to attract an older crowd while Instagram users are younger.

This read-later or on-demand stream is not quite the same as one's primary curated streams. It's more of a holding place for content that makes it past the eight-second filter that may or may not be worth retaining for a longer period of time. Because the information is not yet digested, one may rely on an app, the Notes feature on their phone, or an open web browser tab to hold on to the information until it can be properly consumed. At this point, it could still be filtered out, but it will get more than eight seconds of attention. It may receive thirty seconds or thirty minutes, depending on how long it takes to digest and how well it holds one's interest, but a point will come where the information is either discarded (filtered out) or transferred to a more long-term archive (a curated stream).

Filtering, curation, and *deep dive* are terms that not only describe how Gen Z processes information but how they process absolutely everything. Ask them where they want to eat dinner when visiting a new city, and they're likely to hop on Yelp and find the top-rated restaurant in moments, filtering out all the others. Even though they've never physically been to this city, they may have already curated places they want to eat (or visit) after seeing Instagram posts from their friends who previously visited the city. They may have even done a deep dive into their curated stream and selected the best places to stay, shop, eat, and be entertained long before stepping off the airplane. They don't just show up in a place and decide what to do; it's already been curated into their stream in advance.

It's the same way with relationships as well. Gen Z has curated streams of people; they have streams of friends (which probably include people they've met online but never met in person, who may live across town, or across the world) and streams of people who influence them as well, ranging from Instagram influencers to YouTube stars. In fact, many of them are likely to have more online friends in their stream than real-life friends who live in their immediate area.

Gen Z adds to their curated stream as things catch their attention. They then deep dive into these topics and learn more about them. This process can solidify the position in their stream, or the item or person might be filtered out. Some topics may only be beneficial for a certain period of time and are filtered out when they are no longer relevant to one's daily life. It's the same as cleaning out the garage or basement and removing unnecessary clutter. With so much new information, technology, and products to try, there's little room for a model from two years ago that is no longer useful.

Other topics or items are deemed irrelevant the more one learns about them. Our thought process might follow: I thought I needed this item in my life, but I became less interested as I learned more about it. Or: I really liked this person until I found out they believe this or have done that, and that's not a voice I want in my life.

Both of these scenarios can take place in the context of products and even people—relationships, mentors, and employers as well. If you want to influence Gen Z or simply grab their attention, you must not only find your way *into* their curated stream but find out how to *stay* in it.

> If you want to impact Gen Z, or simply grab their attention, you must not only find your way *into* their curated stream but find out how to *stay* in it.

Another example of this type of thinking follows: I used to really enjoy working for iTech, but now that I see how the CEO treats his team and what he does with his money, I'd rather go work for NewTech. They are a cause-driven company, respect their team members, and support causes I'm passionate about.

This may sound ridiculous and flaky to some, and to some extent it is, but it is literally how this generation thinks. More than nine out of ten (93 percent) of Gen Zers say a company's social impact affects their decision of whether to work there.[1] We no longer live in an age where a Boomer will stay with one company for thirty years even though he doesn't like the management and the work isn't fulfilling just because he believes in loyalty and the job gives him a shot at his own American Dream.

Gen Z does not seem quite as quick to jump ship from a job as Millennials were in their early twenties, at least not from what I have seen. We must remember, this is a generation that grew up in the mid-2000s, in a time of economic recession, increased violence, and uncertainty. They watched their parents lose their jobs in 2008 and recall them being out of work and stressed about it for a while. They have tens, if not hundreds, of thousands of dollars in student loans and are living at home after college—even with a full-time job—because rent is too high. On top of all this, they've now had to navigate a global pandemic. It's not like it used to be where people grow up and settle down in the same place they were born or in the closest major city. Universities are more likely to draw students from a wide range of places. Some may return to their hometowns after graduation, some may stay in the city where they attended university, and others may end up moving across the country to an entirely new place they have little to no connection to.

I know one Gen Z student from New Jersey who graduated from college and got his first job in Phoenix. So he packed up and moved two thousand miles away, leaving his family and girlfriend behind. This may seem unusual, especially when he could find plenty of jobs an hour away in New York, but this story is becoming somewhat of a trend. Gen Z is much more mobile, especially in an age where it's so easy to stay digitally connected. It does, however, have its downsides. If your closest friends in college end up getting jobs in Arizona, Boston, and Miami, and you stay home in Jersey, you just might wind up living at home for a while. This would have been socially unacceptable in years past, but this young adult has expensive student loan payments, so it just doesn't make sense for them to rent a one-bedroom apartment for fifteen hundred dollars a month when they can live at home. In 2016, for the first time in modern history, there were more young adults living with their parents than those who were not.[2]

What is interesting about these two scenarios is that they are polar opposites of one another. You might think, *So you're telling me Gen Z will either move back home after college or move halfway across the country to a city they have no connection to?*

Yes! Even though Gen Z is very risk averse and likes to play it safe, when they do make moves, they tend to go all-in.

When we look at the data, we see that Gen Z is a very conflicted generation. Nearly three-fourths (72 percent) of high school students say they want to start their own business;[3] yet, there are 23 percent less working during high school compared to Gen X.[4]

Of those who are working, 46 percent work in the gig economy with no job security in terms of a guaranteed paycheck or benefits. But they have the flexibility to set their own schedule, freedom to be their own boss, and the potential to make more per hour than at a traditional job. It's a risk, certainly, but it's a risk that appeals to nearly half of young Gen Z workers.

Even though Gen Z is very risk averse, when they do make moves, they tend to go all-in.

So why is Gen Z so conflicted? Why are they likely to move to a city they've never been to for a job but slow to get their own apartment if they work close to where they grew up? Why are they so entrepreneurial and willing to take some risks while the thought of other (similar) risks leaves them paralyzed? Doesn't it seem like Gen Z is growing up both faster *and* slower than previous generations? How can both of these things be true within the same individual?

Takeaway

The eight-second filter challenges the notion that Gen Z has an eight-second attention span. The eight seconds represents the amount of time a person typically spends taking in a piece of information to determine if they are interested. If they are, they will give it their full attention (deep dive), and it could become part of their curated stream. If they aren't interested, it gets filtered out.

This is necessary because we are inundated with tens of thousands of messages each and every day. Gen Z has learned that if they do not filter, they will become completely overwhelmed and end up shutting everything out.

A curated stream can be thought of as the permission someone gives you to speak into their life. You have made it past their filter and are part of the stream of information they are curating. In the context of social media, it's when you follow people and they follow you back, which gives you the ability to learn what is most important to them. You can be an influence in their life.

Because this is permission-based, the ability to be in someone's curated stream is *their* choice, not yours. You may follow them, but if they do not follow you back, you do not hold a place of influence in their life.

Gen Z uses their eight-second filter for absolutely everything. If you have something to say or sell, you must grab their attention in the first eight seconds of your message, or they will become distracted. This isn't their fault for not having a longer attention span. It's your fault for failing to grab their attention. You didn't make it past their filter. The eight-second filter helps maintain the quality of the stream so Gen Z can dive deep into what interests them and ignore what doesn't.

You need to get in the curated streams of your audience or potential customers. One way to do this is by partnering with Gen Z influencers who will advocate for your brand so you can get past the filters of their peers. Once you have made it past these filters and into their curated stream, you must add value and remain relevant to them to stay in their stream. Getting added to someone's curated stream is not a permanent status; we live in a world where it is very easy to unfollow someone or something that no longer interests us.

Z

TRUTH #5
Gen Z Is Growing Up Fast and Slow

Throughout my life, I've seen many changes in technology, but perhaps the most profound change has been how quickly technology has progressed since the year 2000. Before this, new technologies were released much more slowly, so we reacted to them differently. We felt a sense of awe when a new gadget was released. We didn't always know what to do with the latest toys.

Gen Z, on the other hand, was born into a world totally saturated with technology. They aren't blown away by the iPad like we were when it was first released in 2010. For them, it's just a tool they are using to accomplish a task. This fundamental difference changes the way they look at the world and what they expect the world to do. While older generations may view certain pieces of technology as fun but unessential toys, Gen Z views the same technology as an essential tool that is totally necessary and vital for everyday life.

Every component of our world has and is being changed, and we are being changed as a result. Technology now commonly turns off your lights, adjusts your thermostat, and enables your security system—even if you aren't physically at home. Gen Z expects the technology they use to constantly improve and reinvent itself. In this world of endless upgrades,

> Every component of our world has and is being changed, and we are being changed as a result.

companies are always working on a new and improved version of the previous version. The original iPhone that wowed us in 2007 is now an ancient relic; a MacBook from 2011 is now extremely heavy and clunky, and the same goes for the first-generation iPad. They aren't impressed by these upgrades because they are normal. What would be odd is technology that doesn't have a new and improved version release every few years.

Buckminster Fuller, an architect and inventor, lived from 1895 to 1983. Besides having quite the name, Buckminster was also a futurist. He is perhaps most famous for popularizing the geodesic dome (you know, the structure you see when you enter Disney's Epcot), which had been invented by the German engineer Walther Bauersfield a few decades prior. Fuller, however, was the first to secure US patents for this structure, leading to its rise in popularity in the 1950s.

While this may be very interesting to some and irrelevant to others, we're going to talk about what I believe was Fuller's more relevant contribution—the knowledge-doubling curve. He noticed that up until 1900, knowledge doubled about every hundred years. However, by the end of World War II, knowledge was doubling every twenty-five years.[1] Today, it is more difficult to predict the rate at which knowledge is doubling because it is happening so rapidly and there are so many different types of knowledge, but the average rate at which knowledge doubled was every thirteen months in 2013 (nearly a decade ago).[2] IBM has predicted the internet will lead to the doubling of knowledge every twelve *hours*,[3] and I believe we are at that point right now.

Not only is available knowledge doubling at such a rapid pace, we now have access to all information at a very young age. This is why we see two-year-olds that already know how to work Dad's iPhone and Mom's iPad. We are incredibly knowledgeable, and it's only growing. As a result, Gen Z is perhaps the first generation in history to have access to all information that has ever existed. This doesn't mean they *know* everything but that they have *access* to know about *anything* they want to know more about. Despite this unlimited access, they aren't typically mature enough to know how to process everything. They have a voice (through social media) but don't always have the wisdom to know when to use it and how to use it well.

All these advancements and shifts have removed a role that was traditionally played by previous generations. We used to pass knowledge down from one generation to the next through teaching, modeling, and, more recently, through the sage on stage that heavily influenced the Millennial generation. Now, there's no need for that, or rather, Gen Z does not yet see they have a need for that. They believe they can function without the generation that came before them, and this belief appears to be confirmed every time they log on.*

> IBM has predicted the internet will lead to the doubling of knowledge every twelve *hours.* Gen Z is the first generation in history to have access to all information that has ever existed.

This is why Gen Z reacts to not having Wi-Fi in a totally different way than those of us who remember a time without it. For us, it may be a minor inconvenience—or even something we intentionally seek out when taking an unplugged vacation. Gen Z responds differently. They can't fathom a world without Wi-Fi, without smartphones, without an app that performs mundane daily functions, such as banking. To Gen Z, it is a foreign concept to pay for everything with cash or a paper check and a waste of time and gas to drive to the bank to simply deposit money. To them, going to the bank looks less like driving to a building and more like opening an app.

Certainly, most generations regularly use these apps and find them more convenient, but Gen Z thinks they are the bare minimum of necessities. If my banking app or Venmo wasn't working, my first thought might be, *This is annoying. Now I need to go down to the bank and get cash before five o'clock,* but younger generations would not come up with this alternative course of action as quickly. If you told them your house didn't have Wi-Fi, they might stare at you blankly, thinking, *How can this be? What do you mean, 'You don't have Wi-Fi?'* Everyone *has Wi-Fi.* It's not a toy or a luxury anymore. It's a tool, and everyone uses it every day of their lives.

I was unpacking this concept with a friend the other day and, a few days later, he sent me a photo of an MTA bus in New York City. On the back of

---

* Of course, they still need Mom and Dad to pay the internet bill, at least until they start their own business.

the bus were two symbols alerting riders that the bus had Wi-Fi and USB ports (for charging smartphones). To my friend—who is a Millennial—this was out of the ordinary, a novelty. Gen Z, however, thinks it is odd when the bus *doesn't* have Wi-Fi.

As a result of both the increase in knowledge and the ease of access to knowledge, Gen Z is growing up faster than generations that came before them. They are, in essence, CEOs of their lives from a very young age. Rather than having others make all their choices for them, they are more autonomous at a younger age than previous generations (more on this in "Truth #6: Gen Z Is Used to Being the CEO of Their Life"). So they have more choices to make, and they're also exposed to everything the world has to offer 24/7 through their devices, which are put in their hands much earlier than any other genera-tion. In fact, 35 percent of their communication is completely digital.[4]

> In fact, 35 percent of Gen Z's communication is digital.

Gen Z spends 40 percent less physical time with their friends.[5] They don't need to go to the mall with a group of their peers; they can hang out virtually via the computer screen and online shop together (although they are more likely to do this alone and send their friends screenshots of their purchases). They don't need to go out to a movie when they can stream vir-tually any movie ever made on their computer or smart TV with the touch of a button.

Gen Z's world is incredibly convenient because they can experience it without actually going out in the world. Everything is available to them from their bedroom—or wherever they happen to be—now that they have smartphones and tablets that allow them to access the world free from the confines of a computer power cord. This shift definitely includes some pos-itive elements, but as with anything, there is also a downside. Members of Gen Z have exhibited substantially higher rates of anxiety and depression and are more at risk of suicide than any other generation.[6] While they are the most connected generation in history, they are also the loneliest gener-ation at the same time.[7]

All of this time alone has taken away the opportunities other generations were given to practice their social skills through in-person interactions. As a result, some members of Gen Z struggle when it comes to one-on-one, in-person interactions—particularly in the workplace. Even if they are incredibly adept at communicating through a screen, they can experience a great deal of social anxiety when they must communicate in person, even with their peers.

These negative side effects produced by a decrease in real-world socialization have caused Gen Z to grow up slowly while they are also growing up quickly due to the increase in ways they can socialize that didn't exist before. It is quite the paradox, and we could spend a great deal of time diving into many layers of paradoxes here.

Instead, let's take a closer look at the sobering reality that Gen Z is the loneliest generation in history while, ironically, the most connected generation. I recently heard about a man who returned to his alma mater—UC San Diego—ten years after graduation. As he walked down the quad, which had been bustling with activity in his day, he noticed a line of students sitting on a wall. They were spaced a few feet apart, and everyone had their heads down, looking at their phone. (No doubt many of them were on a social network.) Obviously, we see this everywhere, but it struck him how much the world has changed in just ten years. Cell phones existed back then, but smart phones were just coming on the scene. The quad was full of people laughing, talking, and socializing with others around them. Now, it was calm and quiet even though it was full of students.

I'm reminded of old black-and-white photos from a hundred years ago of men in suits, standing on street corners, their heads buried in newspapers. It's really no different than it is today; only the medium connecting us to the world has changed. The more everything changes, the more everything remains the same. The more connected we become, the greater the potential for a sense of loneliness to develop, regardless of the era we are living in.

It would be unfair to compare a college campus of ten years ago to a campus today and conclude there is less social life simply because it is quieter. Rather, the social life has shifted. This generation socializes differently, and because they have the ability to meet and connect with people around the world, even their streams of friends are now curated—to the point that one could have a large network of friends that doesn't include a single person who is on the same campus as they are. A young person could be born and raised in California, attend college in San Diego, and have a tight-knit circle of peers who attend college in Indiana, Florida, Germany, and Dubai. Some of these will probably be people they have never met in person and are only connected to through a screen. Still, they have closer relationships with them than the people they walk past every day on their own campus. This would have been much less common ten years ago and even been a cause of concern for some parents, but it is becoming more and more the norm today. It is no longer strange to hear of teenagers taking international flights to finally meet their closest friends in person.

The other big factor is the amount of time spent on social media. You wouldn't think increased mobility and access to social networks would contribute to loneliness as both appear to open doors to a realm of possibilities. However, a 2020 report by the health insurance company Cigna found that 61 percent of adults say they feel lonely. When you look at Millennials and Gen Z, the numbers rise sharply to 71 and 79 percent, respectively.[8]

It's no coincidence that 65 percent of Millennials and Gen Z are more likely to communicate with others digitally rather than in-person.[9] While there are certainly benefits to digital communication, it cannot fully replace actual, real-world connection; it can only enhance it.

Another study found that Gen Z's loneliness doesn't just stem from social media but from a fracturing of neighborhoods and communities. Young adults today spend less time connecting with neighbors and co-workers than previous generations did, families are becoming smaller, and people are less likely to attend religious services regularly.[10] Even politicians are taking note of this as the study I just referenced was prepared for a US Senator from Utah. The way we live is a factor. Young people are more likely to live in cities or densely populated neighborhoods than previous generations, which means you are far less likely to interact with your neighbors than you would if you lived in a single-family home with a front porch and a yard where your kids play in the street.

I had lunch with a man recently who told me a story about when his son was younger. The son loved computer games and would throw a tantrum when he couldn't play them. This issue wasn't so much the computer games but more of a parenting issue, and the man realized that. You wouldn't let your kids have ice cream for every meal, but at the same time, this doesn't mean you ban ice cream entirely. It's all about helping your kids find balance.

Nearly every morning, this kid would sneak out of bed to play computer games. I've heard of kids sneaking out of bed late at night, but this kid actually woke up earlier than everyone else. One morning, dad walked in to see his kid playing computer games and actually creating his own video within the game.

Fast forward a few years. This kid further developed his video skills as he grew up. In college, he partnered with a friend to do paid video work for companies, and after college, Amazon hired him to work in one of their corporate offices. What started out as a kid misbehaving turned into a full-time job, and I can't help but imagine how this story would have unfolded if his dad had viewed gaming and technology as the issue rather than seeing it as a parenting issue. This was not just an issue to quickly deal with by shutting it down but an issue where what the child needed most was to be taught how to keep his life in proper balance. Many of us hear stories about children and technology that don't end well, so it can be really easy to blame technology and overreact by severely limiting access to it or even banning it entirely.

We will always have someone or something to blame for the negative things we see in the world, but that doesn't make any of it go away or solve anything. When we see these things, if we conclude that technology is bad, we miss out on the many positive aspects new technologies have brought us. Instead, we can recognize that while technological advancement has been largely positive for all of us, it has created some unique challenges for Gen Z, and future generations will continue to face these and new challenges as well. Instead of pointing a finger, those of us who recognize these challenges can help Gen Z overcome them. One of the ways we can shift our perspective on Gen Z is to realize that they are not just easily distracted; they have a highly sophisticated eight-second filter as I discussed in the previous chapter. They effectively curate what is most important to them and deep dive into what intrigues them. They are thirsty for knowledge. They don't ignore the sage on stage because they aren't willing to learn; they are instead looking for a guide to come alongside them on their journey. This shift in our perspective will not take place automatically, but it will determine if we are filtered in as part of their curated stream or filtered out as irrelevant.

Many statistics show us Gen Z's access to social media and technology from such a young age isn't beneficial. At the same time, this access won't go away anytime soon, and it's not practical to simply remove it from the lives of your children entirely. Imagine how their social anxiety, which is already significantly higher than previous generations, might increase if they are the only one in their junior high class without a smartphone.

Instead, parents can be equipped with tools to maximize the positive aspects of this new era and minimize the negative effects. We can teach children how to manage social media well and actually leverage it to their advantage in some ways. We as parents have a responsibility to this generation to help them make sense of this world they were born into.

— — —

Another way that Gen Z is growing up fast and slow has to do with their approach to employment. Interestingly enough, fewer Gen Z high school students are working today than previous generations did at their age: Only 18 percent of Gen Z teens ages 15-17 were employed in 2018, compared to 27 percent of Millennials in 2002 and 41 percent of Gen Xers in 1986.[11]

How can they be more entrepreneurial than previous generations but working less? They seem to have more desire than follow through, which is exactly what I mean by "growing up fast and slow." The energy, the passion, the ideas, and creativity—it's all there, but what is lacking is follow through. Perhaps they don't know *how* to follow through.

The looming risk and fear of failure (and potentially even public ridicule via social media) has led to an overwhelming anxiety that has left Gen Z paralyzed. This is not to say they are lazy or lack initiative; in fact, the opposite is true: 46 percent of Gen Z are now part of the gig economy,[12] where they can work when—and if—they feel like it. This is a high percentage considering only 36 percent of the overall workforce participates in the gig economy as either a full- or part-time job, and 29 percent consider it their full-time job.[13]

The gig economy provides workers an opportunity to be their own boss and get a taste of entrepreneurship without actually taking the risk of starting that business they've been dreaming about. It's an opportunity for them to discover if being an entrepreneur is actually what they want to do or if they would be more content in a more traditional job.

Rather than starting their own business or pursuing traditional employment, some may even find the gig economy lifestyle is an end in itself, not just a means to get to their desired end. One can easily string together multiple gigs to create their own, customized full-time job. They can deliver food through DoorDash or GrubHub during meal times and drive people around with Uber or Lyft between the lunch and dinner rush. One could work from 9:00 to 5:00, noon to 8:00, 9:00 to 9:00, or even a split shift from 11:00 to 2:00 and again from 5:00 to 8:00 if they just wanted to hit peak meal times. The point is, you are in total control; you decide when you want to work with few limitations. The only real limitation is certain times of day and days of the week are more profitable than others; for example, you are more likely to make more per hour delivering food on Saturdays than Mondays, but Monday may be the more desirable day to work, and one may want Saturdays off. You can choose which is more important to you—a better schedule or more money—and you may even make the most money with a schedule that is better for you. You have the freedom to decide to only work the hours where you know you will make twenty to thirty dollars an hour, and you'd rather be working on something else or pursuing recreational activities during the times when you will not make as much. By choosing to work peak hours (which could include nights and weekends), you can make a full-time income by only working part-time hours. Regardless, you have the flexibility and freedom to work if and when you feel like it. This on-demand form of work offers the ultimate flexibility and is also incredibly

> Almost half (46 percent) of Gen Z are part of the gig economy, where they can work when—and if—they feel like it.

103

entrepreneurial. It makes sense that Gen Z would be so attracted to these kinds of jobs since the rest of their lives are already on-demand. (More on this in "Truth #6: Gen Z Is Used to Being the CEO of Their Life.")

The perfect storm has created highly entrepreneurial individuals. In this context, growing up fast has been great for Gen Z. While they may not necessarily have refined the practical and emotional skills needed to succeed in this space, they can bounce their ideas off their peers online, obtain real-world help from their guide(s), and take part in a new and exciting gig economy that affords them maximum flexibility to make a living while they figure out how to launch a successful business. Of course, not all of them will make it to this point and not all will launch their own businesses. As Gen Z transitions out of college and into the workforce, the gig economy also provides a temporary income while they secure a full-time job in their field. Sometimes, it even helps them develop the emotional skills they didn't refine when they took in all the information they were taught in college or from their online peers around the world.

The fact that Gen Z is growing up fast and slow has implications on absolutely everything, not just technology. This undercurrent has repercussions no matter what you do—for parents, educators, employers, and for Gen Z themselves. Even if access to technology is limited, the overabundance of technology in virtually everything we do is not only changing our world, it's changing us and changing the way we raise children in this new world. Sure, you can try to go off the grid, but it is difficult to escape—even the Amish see the value in advertising their furniture online. If this is not an indicator that we have entered a new era, I don't know what is.

In this new era, everything we thought we knew is totally different, including how Gen Z works, how they learn, and *who* they learn from.

Robin Chase, founder of ZipCar, puts it this way: "My father had one job in his lifetime, I will have six jobs in my lifetime, and my children will have six jobs at the same time."[14]

I've witnessed gig workers use message boards like Reddit to communicate with other gig workers and discover the best gigs in their geographic area. They no longer have to rely on co-workers who they may or may not click with for advice on how to improve and make the most of their job.

Instead, they can be mentored by their peers across the country—and even all over the world—who help them solve problems, maximize earnings, and discover hacks that will make them more efficient as they perform their gigs.

So many different gig apps are out there today. I named six in the category of food delivery alone, and surely, there are more—or there will be more by the time you read this book. Of course, Uber and Lyft are also two popular apps that receive the most airtime, but they can also make workers wary of the gig economy all together. You risk a much higher liability with having a stranger in your car than with having a stranger's food in your car, which is why apps like Uber and Lyft rely on community ratings where both drivers and passengers rate each other after every ride. In this case, the company is not bearing the brunt of creating trust. They perform background checks on drivers, but most of the trust is built through ratings of those who use their app to either make money or get a ride. In a similar way, online reviews of products do the bulk of the marketing for the companies who make the products. Anyone can read or write generally unbiased reviews because no one stands to win or lose financially from their review, which gives users a better idea of which product is for them. This also takes away a portion of the burden of convincing a customer to use their product as they have others doing this for them—who often aren't even getting paid to do so.

Uber and Lyft weren't the first to innovate in this space, though they are often synonymous with the gig economy. The idea for what became Europe's BlaBlaCar was born in France as early as 2003 when an entrepreneur was trying to get from Paris to the south of France at the last minute for the holidays. He didn't own a car and couldn't get a seat on a train, but he saw countless cars with empty seats and thought that there must be a way to link up those who needed a ride with drivers who had empty seats in a safe and secure manner that wasn't just an app-based version of hitchhiking. In 2003, before social media was commonplace, this idea was light years ahead of its time.

If you aren't interested in driving as your gig, plenty of other options are out there. You can find gig work walking dogs, doing odd jobs, putting together furniture, or working for a day in a warehouse. The options are endless. Not only do you get to choose the type of work you perform, you can choose how long you perform it for. Perhaps it's a way to supplement your income for the long-term or provide income while you search for a new job or build a business. It could also be a way to earn extra money for something specific, like a vacation or a new guitar. I once received a ride from a singer/Uber driver in Philadelphia who was trying to earn enough money to record an album without taking out a loan.

To be fair, it's not *just* Gen Z doing this, but they are certainly working in the gig economy at a higher rate than previous generations, and it's constantly increasing. A Boomer driving for Uber may be doing so because they are down on their luck in the job market, or perhaps they just want to try something different. They may be retired and trying to earn money to pay for an album like the woman in Philadelphia. The key difference is that they had a traditional job first; they aren't doing this right out of high school or college as a primary means of income. When someone of their generation works these gigs, there is more of a stigma to it, which is virtually non-existent when Gen Z does the same thing.

> The rise of the gig economy is forcing many employers to become more flexible and offer more freedom in order to attract and retain employees.

This will radically alter our workforce. Never before in history have workers had this much flexibility and this many options, which has even bled over into the traditional workspace as many companies are recognizing they must become more flexible if they want to attract and retain top talent from the Gen Z worker pool. This is precisely our key point: Even if you are not part of the gig economy or it's not a direct competition to your business, it will soon become (if it has not already) your competitor in terms of attracting talent. Additionally, employees can more easily quit a job that they don't like because they can begin making money via apps practically overnight, giving them a softer landing if they don't have another job to jump directly into. This will mean Gen Z workers will not stick around in toxic workplaces as long as previous generations did—or even in healthy workplaces that simply don't offer the freedom they desire.

With this in mind, leaders in every industry would be wise to ponder how the gig economy could disrupt their business in terms of hiring and retention, even if it is not a direct competitor. Leaders must then ask themselves how they can make their workplaces more flexible to attract a new generation of skilled workers.

Takeaway

The perfect storm has left us with a generation that is growing up fast and slow at the same time. Ease of access to information has made young people more knowledgeable; however, a disconnect and lack of maturity accompany this knowledge. The younger generation doesn't always have the street smarts to complement their knowledge from previous generations because they have been filtered out and replaced by the internet, by someone on the other side of the world who is more compelling. You no longer need Dad to show you how to change a tire because you can easily find a video on YouTube to walk you through the entire process.

In this new era, everything we thought we knew is totally different, including how Gen Z works, how they learn, and who they learn from. They don't need a sage on stage; they need a guide positioned by their side—a GPS to help them navigate this new world. You don't automatically qualify as the guide by their side just because you're a parent, teacher, or member of an older generation. You have to earn this role; you have to get permission to become part of their curated stream. We will delve into this further in "Truth #9: Gen Z Needs a GPS."

The rise of the gig economy has radically altered our workforce, forcing many employers to become more flexible and offer their employees more freedom. Since Gen Z already lives on-demand lives, it makes sense that they prefer on-demand work as well. They want to determine *when* they will work, *where* they will work, and *how* they will accomplish their work. We will unpack more on this in the next chapter.

Z

TRUTH #6
Gen Z Is Used to Being
the CEO of Their Life

A few years back, a comedian tweeted that his daughter was looking for a summer job and hoping to find part-time work as a CEO.[1] He was being sarcastic, of course, but this statement struck me as more than just a joke—it actually summed up in two sentences what I have observed in this generation.

What we have today is a generation that has more options than ever before; thanks to the internet, smartphones, tablets, and streaming, their options are truly endless, and they are used to having what they want, when they want it. They have no concept of waiting until a particular time for a TV show to come on. Why on earth would you do that when you can stream an entire season of a TV show whenever you feel like it? Why would you wait a week to find out what happens to the characters when you can binge watch an entire season over the weekend? Why listen to an entire cassette tape or buy a CD with ten songs you don't want to hear just to hear the one song you do when you can stream it on-demand?

This on-demand lifestyle doesn't just apply to the way movies and music are consumed. It applies to absolutely everything. This new world is making it easier and easier for them to curate every aspect of their lives. Why wait until the bank opens to complete a transaction when you can do it on an app anytime while you're watching a movie or doing something else? Why even wait for your coffee when you can order it via mobile so it's ready to go the moment you step foot into the coffee shop? Why sit in traffic and waste time walking the aisles of the grocery store when you can order your groceries from home and have them delivered to your door? If you're not sure what to cook, you can order a meal kit that comes with pre-measured ingredients and instructions to cook your own five-star meal. Or skip cooking entirely and order food from your favorite restaurant with an app for delivery in under an hour.

> Since everything is available on-demand, Gen Z is used to functioning like the CEO of their own life from a very young age.

Gen Zers are digital natives. They use apps and the internet for doing life. Everything is available on-demand, and as a result, Gen Z is used to functioning like the CEO of their own life from a very young age. This should not come as a surprise to us; the world they've grown up in has made them this way. They don't have the same carefree attitude of the generations who grew up in a different era; so much more is coming at them today. So as CEOs of their lives, they use their eight-second filter to control what they will pay attention to. Not necessarily because they care less about what is filtered out but because they know they can only focus on so much to avoid being continually distracted and never focusing on anything (or anyone) significant.

Gen Z not only desires to access information and content on their schedule, they also prefer *access* over *ownership*. That may seem crazy to some, but they are the CEO, and this is what they like. Kevin Kelly brings up this point in *The Inevitable* when discussing how the future world will work: "Every year I own less of what I use. Possession is not as important as it once was. Accessing is more important than ever."[2]

A few years ago, a journalist made this striking observation: "Uber, the world's largest taxi company, owns no vehicles. Facebook, the world's most popular media owner, creates no content. Alibaba, the most valuable retailer, has no inventory. And Airbnb, the world's largest accommodation provider, owns no real estate. Something interesting is happening."[3]

There is now a Uber for practically everything—and it works. As Kelly explains, "The promise to customers is that you don't need a lawn mower or washing machine or to pick up flowers, because someone else will do that for you—on your command, at your convenience, in real time—at a price you can't refuse. The Uber-like companies can promise this because, instead of owning a building full of employees, they own some software. All the work is outsourced and performed by freelancers (prosumers) ready to work. The job for Uber for X is to coordinate this decentralized work and make it happen in real time."[4]

Uber isn't just providing opportunities for entrepreneurs to make a living while choosing when and where they will work, they are also changing how transportation works. Airbnb doesn't just allow people with an extra room to make extra cash, they are changing how travelers find accommodations—and increasing one's options.

Access over ownership affects companies, industries, and our own lives in big ways and small ways as well. I think most people today would rather have digital versions of media over CDs or DVDs, but we have seen a significant change in recent years as we've shifted from ownership to access. Most Millennials remember the shift from owning CDs or DVDs to digital downloads, but these physical files still lived somewhere. You would pay to download them, and the file would appear on your device. But now everything is in the cloud, and we pay to access it. We have Spotify for our music, and Netflix for our movies—a new streaming service seems to debut every month. These platforms give you the option to stream as much content as you like, but once you cancel your subscription, you don't actually own anything; you were simply paying to access it. Amazon offers another option where you can buy movies and TV shows that live in the cloud, but you don't receive a physical product. You can watch them on-demand on any device, but you're paying for access rather than purchasing a physical product. The difference is there is no subscription; you only pay once for access to each product.

Access over ownership is becoming more and more prevalent in our culture. You can pay to access office space for a single day or subscribe to a shared office to use when you need it for much less than the cost of a traditional office space. Instead of owning a car or relying on public transit alone, you can use Uber or Lyft to be driven anywhere or a service like

ZipCar to find a car near you to drive on-demand without waiting in line for a traditional rental car. According to ZipCar, An estimated 10 percent of the population will adopt car sharing as their primary mode of transportation by 2025.[5]

> An estimated 10 percent of the population will adopt car sharing as their primary mode of transportation by 2025.

Even if you own a vehicle, you can still benefit from access over ownership. A friend of a friend recently needed to make an out-of-state trip to another city about three or four hours away. But Luke was concerned that his high-mileage vehicle might not be up for the challenge. He decided to rent a car and found a great deal for the one-day trip. This turned out to be a smart move because a deer ran into the side of the car when he was on his way home. He had declined the rental company's collision insurance but only because the credit card he had used to pay for the car offered a collision waiver for rentals.

When Luke turned the car back in to the rental center, he simply dropped the vehicle off and went on his way. It was no longer his problem to deal with; he didn't even have to use his personal insurance.

In this scenario, access over ownership paid off in a significant and tangible way. While most situations will not be this dramatic, as the world continues to move in this direction, we will find that it is easier and more convenient to pay a small fee for access to certain goods instead of a larger fee to own them. In the future, this may become the only way to access certain items.

The list of items one can access instead of owning is constantly growing, and a time may come when we pay to access more items or content than we own, which will significantly alter the way we live and work. This may sound radical or even scary, but if you think about it, we've been doing this for decades with gym memberships. It's just on a larger scale and encompasses more of our lives. No matter your perspective, we are moving toward this reality. At the very least, you should begin asking yourself what it will look like when a generation who has only known the on-demand life becomes the dominant population in your office.

When my kids were teenagers, computer strategy games were very popular: *The Sims, RollerCoaster Tycoon,* you name it. These simulation games made the computer even more of an access point to another world. Well, these games are back, but this time, they're in Apple's app store. It wouldn't make sense, twenty years later, for them to only be available on PC when Mac is a strong competitor, and we now have mobile devices to boot. In fact, many only play games on mobile devices because they want to have them on demand whenever they have a few minutes to kill between other activities. Unless you're an avid gamer, there simply isn't enough time to get lost in a game for hours—or maybe you want the ability to do that anywhere you are. What if you want to build a SimCity while lying on the beach? You wouldn't take your computer or even a laptop out there with you, but you'd almost certainly have your phone with you.

The developers of these games realized they needed to make them more compatible with mobile devices, but they also took advantage of a new way of distributing their games to the users. Instead of paying a onetime fee of twenty or thirty dollars to own a copy of the PC game, they allow you to download RollerCoaster Tycoon to your phone for *free.* This may seem counterintuitive, but it's actually genius. You see, once you get hooked on the free game, you'll find paid extras you can download to enhance the gameplay. It's very easy to spend ten, twenty, fifty, and even a hundred dollars to unlock new aspects of the game that cost money. Rather than a onetime fee, the developers are now making money from the same people on a recurring basis. It doesn't matter that some people will never buy the extras because they make more money by giving the game away for free and charging for unlimited extras than they do by charging everyone a flat price for the game a single time.

More and more games are using this model. There's no risk to join, and once it's a part of your stream, you can pay for special features if you choose to do so. It's the same concept as access over ownership—you don't receive a physical disk containing the game; it comes from the cloud. The business model invites everyone to download the app. Everyone can play for free, and most will. Others will pay a bit but not much more than the cost of the game in its former disk format. However, a third group will pay that much many times over. The game developers have successfully built a relationship and figured out a way to monetize that relationship on a recurring basis. Your business must learn to do this as well to thrive in a changing economy.

— — —

Endless options, on-demand lifestyles, and access over ownership have caused Gen Z to grow up faster than previous generations—but if you recall, Gen Z is growing up fast and slow at the same time. They sometimes allow items through their filter that they would be better off to filter out, and they sometimes filter out important items. They may also get more caught up in a task or goal and forget to nurture personal relationships. This is why statistics consistently show Gen Z more prone to experiencing loneliness than previous generations. They are the most connected; yet, at the same time, they are the loneliest generation in history as we have already discussed in the previous chapter. In spite of this, they have a global network and are more likely to be mentored by peers around the world than the adults in their local community (which we will discuss in "Truth #7: Gen Z Is the First Generation Mentored Primarily by Their Peers"). They understand the power of influence and know that if you don't have this commodity, you won't get very far. (We will discuss this at length in "Truth #8: Gen Z Understands Influence Is Today's Most Powerful Currency.") All these factors have created this new kind of human—this alien of sorts—who functions as the CEO of their own life, which, of course, impacts the way they work as well.

Many workplaces have recognized the shift Gen Z has brought about and began making work more flexible. These companies will find, a few years from now, that this move has actually future-proofed their businesses, giving them a leg up over the competition that requires work be performed on-site, in a downtown office building, between the hours of nine to five. This traditional model has forced many to choose between spending one to

> Endless options, on-demand lifestyles, and access over ownership have caused Gen Z to grow up faster than previous generations, but they are also the loneliest generation in history.

two hours (or more) commuting or paying sky-high downtown rent prices. Previous generations seemed to accept that this was just how the world worked. If you wanted a nice home for your family in the suburbs, you needed a decent job downtown, which ironically meant you had less time with your family in the suburbs. Not every scenario played out exactly like this, but it was widely accepted that a good-paying job often meant a long commute. Gen Z has been the first generation to challenge this status quo en masse. While some will follow the traditional methods, many more will seek jobs that work with their schedule, whether in the gig economy or for a company with more flexibility that allows them to work from home on their own terms.

We are in a transition period here, too, as many companies have been slow to evolve in this area. Since Gen Z grew up during the great recession of 2008, they understand that jobs are scarce and a limited number of positions are available in their desired field. So they will actually compromise in this area. Out of fear of not having a job, many will accept jobs that offer less flexibility or that go against what we just discussed. However, they will not stay at these jobs long-term. When an opportunity with more flexibility comes along, they'll jump on it; just because your open positions are filled with Gen Z workers today doesn't mean they will be a year from now. The best way to future-proof your business is to ensure that your structure aligns with what Gen Z has come to expect, and this can be done without sacrificing bottom-line results. This is crucial because this generation doesn't just make up your employee roster; they are also your largest customer base.

I once spoke with a student after he finished his first day of nine to five work, part of his college internship. He was exhausted and a bit disillusioned. "I've never experienced this before," he told me. "I've never worked this much all at once. How do people do this? How do they focus on one thing for eight hours straight?"

> The COVID-19 pandemic greatly accelerated changes in how work is performed. This is the way of the future and not just a temporary change. Not all jobs will make this shift, but many will become much more flexible than they were before 2020.

I chuckled a bit internally, as there are many days where I would love to work only eight hours. He went on to explain that at least his college classes were split up with a break in between them, whether a few hours or a whole afternoon. But he didn't attend eight straight hours of classes. Many students have class in the morning and class in the evening with a large gap in the afternoon to do as they please. Some use this time to work a gig or a job on campus. Others will use it to clean their dorm and do laundry. Still others do homework. But perhaps most will use it to watch Netflix, take a nap, or hit the gym. Some students may even use the time to do all of the above: take a quick nap, catch up on their favorite TV show while they wait for their DoorDash to arrive, throw in a load of laundry, head to the gym, or deliver DoorDash themselves for a few hours. The point is, they are used to an on-demand lifestyle, and doing one thing for eight hours straight is difficult to fit into that. Sure, they may show up and be physically present in your workspace for eight hours, but that doesn't necessarily mean you're getting eight hours of work out of them. You may actually find that they produce more working from home for eight hours on and off within a sixteen-hour period or that they can do eight hours of work in six hours from their living room or a coffee shop. Just the fact that they didn't have to sit in traffic for an hour with another hour-long commute waiting for them at the end of the day may give them the spark they need to accomplish more in less time.

While some jobs must be done on-site for a certain period of time with little more than a lunch break, many jobs are, in truth, more flexible than we have traditionally made them. As a new generation floods the workforce, will we be hung up on how we've always done things? Or will we be willing to make adjustments if it means we can attract the very best Gen Z talent? Once we hire them, will we be willing to relinquish control and give them a say regarding when and how they work? As long as we find ourselves in a time of economic prosperity and an abundance of jobs, we will *have* to become more flexible if we want to keep the talent we attract.

Many jobs are more flexible than we have traditionally made them.

Think about it this way: From a very young age, we have taught our young people to live this on-demand lifestyle through the way they attend school. Regular school classes through grade twelve are quite structured and all revolve around preparing kids for college. There, they are given the opportunity to pick their own classes, set their own schedules, and write their thesis on whatever topic they like. Everything is customized and tailored to the individual throughout their college experience. Then they graduate, enter the workforce, and are now told that they must produce according to our schedule. Almost overnight, their entire world is different, and the part-time jobs they had in college insulated them from the full weight of this reality. No wonder we have so many students who have worked hard for years at school and their part-time jobs but end up struggling when they land their first "adult job."[*]

We look at them and say they are having a difficult time transitioning to adulthood, yet we (collectively) created the world they were raised in. We unknowingly taught them to have completely different expectations than what they will ultimately experience.

Until now.

Gen Z is the first generation that has stepped up on a large scale and demanded that the world adjust to them rather than them adjusting to the world—and the craziest part is, it's actually happened.

The world has changed for all of us, so now, schools, workplaces, and even the home must adapt to this on-demand, siloed life that Gen Z has been living almost from day one—where they can eat when they want, work when they want, get an Uber to take them where they want to go (no more waiting on a parent)—and each one of these is customized to suit the needs of the individual at the moment. They can select the type of Uber they want, or they can use a car-sharing service to select the exact make, model, and color of car they are in the mood for. Not only do they exempt themselves from the hassles of owning a car, they can have a new car every day. But they can also get by without a car because they have apps that give them access to every restaurant in town for food delivery, or they can have

---

[*] One way that leaders can leverage the strength of their Gen Z employees is to adapt their already well-refined work styles. Harness instead of change. Essentially, educators have spoken about this concept forever. Kids are so creative when they are young, but when they reach school age, they slowly but surely lose this creativity. They assimilate and adapt to their environment because they want to fit in.

groceries delivered if they prefer to cook themselves. Many of these apps are beginning to offer delivery from other types of stores as well, so one can now get lunch, groceries for dinner, and dog food delivered on-demand.

Restaurants also offer far more options than in the past and will make food just how a customer likes it—so they can have mass customization on top of endless options. Fast-food restaurants have developed apps that make it simple to customize a meal to suit their every whim. This is why they are so outraged over seemingly small matters or when something doesn't turn out exactly as they requested it because their expectations have changed and are now much higher.

This doesn't just affect how they order a hamburger but how they want to work as well. This is why they prefer jobs that give them ultimate flexibility, and some of these app-based gigs even spell out the exact nature and estimated amount of time it will take to complete the task and then give the person who will potentially perform the work a minute or two to decide if they actually want to do it. The gig economy is again a sign of a mindset shift and an indication that Gen Z is already changing the world around us in ways we would never have anticipated. While these are physical actions, I am trying to highlight a mindset: The world is structured to serve me, and I am able to determine the schedule.

This is why it is much more difficult to pigeonhole Gen Z than even Millennials because their world is so customized to them, and they are encouraged to be their own customized selves. Every aspect of their lives is customized; they are their own boss, their own CEO. It can be difficult for Mom and Dad to limit their options in a world that gives them so many choices and the ability to customize virtually anything to their liking.

Burger King's marketing team must have been made up of futurists because they caught on to this mindset shift decades ago when they introduced the slogan Have It Your Way in the 1970s. Now, it's even easier to Have It Your way at virtually any fast-food restaurant because the app shows you all the different options when you place your mobile order—even the secret-menu options.

We also see this with banks that are open past five and seven days a week. I never want to go to the bank anymore, and neither does Gen Z, but these companies understand they must adapt to a changing world in order to remain relevant to their largest potential customer base.

The movie *City Slickers* (1991) includes an early scene where the characters played by Billy Crystal and Danny DeVito are doing a show-and-tell presentation at their kids' school. Mitch—played by Crystal—is going through a mid-life crisis exacerbated when he begins telling the kids about his job and he realizes how boring it is and how he has no real autonomy or authority. His advice to the class is to "value this time in their lives" because while they are still young, "they still have their choices." He then goes into a lengthy monologue about how, for the rest of your life, others will make your choices for you.

Mitch is a Boomer with a cynical outlook that is more common amongst Gen Xers, but the cynicism of some in these generations is certainly based in reality. This, however, is not the case with Gen Z; they are actually presented with more choices the older they get. Unlike Mitch, who is lamenting the loss of his options, Gen Z is actually happy when their choices are pared down for them and they don't have to rely so heavily on their filter. If anything, they suffer from too many choices rather than a lack of choices, absolutely affects the way that they work.

> Gen Z suffers from too many choices rather than a lack of choices.

As you can imagine, all this is setting Gen Z up on a collision course as they enter the workspace with the generations that came before them. One executive was struggling with an employee who wanted to work on multiple screens and at their own pace. He wanted to work when he wanted to, which happened to be after dinner and into the night when he felt most creative and focused. He wanted to work on demand and how he wanted, and he always got the work done, so his boss gave him a lot of rope once he proved himself. He checked all the required boxes, so his boss gave him grace with the how. This was a big risk for the boss to take, as this wasn't common at the time. But for the employee, this was his normal and how he functioned best. He had always rolled this way, and the old rules and customs of a traditional office environment made no sense to him. He did understand that some things had to be done a certain way and he had to do other things outside his normal for the sake of the company culture and team dynamics. He was open to listening and doing his part in the process and didn't want to be told, "Just do it *this* way." The results spoke for themselves, which is what those he reported to were looking for. Plus, he was happy. It was a win for everyone.

This will not work in every situation, but Gen Z is currently the only generation entering the workforce for the first time, and as more and more of these CEOs start out in entry and mid-level positions, we will need to be more and more flexible if we want to pull the best out of them. Amazingly, small adjustments—that may seem radical because they have never been done before—by leaders will make a world of difference in making Gen Z feel more comfortable as the workplace begins to align more with how they have been taught to live and what they have come to expect.

Some executives are concerned that if they give their employees too much freedom, they will only get the bare minimum in return. This may be true in some cases, but these employees are not people you want on your team to begin with. Find the right employees and give them some rope. As long as they are performing and the end results are where they need to be, is there really a problem?

— — —

We've been using the phrase *a new era* to describe the time we are stepping into for a few years now. I used to call it *the new normal* until this expression became terribly overused during the COVID-19 pandemic. It was often used to say, "We really don't know what's going to happen. We know it will look different, but we don't know how it will look different. We don't know how long life will be this way, and we really don't have a clue what's going on, so we'll just call it 'the new normal'—which just means we don't know a whole lot about what is happening."

The new era we are transitioning into became even more pronounced in 2020 when we saw even more accelerations in technology as many office workers transitioned to a new way of working remotely. Some of these changes will surely only be temporary, but more and more companies will probably become more flexible with how their employees work in the future. While some are looking forward to returning to the office and their normal routines, others have found that they don't miss the commute, they enjoy more time with their families, and they are perhaps even more productive at home than at the office.

Regardless of where you fall on the scale, as companies have been forced to allow their teams to work from home, many have found that it didn't hurt their bottom line—and, in some cases, it even enhanced it. At the end of the day, it comes down to two things: trust and normality. If I don't trust an employee to do their work at home and require them to be in an office where I can keep an eye on them, I probably shouldn't hire them in the first place. Sure, many folks truly are more productive in an office environment, but that isn't the primary reason why we work in offices. For many companies and leaders, it's about control. So when younger workers want the freedom to work remotely, their desires are often quickly dismissed by their (often older) bosses. This has largely been true even at cutting-edge tech companies in Silicon Valley where the bosses are Millennials. They certainly offer more freedom than a traditional workspace but not the level of freedom Gen Z craves as they have been conditioned to be autonomous from a young age. It's not just entitlement—the perfect storm made them this way, and we as parents helped at times.

Please understand, I am not saying any boss who wants their team to work in the office for forty hours a week is an egomaniac or controlling. Every industry can't allow their workers to work from home, and not every job can be performed from home. Thus, just because one requires their workers to be on-site does not mean they don't trust them. Another factor at play, which is arguably a larger factor, is what society considers normal. Working in an office is normalized, and those who work from home full-time are often outliers. This has been our normal for many years. But in 2020, many of us were suddenly thrust into a new normal, and not every change that took place was a temporary change to combat a virus. COVID forced many companies to temporarily innovate, but as these innovations become permanent, companies in all fields will be affected. This could very well be a tipping point that leads us into a new era that has absolutely nothing to do with a virus but more to do with a newfound way of working that cuts costs, increases loyalty and morale, and gives access to better pools of talent—all without sacrificing productivity. We were already transitioning into this new era before 2020, but this was the year the process was suddenly accelerated.

Let's take a look at Facebook. Prior to 2020, they—like most big companies—were office-centric, offering perks like free cafeterias, the ability to work with colleagues in multiple shared spaces throughout the building rather than being confined to a desk in a single location, and even dry-cleaning services "to give employees little reason to go home, let alone avoid the office."[6]

As one journalist noted: "Tech executives have long believed that person-to-person communication was a big part of the creativity that went into generating popular products. They built giant campuses that reflected that belief, from the trendy and elaborate offices of Apple, Google and Facebook in Silicon Valley to the new Amazon headquarters in Seattle."[7]

Facebook's Bay Area headquarters, made up of more than thirty buildings that span both sides of the Bayfront Expressway in Menlo Park, is a sort of city within a city, boasting more than 15,000 workers in a community of 32,000. Two of the most prominent buildings were designed by world-renowned architect Frank Gehry to create a modern and fun atmosphere that would appeal to workers of all ages. In 2015, Facebook even offered workers cash payments of up to fifteen thousand dollars to move within ten miles of the office. Granted, this isn't much when one takes into account the price of housing in that area, but it demonstrates that Facebook placed a high value on the presence of workers in the office environment. At least they used to. COVID changed all of that.

"Before the virus happened, a lot of the discussion about the tech sector was about how to bring people to work sites and create affordable housing," a urban and regional planning professor in Buffalo, New York, stated.[8]

In March 2020, even before local shelter-in-place orders were issued, Facebook and other tech companies transitioned their teams to working remotely. By May, they were pleasantly surprised to learn that their employees performed better than expected, which is especially striking when one considers how stressful this period of time was. There was already chatter that tech workers preferred remote work, but businesses were forced into this radical change, which caused them to see this conversation through a new lens. So they asked, "What if we made this the new normal even when there's isn't a public health emergency? We can give workers more flexibility, increase morale, decrease costs (of large office spaces), and recruit from a larger pool of top talent who want to work with us but don't want to relocate to Silicon Valley, no matter how much we offer to pay them."

Sister companies Twitter and Square (now Block) were among the first to make this game-changing move, announcing that their employees would be allowed to work from home indefinitely. After this announcement, Google Trends reported a spike in searches for "Twitter jobs."[9] Facebook followed suit, announcing in May that as many as half of the company's 48,000 employees would be working from home within ten years.[10]

While making this announcement, chief executive Mark Zuckerberg stated: "It's clear that COVID has changed a lot about our lives, and that certainly includes the way that most of us work. Coming out of this period, I expect that remote work will be a growing trend as well."[11]

If other tech companies follow suit, we will probably see a decentralization in tech jobs. Workers will no longer need to be in Silicon Valley, New York, or Austin, and tech companies will have access to talent they would not previously have had access to. If the best worker for the job is in Indiana and has no problem leaving, that will not be a big deal, although companies will probably adjust starting salaries to fall in line with the cost of living locally for individual workers, much to the disappointment of those who might like to collect a high coastal salary but live in Middle America in order to maximize their disposable income.

If this happens, what will happen to these big corporate campuses? They may just get rid of them. I'm sure they will be happy to shed the extra expense of maintaining these facilities. Perhaps once a month, they will rent a space and bring everyone together for a day, but you don't need to maintain an entire office complex to do this. We may soon see a day where office parks sit empty and fall into disrepair, much like the abandoned warehouses and former factories of the Rust Belt and many cities in the Northeast—until a new generation decides to turn them into hip and trendy lofts.

Will what is taking place at Facebook, Twitter, Square, and other tech giants become the new normal? Or will it merely be a temporary normal?

For tech companies, it seems as if these changes will, at least in part, become a new part of their company culture. But whether this trend becomes widespread will be determined by whether a tipping point is reached. It is also possible that a tipping point could happen within the tech industry, leading to a new normal of decentralized workspaces, but traditional industries could largely revert back to the former ways of running businesses. We may even see some businesses adopt a hybrid model that blends both the old and the new, and we are indeed already seeing this.

I know one business owner who thinks that remote work is not a positive, even after a year of it working pretty well at his company. He thinks that everyone needs to be in the office to get the best out of them and that his employees will be more productive in an environment where the boss is on site and can pop into their offices at any time as they work on projects.

This model has been our normal for so long because we aren't always organized. When we get our teams started on new projects, we don't have everything ready to go, so we just start moving and lay out expectations and guidelines as we go. This requires everyone on site so we can monitor the course and help steer the ship in the right direction. So many managers function this way, and they have to because they have not mapped everything out for their team in advance. But if they became better organized and rolled out all the expectations, goals, and metrics that will be used to measure progress up front, everyone would know exactly what they need to do and could do it from anywhere. They might even function better in an environment that doesn't have the distractions of people popping in and out of the room as they work. The course is mapped out and clear, so the boss doesn't need to be there to help create the map as they go because it's already been prepared for them.

The trickiest part about the fully remote workspace is building a healthy culture within the organization. This goes beyond being organized and making expectations clear. The truth is, many organizations don't intentionally build a healthy culture. They may have a mission statement or some bullet points written down somewhere, but it is all they can do to get through the day and accomplish whatever it is their organization is tasked with accomplishing in order to survive. The emphasis is on the day-to-day, and little thought is given to the long-term health of the organization and employee culture as all the long-term thinking tends to be taken up by products and profits. Sometimes, these organizations end up being relatively healthy by default due to the health of their leaders, but as organizations struggle to pull this off without a degree of intentionality as they grow larger. Remote work makes this task more difficult because it's tricky to ensure everyone is on the same page when they aren't in the same room or the same building.

Rather than making a decision for everyone based on the productivity habits of the few, leaders must treat everyone as individuals and help them make the needed adjustments so that they function at their best. This is true whether the employee is working from home or in an office. Everyone has areas where they excel and areas where they need coaching, and leaders can effectively learn to manage this tension if they lean into it.

The bottom line is, if we are willing to look past the how and just focus on the what and when—what will be accomplished by the deadline—how the tasks are accomplished will become irrelevant. The only thing managers need to do is make the expectations clear so everyone knows what is expected of them. Then, the employees can figure out how they want to accomplish the tasks. (And shouldn't this always be the process anyway?) Maybe this means they take some time at the beginning of the day to work on personal projects, maybe it means they take a break in the middle of the afternoon, or maybe it means they start at the traditional time but finish all their work sooner and have additional time to manage their personal lives and connect with their families. Regardless of the avenue the employee chooses to accomplish their work, the end result is the same: happier, more creative, and more productive humans. This is good for everyone.

We all have a unique way of working that works for us, and the truth is, most people do not want to disappoint you. It may be the eleventh hour before something gets done, but if an employee can navigate managing this kind of stress and works best under pressure, let their results speak for themselves. Some people are most productive when they wait until the last minute.

This new way of working will probably not remain within the tech space. The forced experiment of remote work has had amazing results, and many businesses are finding they can't argue with productivity and profitability, even if they dislike the idea of everyone working from home.

Two key factors will be at play, affecting businesses in the future. Businesses will have to compete with other companies in their industry who allow their employees to work from anywhere, but they will also have to compete with the gig economy as it continues to evolve.

As the war for talent becomes more and more competitive, those who resisted adopting this new way of operating will find that they have lost their competitive edge. Businesses currently have a profound opportunity to follow the lead of the big tech companies and innovate before they're forced to by making temporary changes permanent.

If your business can do this, why wouldn't you want to be on the front end of this tipping point as it begins to tip? (Hurry—it's tipping!) This could be one of the best decisions you make to future-proof your business. It will give you access to some of the best talent in the world as the most skilled person for the role may not live nearby and may not desire to relocate. This impending tipping point didn't emerge from nowhere. The world was already moving in this direction before the pandemic. Like the exponential growth in technology that we have seen in the last decade, COVID-19 simply sped up these changes and moved us closer to the tipping point.

We have already discussed this in "Truth #2: Gen Z Is Growing Up in a World that Has Never Existed Before," but here is the visual to refresh your memory:

INNOVATION ADOPTION CURVE

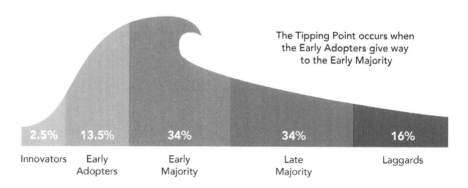

The Tipping Point occurs when the Early Adopters give way to the Early Majority

| 2.5% | 13.5% | 34% | 34% | 16% |
| Innovators | Early Adopters | Early Majority | Late Majority | Laggards |

Personally, now that we are well into 2022, I believe the way of the future is not fully remote. I think we were trending in this direction in 2020, but employees of all ages began to miss the camaraderie and team building that unfolds naturally in a centralized workspace. However, this probably won't mean that we revert back to the old ways of being in the office every day. Instead, the workspace of the future is a hybrid workspace, which will unfold in a myriad of different ways, depending on the company and industry. It could look like working from home Monday/Wednesday/Friday and being in the office Tuesday/Thursday, alternating home/office every other week, working mostly in the office with the option to work a day or two each week from home, or mostly working from home but coming together in a central location once a week or once a month. (This space may not even be a traditional office complex but a neutral space the company rents out one day a month, which serves both the purpose of bringing everyone together while cutting down on rent and utilities.) Regardless of how it will look, I predict hybrid will become the way of the future—not because COVID-19 changed our world but because it caused us to innovate and find new ways of operating that benefit both the company and its workers.

The perfect storm has modified the world we live in, and COVID-19 has accelerated and amplified these changes. While many have tried to resist this change—at times, successfully—this will soon be the way of the future for all of us. Some things will never go back to the way they were once the pandemic is over because the pandemic was not the primary reason for the change—it simply sped up the change and created the conditions so that more and more people from the middle of the tipping point spectrum (the late majority) moved into the space with the early adopters and early majority.

> The workspace of the future is a hybrid workspace.

Under normal circumstances, the laggards would have likely held out longer because they tend to have more money and influence, especially in powerful corporate positions and even in government. They have been able to delay the speed at which we approach the tipping point even if they are only hanging by a thread. The pandemic changed all that and tipped the tipping point. No matter what you think of this, it is the reality we are dealing with. This was not some sort of conspiracy; we would have eventually reached this point anyway.

This doesn't mean that those who have resisted change will be left behind or put out to pasture. There is a place for everyone in this new world—some of us just arrive earlier than others. Some are early adopters, most of us are in the early or late majority, and some of us are laggards. Regardless, we are all moving forward; it's simply more difficult for some of us because we don't want to let go of what we had before. We don't want to embrace a new way of doing things. You might even find yourself here, and that's okay. What is important is that you don't stagnate because if you continue to resist these changes, you will miss out on the opportunity to play a role in positively influencing this generation and the generations to come.

One day during COVID, my friend Dean Minuto told me that in times like these, legends are made, and this is true for both individuals and businesses. We are living in a time of great uncertainty. Some industries are suffering while others are growing by leaps and bounds. New industries are emerging while others become nearly obsolete, and many are wondering if they'll ever go back to the office. These are the times in which legends are made, the times in which the Fortune 500 companies of tomorrow are born.

Takeaway

We live in a world of seemingly endless options, with nearly everything at our fingertips when and how we want it. Since this has been Gen Z's reality from a very young age, they have grown up functioning as if they are the CEO of their own life. This on-demand, siloed lifestyle has led to curation of nearly every area of life, and there is now a higher value for access over ownership in many arenas. Schools, workplaces, and homes are adjusting to this new way of life and have been for some time.

All this rapid change has caused Gen Z to grow up faster than generations before them (and has also caused them to grow up slower at the same time). The COVID-19 pandemic has accelerated this rate of change dramatically.

Prior to COVID, I predicted that the workplace of the future would allow people to be more mobile. One would be able to work in different parts of the office rather than sitting behind a desk all day. Additionally, I predicted that remote work would become more normalized and employees would be able to set their own schedules. Some may want to get a very early start, while others will prefer to sleep in and work afternoons and evenings.

Some are night owls and like to begin their workday around dinnertime and work until after midnight, and others prefer a more traditional 9:00–5:00 schedule—they just want the flexibility to work from home or a coffee shop a few days a week. I predicted there would be much greater flexibility than what we saw prior to COVID, and we would reach a point where certain jobs would not require employees to work eight hours a day or forty hours a week as long as the job was performed well and expectations were met.

One way that leaders can leverage the strength of their Gen Z employees is to adapt their already well-refined work styles. Harness these instead of trying to change them. Educators have spoken about this same concept forever. Kids are so creative when they are young, but when they reach school age, they slowly but surely lose this creativity. They assimilate and adapt to their environment because they want to fit in.

When COVID hit, it wasn't so much that it changed the way we work without warning. Rather, it accelerated changes that were already taking place behind the scenes. As such, these changes will be more permanent than temporary. Not all jobs will make this shift, but many will become much more flexible than they were before 2020, and as we come out of COVID, the new normal will be a hybrid work schedule that splits time between working from home and the office.

This entire book is about giving you a new lens to see Gen Z differently. Once you see differently, you can change the way you interact with, lead, and parent this generation and the generations to follow. In this spirit, what if you shifted your perspective when it comes to big changes in the way work is done. What if, rather than seeing this as something you begrudgingly have to do to accommodate Gen Z or a COVID thing, you saw it as an opportunity to recruit the best talent possible without regard to geography? Now, your top candidate doesn't have to live in your market or be willing to relocate. You could be based in California and your best worker logs in from a small town in Indiana. You may even find they live in another country entirely.

Seeing through this new lens will change the way you lead and give your organization a competitive edge in this new world.

Z

TRUTH #7
Gen Z Is the First Generation Mentored Primarily by Their Peers

One of the things I love about this new generation is they are not afraid to speak their minds. While they value harmony, tolerance, and everyone getting along, they are not shy about speaking up when they disagree. This could seem annoying at first, but I find it quite refreshing.

As a Gen Xer, I've experienced the Abilene paradox. If you're not familiar with this phenomenon, it happens in a group when people think everyone else wants to do something, so they all jump on board only to later find out that no one actually wanted to do that at all.

This phrase was coined in 1974 by Jerry B. Harvey,[1] a leader in the management space. He told the story of a family from a small west Texas town who drove fifty miles to Abilene for a dinner that was less than enjoyable only to later find out that everyone in the group would have rather stayed home. But because they all thought other members of the family wanted to go to Abilene, they went along with it.

Of course, this happens all the time in the workspace, particularly when a leader is trying to do something for their employees, but none of them are interested. But because the boss wants them to do it, they feel obligated to say yes.

Just the other day, a friend of mine told me about an annual summer picnic where the leader of a company told everyone he had a special surprise for them and instructed them to wear closed-toed shoes. My friend grew quite anxious as the picnic approached because he knew he would have to participate in the activity, no matter what it was. *What will he make us do?* he kept asking himself, a sense of dread nearly overtaking the excitement of a fun day with his co-workers.

When the day of the picnic finally came, it turned out the surprise was axe throwing. The boss had rented a mobile trailer, and he was really excited about it, but my friend was not. "I'm not very coordinated," he told me. "I can barely throw a football straight—and he wants me to throw an axe? This is not going to end well!"

My friend tried to exempt himself from the special activity, but at one point in the afternoon, he crossed paths with his boss. "Did you see the surprise?" the boss asked. "We've got axe throwing! Have you done it yet?"

"Not yet," my friend replied. "But I will."

At that point, he knew he had no choice. He took part in the activity and as it turned out, he wasn't good at it, and he certainly didn't like having to do it to make the boss happy even though from the boss's perspective, the activity was a fun gift to the employees. While I'm sure many of the employees enjoyed this activity, some—not just my friend—only did it because they didn't want their boss to feel bad about the choice of activity.

The point of all this is we are influenced by the people around us every day, but this influence isn't always intentional or helpful. My friend's boss wasn't intentionally trying to make him feel obligated to participate in an activity he wasn't comfortable with; he was just trying to do something nice for his team. I'm sure some genuinely enjoyed it. At the end of the day, however, this story illustrates something we see at work all the time: a boss doing what he thinks the team will like rather than figuring out what they actually like. Given enough time, this boss is sure to plan something that no one likes, but they will go along with it and pretend that they do because they don't want to let the boss down.

My friend who went along with the axe throwing is a Millennial. Caught in the middle, he ended up doing what he thought would make the boss happy (and it did). His boss was happy to see him having a supposed good time even though inside my friend was a nervous wreck, and his participation in the activity was a bit forced. Gen Z is not like this. They would much more quickly say, "Oh yeah, I saw that axe throwing is an option, but I'm not doing that."

At this point, the boss may be a bit taken back, especially if he paid for everyone to participate in the activity. But this doesn't faze the Gen Z employee. "Thanks for doing that, but I'd rather do this instead."

Gen Z knows how to break free from the Abilene paradox and harness peer-to-peer influence in ways unlike any previous generation. They are not afraid to rock the boat, to speak up, and to let their voices be heard.

Millennials, who were primarily raised by Boomers, often found Gen X— the bridge generation—to be their allies. This generation was typically less hard on Millennials as they understood that the world was going through a rapid series of changes, and the younger generation was doing the best they could to adapt. This is why, in the classroom and workspace, Gen X largely found success in teaching and leading Millennials even while their Boomer parents struggled to connect with them.

The Boomers in the office struggled to connect with Millennials as they often misunderstood them and were unnecessarily harsh to this new generation, perhaps because they viewed them as inefficient and unprepared for life. Now we find ourselves at the place where the tipping point has tipped. The old rules no longer apply, and we no longer live in the Boomer's world, especially as Gen Z begins to join Millennials as the largest bloc in the workspace. In fact, Gen Z is currently the only generation of young people entering the workforce, and many of them are already in leadership positions.

Unlike Millennials, however, who still looked to Gen X and Boomers to guide them, Gen Z isn't looking to the older generations for guidance. While previous generations learned from the generation that came before them, Gen Z is mentored almost entirely by their peers.

This could be because Gen Z is tired of older generations (Boomers in particular) looking down on them. This happened first with Millennials, who seemed to be the generation everyone loved to hate. You don't have to look too hard before you'll hear someone quipping about "kids these days." Millennials tend to just ignore these remarks, but Gen Z is fighting back. They are fed up with older generations stereotyping them and doling out unsolicited advice, so they've come up with a witty comeback that *The New York Times* described as the digital equivalent of an eye roll: Ok, Boomer.

This phenomenon has spread like wildfire with the catchy phrase making its way onto stickers, T-shirts, hoodies, hats, water bottles, New Zealand's Parliament,[2] and even the US Supreme Court.[3] One nineteen-year-old girl designed a hoodie that repeated the phrase multiple times in the style of those retro "thank you" plastic shopping bags. She unveiled her design on TikTok and immediately had ten thousand dollars' worth of orders.[4] Another eighteen-year-old opened an online store selling "Ok, Boomer" products and plans to use the money to pay for college, and he's not alone. Many teens are cashing in on the frustration their peers feel toward the older generations.[5]

> Gen Z recognizes that they don't need adults for things that you and I needed our parents for.

The phrase "Ok, Boomer" has become, as *The Times* puts it, "Generation Z's endlessly repeated retort to the problem of older people who just don't get it, a rallying cry for millions of fed-up kids. Teenagers use it to reply to cringe YouTube videos and basically to any person over thirty who says something condescending about young people—and the issues that matter to them."[6]

As you see here, one does not need to actually belong to the Baby Boomer generation in order to be a "Boomer"; it's a state of mind, and one thing is clear: Gen Z is not tolerating the stereotypes older generations attempt to label them with.

More practically speaking, Gen Z recognizes that they don't need adults for things that you and I needed our parents for. They are mentored, primarily online, by vast networks of their own peers—sometimes peers they have never actually met but follow on Instagram or YouTube. I might also add that these peer networks are global. It's not just their friends from school or in their hometown. It's perfectly normal for two college students on opposite ends of the country to collaborate on a song remotely, and young people from all over the world are connecting with one another daily online through a myriad of platforms. They learn from each other, offer advice, and help one another out as best they can. In many cases, it works very well. For example, you may see teens asking other teens about cryptocurrency even though Dad is a successful banker. He has a career in the field, but he doesn't believe in crypto and might as well be living on another planet.

When we say Gen Z is mentored by their peers, "mentorship" implies a deep connection and transfer of knowledge, but we are also talking about everyday topics and activities here, such as checking the reviews of a restaurant before deciding whether to eat there. The Gen Zer might say, "No thanks, Mom, I don't want to go there. I know you like it, and I have never been, but I looked it up, and it doesn't have good reviews."

Investing in cryptocurrency versus stocks would be another example. It's not necessarily in depth. One could be mentored by a peer who encourages them to look into crypto as opposed to more traditional methods, but they aren't necessarily coming alongside them for hours and offering detailed investment advice. Instead, advice is often given in passing: "You should really look into bitcoin. I've heard of several people who have made a lot of money with it." The peer points them in the right direction, and they do the deep dive on their own. With everything online, they can easily find and review recommendations from people all over the world who have walked the path they are contemplating.

Some collaborations are just for fun, such as two college students in California and Vermont who came together on their computers to write and mix an "Ok, Boomer" song that made the rounds on TikTok and ended hitting the number three spot on Spotify's U.S. Viral 50 chart with more than a million streams.[7]

Peter Kuli, the student in Vermont who put the song together using clips his friend in California had recorded, had debated whether he should go to college at all before the song went viral during his sophomore year. He was already recording music and settled on Champlain College when he discovered they had a program that would allow him to specialize in sonic arts. This extremely niche form of art has been around since the 1970s but didn't begin to take off until the 2000s when technology became more advanced.[8]

Kuli wasn't trying to go viral; he simply took what he was interested in and what was trending and blended the two. He had seen the ways social media and streaming changed how artists write music.[9] For example, because TikTok relies on short soundbites, many songwriters are putting the catchiest lines of their song at the beginning instead of waiting until a minute in to drop the chorus.

> Going to college definitely helped launch Peter Kuli's career, just not in the way he expected.

"Between classes, hanging out with friends, and other standard nineteen-year-old activities," a Vermont newspaper wrote, "Kuli is sitting down for coffee with reporters and signing record deals."[10]

Yes, you heard that correctly. This simple project involving two friends living on opposite ends of the country not only ended up going viral but led to the beginning of a career. A record label purchased the rights to distribute the "Ok, Boomer" song and perhaps future music the student creates. Going to college definitely helped launch his career, just not in the way he expected.

Kuli described the record deal as "an interesting turning point" to Seven Days Vermont. "No matter what I decide to do, it's going to give me a lot of leverage," he said. "If this stupid song worked, then just about anything can."[11]

— — —

In the on-demand world, mentorship can be streamed without either party actually coming into direct contact with each other. When one filters something into their curated stream and wishes to deep dive into it to learn more, they can quickly search the internet or social media to find experts on this topic. After following these influencers for a while and absorbing the free content they offer, they may find that those they are learning from are offering paid content as well. Here, the mentorship is streamed on a subscription-based model for one to deep dive into the exact thing that interests them or that they desire to learn how to do.

A huge market is now available for these online courses, so much so that the e-learning industry was valued around $107 billion in 2015 and expected to grow to a $325 billion industry by 2025.[12] Some of this e-learning is being offered by large companies, but a huge number of individual influencers are also building and monetizing their brands online—not just through ads and views or selling physical products like books. Many are figuring out how to build relationships by offering something of value for free, then monetizing those relationships. Choosing online courses is genius, because if you only sell a book, you're looking at a onetime sale to each individual. Getting a second sale would require a great amount of time and energy to create a second product, not to mention the initial monetary investment that requires.

Creating an online course opens up an entirely new world, and it's becoming more accessible for the average person. Influencers can subscribe to services that will assist them in creating their courses (note they are "subscribing" to something that aids in creating their own subscription model), and generally, the only other thing they need is decent audio/video equipment to film themselves for the course. Everything else is built within the platform that helps them create the course. They upload the video content and build out modules, and it's ready to go to market. There's still a front-end investment, but now the power to teach others and profit from it is no longer in the hands of large institutions. Average people who have built niche online followings that have become brands can now become guides to others through online courses, and this is their full-time job. In fact, many are earning six-figure incomes from these roles that require zero higher education.

Forbes is correct in declaring "e-learning is the future,"[13] and colleges and universities are realizing they need to dive into this space to become relevant. Millennials believed their parents when they told them, "You need to go to college so you can get a good job," but Gen Z responds quite differently. If you were to tell them this, they might look at you and simply ask, "Why?" They are not swayed with "because I said so" or "this is the way it's always been done" arguments.

In spite of this, Gen Z is on track to become the most educated generation. Among eighteen- to twenty-one-year-old high school graduates, 57 percent were enrolled in college in 2018, compared to 52 percent of Millennials in 2003 and 43 percent of Gen Xers in 1987.[14]

As you can see, this change in attitude has not fully manifested in a change of behavior for Gen Z. This is likely because they grew up during a recession while Millennials came of age during a time of economic prosperity. Gen Z knows great jobs are not automatically available to everyone who wants one, and as I mentioned earlier, though they have a strong desire to start a business, they are also quite risk-averse, so taking this leap can be difficult for them. This could be why we see them giving in and pursuing a college education at the same rate as the generation before them. However, what Gen Z expects in college and eventually in the workplace is different from Millennials. They expect new technology to be a part of the learning experience and utilized at work as well, and they will consistently challenge the status quo in both spaces. This is why some colleges and universities are realizing they need to change the way they have been doing things in order to remain relevant to a new generation of "customers" in a world where all knowledge is essentially available to anyone online. We have yet to see significant change in this space, but this will quickly come to light in a post-COVID world.

Takeaway

Those who belong to more established generations often assume they know what Gen Z needs, and they are typically not afraid to offer their unsolicited advice. This advice is often met with sighs and eye rolls, akin to the "Ok, Boomer" phenomenon.

The reality is, in today's world, younger generations do not have to rely on older generations for wisdom. All the knowledge in the world is available to them at their fingertips and on-demand. In the on-demand world, mentorship can be streamed without either party actually coming into direct contact. As a result, Gen Z has become the first generation to be mentored by their peers rather than by the generation before them.

When one filters something into their curated stream and wishes to deep dive into it to learn more, they can quickly search the internet or social media to find experts on this topic. Often, these experts are their own age or not much older than they are. Like with most generations, they relate more easily to their peers, and young people today have a platform and access to more knowledge, which has allowed them to grow up faster than previous generations.

As this practice becomes more common, it becomes more difficult for older generations to play an important role in the conversation. This is why the model has shifted from sage on stage to guide positioned by the side, from SOS to GPS. (We will delve into this further in "Truth #9: Gen Z Needs a GPS.") This requires one to change their perspective, which will always lead to a change in behavior. Parents and leaders must come alongside Gen Z and enter into their world rather than expecting them to eventually grow up or come around and adapt to our world—because our world is now their world thanks to the perfect storm.

One of my main arguments is that businesses and parents alike should pay attention to all the social channels that young people use today, even if they do not engage on these platforms themselves. Businesses really have no choice but to engage if they want to stay in business. Even if a generation is not old enough to buy your product or service, they are your future customers, and you need to begin telling them the story of your brand now. (Yes, that's right—the story of your brand, not just what you have to sell.)

Even if one is not active in adding to the conversation on these social channels, these powerful listening tools will give you a window into what Gen Z values. You will learn what they believe in, what they struggle with, and how they communicate. This will allow you to build a strategy to come alongside them and add value to their lives. For businesses, this will look like connecting them to your brand and showing them how it can solve the problems they face. For parents and mentors, this will allow you to help them become the best version of themselves without being the Boomer in the room that is met with eye rolls every time you speak.

When successful, this approach will shift Gen Z's perspective to see the wisdom and insight the older generations can offer. This will get you curated into their stream because you have proven you have something to offer and can add value to their lives. It works the same way with a brand, product, or service as well.

TRUTH #8
Gen Z Understands Influence Is Today's Most Powerful Currency

Influence is the new currency and probably the most valuable commodity in our world today. Just like someone who works in marketing or customer relations knows that spending five dollars to keep a customer happy can result in five *hundred* dollars in positive PR, Gen Z understands that if you don't have influence, you won't be heard.

Influence is equivalent to a healthy company culture. It allows one to share feedback, make suggestions, and speak into someone's life without rules. When you have influence in someone's life, you can bypass their typical filters because you are already prequalified. You're part of their curated stream, or as others have put it, you've earned the right to be heard; you've built a bridge that can bear the weight of truth. You can say things that might be upsetting to someone if you didn't have relational equity.

Lyle, a friend in Nashville, recently shared a survey with me that listed the top ten jobs that kids want to hold when they grow up.

TOP TEN JOBS KIDS WANT TO HAVE

Rank	Job	Percentage
1.	YouTuber	34.2%
2.	Blogger/Vlogger	18.1%
3.	Musician/Singer	16%
4.	Actor	15.7%
5.	Filmmaker	13.6%
6.	Doctor/Nurse	13.4%
7.	TV Presenter	12.4%
8.	Athlete or Teacher	11.9%
9.	Writer	8.4%
10.	Lawyer	6.4%

*Source: Daily Mail UK; survey by First Choice Travel

As already stated, 65 percent of first graders will end up working jobs that do not currently exist.[1]

The kids surveyed in this 2017 study were able to select more than one option, which is why this data adds up to more than 100 percent. The research also revealed that Gen Z would rather learn how to use video editing software than study math and history, and a third desired to increase their knowledge of computer programming.[2]

You'll notice that the first two professions have to do with writing blogs or making videos, and the first five have to do with entertainment, as does number seven. In days past, the proverbial "good job" was a doctor or a lawyer, and while those still rank, they do not rank nearly as high as they did in previous years. They have been pushed out of their top spots by jobs that have, for the most part, just come into existence—or have been revolutionized—in the past decade. If you think about it, every job on this list has to do with influence of some kind.

Influence isn't all about offering suggestions for improvement or helping correct someone's mindset or behaviors. It also encompasses simple, everyday things that are far less consequential. When a friend recommends a certain book, movie, car, or stock pick, you are more inclined to go along with it than if someone you weren't as close to made the same recommendation. You'll also be more likely to change what you were planning to do when someone you trust recommends something else. You scrap your original lunch plans to eat at the restaurant your friend recommended. You don't buy the car you were going to buy and instead buy the same model as your trusted neighbor. You decide to apply for one job over another when you were previously torn between the pros and the cons.

> Influence isn't all about offering suggestions for improvement or helping correct someone's mindset or behaviors.

I experienced this firsthand while running one of our summer programs. Maju, a young influencer who I had met in Brazil, had agreed to be a part of our summer staff, and at one point, she posted about her upcoming camp job to her 5.6 million Instagram followers.[3] Within minutes, our channels blew up with hundreds of applications and queries about working for us the following summer.

What is most interesting about this is she didn't mention anything about employment. She briefly mentioned something she was involved in, and her followers wanted to be a part of it as a result. We continued to receive applications from young people across the world for some time—in fact, I would say we received even more applications unintentionally than we had through our intentional marketing and recruiting efforts. The craziest part of the story was we never asked her to do this. It was all organic and perfectly illustrates the power of influence that Gen Z has in shaping the decisions of their peers.

In the past, our influencers were primarily celebrities, politicians, musicians, and well-known leaders in the corporate space or various fields. Social media, however, has changed all this. Now, ordinary people—moms with small children, young adults, high school students, and even children—are becoming influencers as well. Some of these have become household names, while others are famous within their unique fields or subfields. Being an influencer is not about fame; it's about the value you add to people's lives. Influence is not a strategy but an outcome.

Gen Z is highly creative, so much so that I call them *contagious creators*. Unlike previous generations—where "being creative" might have meant creative writing or painting or playing music and songwriting—much of Gen Z's creativity encompasses the digital space. Their technology, as we have discussed, is the tool they use to create all sorts of things. They consume content, which they input through their eight-second filter into their curated stream for on-demand deep diving, but they also output a good deal of content as well.

> Being an influencer is not about fame; it's about the value you add to people's lives. Influence is not a strategy but an outcome.

One obvious way that Gen Z outputs content is through social media, primarily Instagram, Snapchat, YouTube, and TikTok. (Facebook is far less popular because that social network has become overrun by their parents and grandparents.) This is not revolutionary by any means, but what is revolutionary is how Gen Z uses social media as a tool, not just a toy. It can be a tool used to find things (such as a restaurant), learn things (through quick soundbites about current or historical events), discover things (a new place to vacation or take a day trip), or purchase things (clothes, a new watch, and even deodorant). They use social media for validation, personal encouragement, building their soft skills, reading self-help blogs, and watching videos giving physical and mental health advice. It can also be a tool used to build a career. To be clear, this is not to find a job but to create a job—a full-time job with work performed on-demand earning an income of six figures or more. I'm talking about being a digital influencer. It is not just a hobby but a legitimate way to earn a living, and more and more ordinary people are doing it.

Previous generations followed celebrities. Gen Z follows influencers. Back in the day, we had to have the shoes that Michael Jordan wore or the same style of clothes as a famous actress or use the same musical equipment as our favorite band. Of course, many of today's celebrities *are* influencers in their own right. The difference is, a celebrity can have a large following and influence, but both are based on outside accomplishments. People follow celebrities because they're famous, but influencers are famous because people follow them. This is the key difference with the type of digital influencers we are talking about as ordinary people build large followings on social platforms where they create content about things that interest them.

Much of this is very intentional. It is, in fact, why I used the phrase "create content" in the previous paragraph instead of "posting content." Influencers don't typically flip through their camera roll, find a photo they like, and think "I'll post this one." It's more intentional, more planned out. They may do something cool, such as spend a day hiking a mountain or exploring a city. They take several photos and post those in the days and weeks that follow—often spread out with other posts in between. In the same way a company may plan out their social media calendar, these influencers create quality content, plan when they will post it, and create specific calls to action. It isn't just spontaneous, even though hours may be spent to make it look as if it is. This is because Gen Z highly values authenticity, which doesn't just mean being raw and unfiltered. Sometimes, it requires careful thought and planning—especially when one is an influencer with a large following. The process of content creation might not be authentic or organic, but the intended message is.

> People follow celebrities because they're famous, but influencers are famous because people follow them.

Most of the content these influencers post is professionally produced, either by themselves or others. Some of this is done directly on their smartphones, thanks to an abundance of powerful apps, but some of it is created on their computer, like how a marketing agency may create high-quality graphics for social media or record and produce a television ad.

For an influencer, social media is their platform. The larger the platform—the more followers they have—the more time is spent creating the content that is posted on their platform. Some serial influencers even have teams of people who produce the content they post.

Sometimes, the purpose of the social content is to send us somewhere. The influencer has a blog, a website, a YouTube account, or a podcast. It doesn't matter what it is, but they want us to end up in a certain place. So they create a stream of content around their subject with the intent that we will move from following them and liking their posts to clicking on their links and watching their videos, listening to their podcast, or purchasing their products.

Other times, the social media feed is an end in itself. Companies send free products to influencers (sometimes referred to as "brand ambassadors") so they will promote the product on their stream. This is usually done very subtly, but sometimes more overtly—in a similar way to how an athlete would wear the clothing of their sponsor. I refer to these influencers as lower-tier because they have much smaller followings—sometimes in the hundreds or low thousands. Most of the time, they don't have a following of two million or even twenty-five thousand. They are much more ordinary but still have a great deal of influence within their social circles.

Higher-tier influencers are actually paid by companies to promote their products to their audience. Say, for example, an influencer is an avid hiker that is always posting photos of themselves in the mountains. The photos are beautiful, and that's what draws people in. Perhaps they even think, *I wish I could go hiking all the time like they do. Instead, I'm stuck in this office. What do they even do for a living that they can do that?* We don't realize that taking those photos is actually the influencer's full-time job. They've built up to one hundred thousand followers on Instagram, and now companies that sell outdoor products pay them for ad space. It's the new way of advertising. It's much more subtle than a TV commercial, and rather than blasting your ad out to everyone, you target the niche audience that has already expressed interest—for one reason or another—in this active, outdoor lifestyle. Plus, consumers are more likely to trust the influencers they have allowed into their curated stream than they are to trust the company itself if they saw or heard a direct advertisement. So the influencer posts about the hiking shorts they're wearing, about how comfortable and breathable they are, about how perfect they are for a long hike. Or perhaps they post a photo on a mountain peak with a sleek watch strategically positioned on their wrist. You think it's just a photo of someone who climbed a mountain when the whole post is actually a watch ad. You want the watch because the influencer you trust is wearing it while you might scroll right past it if the same watch ad from the manufacturer appeared on Facebook.

For a digital influencer, building a platform is just the beginning. The ultimate goal—if they are to turn it into a full-time income—is to build a business off their platform. Some influencers spend years building their platforms while working an outside job before they earn a dime. Others earn small incomes but never enough to quit their day job; it's more of a hobby, but they don't mind. Most influencers focus on doing what they love,

> One organization found that 92 percent of consumers trust an influencer more than an advertisement or traditional endorsement.[4]

and if they gain a huge following and it turns into a job, that's a bonus. Unlike a modern office worker, you will rarely—if ever—hear an influencer say, "I don't like what I do, but the money is good," which is especially important for Gen Z because they are so cause-driven and desire to find meaning and purpose from their work.

Take running, for example. Many people consider themselves runners, run regularly and take part in races, and post about their runs on social media. But there is a big difference between the hobbyist runner, who likely also posts photos of their kids, pets, and vacation; and the influencer runner, who posts almost exclusively about matters related to running. They've found their niche and gathered a following, attracting the attention of sponsors, and running is either supplementing or providing the majority of their income.

A catalyst often causes influencers to shift from hobbyist to entrepreneur. Sometimes an inciting event makes them an overnight success, such as a post going viral. Other times, it's a slow build. With both, they will find a tipping point where continued growth becomes inevitable. I have seen some influencers posting content to one hundred thousand or more followers and seen other influencers posting similar content of the same—or better—quality to less than a thousand followers. The person with less followers likely followed the person with more followers first, saw their success, and was influenced to follow in their footsteps. This is what I mean when I say Gen Z's creativity is contagious. The difference is, one influencer has reached a tipping point where all they have to do is keep doing what they're doing, and their influence will continue to grow. The other is in a building phase. Both require a good deal of intentionality and hard work, which is why most people follow influencers rather than becoming one.

—— —— ——

Influencers do not necessarily need massive followings in order to be successful. It all depends on their niche. A friend of mine recently told me that he and his wife are in the process of adopting a Cavapoo puppy, a designer breed that is a part Cavalier King Charles Spaniel and part Poodle, in case you were wondering. They searched for months to find a reputable breeder and finally located one in Utah, a mother/daughter team. They filled out the application and received an email from the daughter telling them they were approved and simply needed to pay the deposit to reserve their place on the waitlist. My friend responded and asked her how he should pay the deposit, expecting to receive a web link to put in his credit card information or perhaps an address to send a check to. Instead, he received an email saying he could Venmo his deposit to an account that had the daughter's first and last name as the username.

What is this, some type of scam? my friend thought. *You really think I'm going to just Venmo five hundred dollars to some girl in Utah?*

This was after he and his wife had spent months searching for a reputable breeder, contacted others that weren't a good fit, and kept returning to this one in particular. However, it was his honest, gut-level reaction.

Hesitant, he typed the girl's name into a search engine. He didn't see anything negative and found her personal Instagram account. *Okay, so she's a real person,* he thought, only to click on her profile and find less than ten photos. *Or is this a real person? Did they just create this account and throw up a few photos of themselves with cute puppies to rip people off?*

He then clicked on her Instagram Story and saw a graduation photo with a caption that read Class of 2020.

Oh! he thought. *She's eighteen. She's Gen Z. To me, asking someone to Venmo them a large amount of money as a deposit is questionable, but to her, it's perfectly normal. How else would she get the money? Check? It could have insufficient funds. Cash? It could be counterfeit. Even if it's legitimate, it could get lost in the mail. Credit card? Who wants to pay those fees?*

Venmo was the obvious solution, but he didn't see that right away because he was looking at the situation through a Millennial lens rather than a Gen Z lens. I can't imagine how this would have transpired if his lens had been Gen X or even Boomer. We may think certain approaches by this new generation are crazy at first when they are only following their natural instincts and using technology as the powerful tool that it is.

This young puppy breeder in Utah had 7,670 followers on Instagram in the summer of 2020, and that number had nearly doubled to 15,100 followers by the winter of 2021.[5] But she doesn't just have an Instagram account; she has her own business—her Instagram profile is simply a powerful tool that makes her business as successful as it is. With puppies selling for around four thousand dollars each and a waitlist a few dozen families long, I would have to guess she is making a six-figure income, which is quite remarkable for someone so young. I was pretty independent at her age, but I certainly didn't have a business doing what I loved and turning an impressive profit. This particular breed of dog didn't even exist back then in the same way that Instagram and other modern technologies didn't exist either.

I would consider this breeder to be not just a businesswoman but an influencer in the designer dog space. She has found a very specific niche on social media and leveraged it to promote her business. She posts photos of adorable dogs she is raising, and many people want one. That is the whole point of her Instagram, and it goes far deeper than "I like sharing photos of cute dogs." It is very intentional and strategic.

If she only had a website, I doubt people would log on several times a week unless they were actively considering a purchase from her specifically. But people will follow her Instagram account, which is a lower investment of their time, and her posts can drive their behavior. They may follow her because they are interested in this specific type of puppy (and they likely will follow several similar accounts as well), or they may just run across it one day, perhaps because a friend follows it. They think, *Oh my goodness, their puppies are adorable!* and then hit the follow button.

Without Instagram, she may sell a few puppies locally, but she is making such a high income because people are flying in from all over the country to buy this specific type of puppy, and they find her on Instagram. The website acts to legitimize the Instagram account and close the deal, but make no mistake—the majority of her business is happening on social media.

It's the same way for Maju, who I mentioned earlier in this chapter. She is not selling puppies, but she does leverage her social media to sell products and sign advertising deals with various companies. I think it would be accurate to say her social media is, in itself, her business. With millions of followers on Instagram and YouTube,[6] she has a legitimate job with a legitimate income, not just something she does on her phone when she's bored. She's doing what she loves and making a living at the same time.

Maju has been featured in ads for various companies, both in Brazil and around the world. When she was working with us in Philadelphia, we were discussing her social platforms, and she mentioned that she has over one million subscribers on YouTube but never posts any new content. I was shocked. I told her she should be taking advantage of this audience, but she explained that she has even more followers on other social networks, and she's so busy with those that she doesn't have time for YouTube. If she were to invest time in this secondary social network, the engagement level on her primary social network would slip, and she cannot have that because her Instagram account is the linchpin of her career.

I visited Maju's channel recently and saw that while she has been posting new videos on YouTube, her presence on Instagram is still significantly stronger. Who would have thought ten years ago that Instagram would actually be someone's career one day? It really is remarkable, to say the least.

━━ ━━ ━━

Another YouTuber influencer I would like to highlight briefly is Jimmy Donaldson, better known as *MrBeast*. This twenty-three-year-old has the number one YouTube channel owned by an individual in the United States with more than eighty-three million subscribers—substantially more than Justin Bieber, Ariana Grande, Ed Sheeran, and Taylor Swift. More than a quarter of those subscribers were added in 2021 alone.

Donaldson uploaded his first video at age thirteen and dropped out of college after just two weeks, stating, "I'd rather be poor than do anything besides YouTube." This would lead to his mom forcing him to move out of his family home.[7]

At this point, Donaldson had been uploading videos for several years, but he was not yet an internet celebrity. Out of a desire to turn his hobby into a full-time job, MrBeast recruited his friends to help him figure out YouTube's algorithm. "I woke up, I studied YouTube, I studied videos, I studied filmmaking, I went to bed, and that was my life."[8]

A few months after dropping out of college, he was convinced he had figured it out. In January 2017, MrBeast uploaded a video of himself counting to one hundred thousand. The video was originally more than forty hours long but had to be sped up to meet restrictions. Still, the finished video is almost twenty-four hours long, and MrBeast doesn't appear to take a break. The stunt was a success, and nearly five years later, the video has nearly 24.5 million views. Donaldson had cracked the code—people wanted to see ridiculous, over-the-top videos. So he continued to make more videos in this genre, and before long, he went viral. By November 2017, he had grown his channel to over one million followers.[9]

Most of his videos feature similar attention-grabbing stunts, such as giving away large sums of money, purchasing the entire contents of a video game store, or opening a car dealership that gives away cars for free. Many of these videos have corporate sponsorships attached.

Today, Jimmy Donaldson is not just a guy in his early twenties who makes YouTube videos. He is the owner of a successful business that employs more than thirty people, including some of his childhood friends. He's partnered with other YouTubers to raise nearly forty million dollars in the past few years alone to clean up oceans and plant trees with large corporations signing up to donate to the causes spearheaded by this Gen Z YouTuber. He's even held "Finger on the App" contests where people attempt to hold their finger to their phone screen with his app open without removing it with a twenty-five-thousand-dollar cash prize going to the last person standing.[10]

This was so wildly popular he did it a second time with servers crashing because so many people downloaded the app to sign up. The prize this time was one-hundred thousand dollars. Over one million contestants were initially in the game, which was eventually pared down to 9, at which point MrBeast offered them each ten thousand dollars to give up. Four players accepted this offer, and a nineteen-year-old, who kept his finger on his phone screen for more than fifty hours, ultimately won the contest.[11] When he announced the winner via Twitter, Donaldson also said he felt bad for the second-place finisher, perhaps because others had been give ten thousand dollars to quit sooner, so he ended up giving that person twenty thousand dollars as well.[12]

During the COVID-19 pandemic, Donaldson created a new YouTube channel in August 2020 called *Beast Philanthropy* and started a charity—a food bank in North Carolina that delivered almost sixty-thousand holiday meals by the end of the year. The twenty-three-year-old hired an experienced executive director to run the day-to-day operations, and Donaldson donates all the ad revenue and brand deals from this channel to the charity. "Every view on this channel is literally putting food in people's mouths."[13]

While he was giving away all these holiday meals, Donaldson also created a for-profit food venture called MrBeast Burger. This franchised digital ghost kitchen launched in December 2020 with three hundred locations.[14] In typical fashion, the announcement came with a video that received millions of views and the #1 spot on YouTube. The announcement video, titled *I Opened a Restaurant that Pays You to Eat at It*, was filmed the previous month at the only physical MrBeast Burger location, a temporary pop-up in Wilson, North Carolina, where Donaldson gave away free food, cash, iPads, and even a new car to drive-thru customers.[15]

At one point, the line grew to more than twenty *miles* long. The crowd quickly became too much to handle and at the request of the local police department, the drive-thru line was closed.[16]

When the video aired on YouTube, it triggered a massive number of downloads of the MrBeast Burger app from the Apple Store and Google Play to the point that their servers were temporarily overwhelmed. For those who were able to download the app and place their orders, nearly every location ran out of food on the first night. In less than three months, MrBeast Burger surpassed one million burgers sold. Within the first year, the chain grew to more than one thousand locations across the United States and Europe.

While other fast-food chains took decades to expand to this volume, this twenty-three-year-old managed to do it almost overnight because of his unique business model—which likely would have failed epically just a few years ago. However, food delivery is now totally mainstream, and we now have this trend of ghost kitchens. If you have never heard of this, don't feel bad. They are not haunted; rather, this new phenomenon has emerged in the last six years and grown by leaps and bounds during the pandemic. One article written in October 2020 claimed the demand for ghost kitchens has accelerated their growth by five years in three months, and they are on track to become a one-trillion-dollar industry by 2030.[17]

The difference between a ghost kitchen and a regular restaurant is minimal from a user interface point of view. MrBeast Burger uses multiple third-party apps, such as DoorDash and Uber Eats for their deliveries, and the restaurant is 100 percent delivery only. The big difference is there is no physical location where you can drive-thru and place an order; the original one in North Carolina was more or less a stunt for the video that introduced the business itself. (In other words, it was all advertising.) This is what makes it a ghost kitchen—the lack of a physical restaurant with a sign out front. Of course, the food is prepared at a physical location, but there is no drive-thru, front counter, or dining room. Some ghost kitchens operate out of warehouses or community kitchens where multiple brands share space. MrBeast Burger products are cooked in the kitchens of existing restaurants. That's right, actual restaurants are also serving their own dine-in, takeout, and delivery customers while simultaneously cooking MrBeast products. The restaurants have little need to update their existing kitchen equipment and minimal training is required. They also use a standardized recipe so that everything tastes the same at any MrBeast franchise—or at least, it should. Some users reported vast variances in quality since Donaldson himself has very little control over anything other than the brand, and it depends on the local restaurant.[18] To an extent, this is true of any fast-food franchise, but a ghost kitchen has even less quality control since it relies on independent contractors to deliver the orders since customers cannot pick up their order at the ghost kitchen even if they want to.

I liked the way *The New York Times* put it in an article titled "You've Heard of Ghost Kitchens. Meet the Ghost Franchises." It went on to describe them as "virtual food brands, driven by real celebrities" with MrBeast Burger as an example.[19] The idea of a celebrity lending their name to a restaurant is nothing new, but the ghost franchise model enabled MrBeast Burger to open three-hundred locations all at once. For the sake of comparison, Shake Shack has been open since 2004 and is just now approaching three hundred locations (which is actually pretty fast growth for this industry), and In-N-Out Burger has taken seventy-three years to reach almost four-hundred locations.[20]

It is remarkable and a bit awe-inspiring that the whole concept is digital and app-based. New franchises can open almost immediately. There is no real estate to secure, no building to build. The kitchen and cooks are already in place. It doesn't require additional servers. And when the actual restaurant (the one with their sign outside the building) is slow, they can stay busy by fulfilling digital orders for their second brand. They don't even need to do anything once they prepare the orders because the third-party delivery companies take care of that as well as handling any customer complaints that may arise.

I personally ordered from MrBeast Burger via DoorDash and had a fantastic experience. The burger and fries (which I reheated in my oven before eating since they were cold from the delivery) were high quality and delicious—although I will say the food is the opposite of healthy and not something I would eat every day. My order was prepared in the kitchen of my local Bertucci's, a struggling outpost outside a mall that has seen better days. To be frank, I am surprised both the restaurant and the mall survived COVID, but now they have new life breathed into them by a kid who has less experience in the restaurant business than nearly everyone working in their restaurant.

Ghost brands have helped restaurants survive the pandemic, especially as more and more people are using apps to order delivery. One MrBeast location near Dallas made seven-thousand dollars on their very first day, and I loved *The Dallas Morning News* headline that read, "YouTuber MrBeast brings delivery-only burger chain to Dallas area."[21] If that is not the most Gen Z headline, I don't know what is.

In Manhattan's East Village, a bodega was operating more than ten ghost brands, and it doesn't take long to get them up and running, even for independent restaurants.[22] MrBeast Burger appears to be working more with medium-sized chains, especially since getting in with one of them probably means getting in with all of them, but some MrBeast outlets are based in independent restaurants. Two chains that have quietly adopted the MrBeast ghost brand are Bertucci's Brick Oven Pizza and Pasta, which has shrunk down to just fifty-two US locations in recent years, twenty-seven of which are in Massachusetts, and Brio Italian Grille, a once-successful Italian eatery with just thirty-six locations remaining in fifteen states. Both of these chains were much more popular, but partnering with MrBeast has made them cool again. I am a Gen Xer, and when I think about ordering food delivery, I honestly do not think of Bertucci's at all, but I enjoyed the MrBeast Burger they cooked for me. Certainly, Gen Z has nearly rejected these old-school chains outright, but ghost franchises have made them cool once again.

What is most remarkable about this young man is that even though he became an overnight sensation, it took hard work and persistence to figure out YouTube's algorithm, which is what ended up making him famous more than pure luck. Quite a bit of trial and failure and resilience were involved. He eventually cracked the code and has built a successful business around it, given away millions of dollars, and become a serial entrepreneur. It's no longer just about YouTube; they are just the vehicle for his personal brand. Oh, and he's accomplished all this by the same age one would graduate from a four-year college if they take a gap year. But here's the thing—he didn't start his career at twenty-two or even eighteen; he started it as a thirteen-year-old teenager uploading YouTube videos. This is a lesson for all of us to not underestimate Gen Z. What might seem like a total waste of time from our perspective may just be the next million-dollar idea.

> You don't have to overhaul everything and alienate other generations to be more Z-friendly.

Finally, restaurants like Bertucci's and Brio, which typically cater to an older clientele, figured out how to reimagine themselves while retaining their original brand. They didn't have to overhaul everything and alienate their loyal customers; they simply created a brand within a brand that targets a younger audience—and it worked. They are still functioning as usual, but a new thing is taking place behind the scenes. This is a splendid example of how the multi-generational workspace functions at its best. You don't have to overhaul everything and alienate other generations to be more Z-friendly; it's possible to have a culture within a culture at your company so that no one gets left behind.

— — —

For some of you, this may feel like drinking from a fire hydrant. Perhaps you were totally unaware of the influencer phenomenon (though you have likely seen them on social media), or perhaps you *were* aware of it but simply had no idea how much it entailed. Regardless, let's bring this closer to home and discuss how it relates to business.

Members of Gen Z are wired to be contagious creators and easily listen to influencers they trust enough to allow into their streams, as this can affect their offline behavior as well. You have to think of every member of this generation who works for you as an influencer for your business and product.

One entrepreneur owns a Chick-fil-A franchise and incorporates these principles into his business. His restaurant, located about an hour outside Atlanta, doesn't sell any products online. However, they use Facebook and Instagram to connect with their customers and engage their employees. For them, social media isn't just an extra thing they do; it is an intentional strategy in their business. They use it to promote products, drive customer traffic into the restaurant, recruit new employees, and shine a spotlight on existing ones. They use it to convey important information to customers and recover unsatisfied customers so they continue to return to their business. Recently, they have also begun to explore how they can incorporate technology into their business instead of banning it outright when employees are on the clock.

> They use social media to promote products, drive customer traffic into the restaurant, recruit new employees, and shine a spotlight on existing ones.

Many businesses that are customer-facing (quick-service restaurants, coffee shops, movie theaters, and grocery and retail stores) are critically aware of the tensions with technology. They want their young employees to understand that they come to work to serve customers, not to spend time on their phones. They certainly don't want customers to approach the counter and find they are competing with a phone for the employee's attention. Many of these businesses have adopted the approach of banning technology outright. They might state, "Leave your phone in your locker. Better yet, don't bring it into work at all; leave it in your car." Others will allow the employee to have their phone on them, but they don't want to see them using it unless the employee is on a break.

None of this is wrong by any means, but is it possible that companies that do this are not harnessing the full creative potential of this generation? Is it possible that their creative power and influence could actually have a positive effect on the business?

Obviously, a business needs boundaries and all that. And yes, it may be difficult to manage the content and storyline of what people post, but the potential value is worth the risk. Rather than shying away from technology altogether because you cannot control the narrative, senior leaders can have their mid-level managers work with their entry-level employees to help guide them toward a productive, safe, and brand-aware way to communicate online.

This Chick-fil-A restaurant owner has also implemented a program where employees who have ideas to improve the business can take photos or videos that are then posted on the team GroupMe app. Sometimes, this content is captured on the employee's personal phone (when it doesn't interfere with their work, of course), but a store smartphone is also available at certain times for the employees to capture their videos.

Do you see what is happening here? The employees are actually mentoring one another through videos. Sometimes, an upper or mid-level manager shares content that serves as a sort of digital mentorship. Other times, employees who are on the same level of the organizational chart are inspiring and mentoring each other. This owner is capitalizing on the fact that Gen Z is mentored by their peers. It's one thing for a manager to tell them how to do something but another thing entirely when their peer presents the same idea, which they are far more likely to accept and adopt into their everyday behavior.

The owner of this quick-service restaurant also uses technology when he has messages to convey to his team. Instead of requiring employees to come to all-team meetings (which Gen Z often finds boring), he posts videos on GroupMe that his employees are required to watch. However, they can watch this content on-demand, when it suits them, which makes them more likely to absorb and retain the information that is being presented. During the COVID-19 pandemic, he found these videos were absolutely critical in keeping everyone informed of changes that occurred in the business on a daily basis, and he also began doing Zoom calls with his team every other night for those who wished to stay even more informed on the changes that were taking place—how it affected their work and how it affected them personally as well.

No matter what business you find yourself in, ask yourself how you can incorporate technology your team is already using into work. This will become very important in future-proofing yourself—setting yourself apart from your competition and giving you a leg up in recruiting—as more and more of your positions are filled by members of Gen Z.

A quick-service restaurant will probably have to learn these lessons faster than an office. However, all industries will do well to ask themselves these questions and put new policies and ideas into practice. In an office, imagine what it would look like if phones and apps were harnessed as tools to enhance your business and not just as distractions from work. Even though these industries' phone policies are not as strict, countless hours are lost each week due to employee distraction. Or perhaps they are already disengaged with their work, so their phones become a welcome distraction. Either way, by proactively harnessing this technology, you can use it as a tool to your company's advantage.

Thousands of different ideas could work here, but perhaps it could be as simple as starting an Instagram page for your department or team. Or figure out how you can communicate using apps to reduce the bombardment of emails and allow employees to be more socially connected with one another. Not every approach will work for every type of business, but nearly every type of business can find a way to incorporate technology into their business in practical and productive ways. This will not only improve morale, but you may just find that you inadvertently tap into the contagious creativity of Gen Z—and that creativity could spawn your next big idea and spread to the other generations on your team as well.

— — —

Hopefully, you see how valuable influence is and how it can be used to make an impact, both at home and at work. Many people do not feel as if they have much influence, but the reality is everyone is an influencer to someone. At least, they should be. Sadly, many people struggle to connect with younger generations or attempt to connect in ineffective ways and find themselves filtered out of the curated streams of those they are trying to reach.

At the same time, if you do not play a deliberate role in influencing the young people around you, someone else will (and probably already is). You do not have a choice but to understand how influence works in the modern world and contribute to what already influences Gen Z. The good news is you do not have to be a slick and savvy influencer to have influence. You can cultivate this as you build cross-generational relationships that will give you an opportunity to speak into the lives of the younger generation, which starts with seeing them through a new lens. In turn, when Gen Z experiences this and realizes they can benefit from the wisdom the older generations share, the relationship will encounter a level of synergy, which is ultimately what we all desire.

> If you do not play a deliberate role in influencing the young people around you, someone else will.

If you have found it hard to connect with younger generations in the past, I would invite you to continue reading the next important truth, where I will provide some practical steps that you can use to begin building influence that will impact the next generation.

Takeaway

Influence is the new currency and probably the most valuable commodity in our world today. Gen Z understands that if you don't have influence, you won't be heard.

Influence is based on trust, and trust is built in part by the value you bring to a relationship. Gen Z does not yet fully appreciate the value that older generations can offer. Once we establish trust with them, we can influence them, and they will positively influence us as well. Whether at home or in the workspace, trust allows those from other generations to be a part of Gen Z's journey, which is not the default setting.

I experienced this when a young influencer from Brazil who was staffing one of our summer programs posted about what she was doing to her millions of Instagram followers. We didn't ask her to do this, and she never mentioned that we were hiring, but within minutes, we received hundreds of applications from young people who wanted to work with us the next summer, which was more than a year away.

The perfect storm has positively affected our world in the sense that it has allowed ordinary people to become entrepreneurs through social media. It was the original "work from anywhere" remote work before remote work became popular. Social media has allowed young people to amass huge followings, earn six to seven figures from ads, and develop their own brands that have led to the creation of real-world, off-social-media businesses worth millions, like when YouTuber MrBeast launched MrBeast Burger.

Rather than banning technology altogether from your workspace, how can you incorporate it into the workplace and leverage it? How can you meet Gen Z where they already are; how can you enter into their world and earn the opportunity to influence them? In other words, what can you do to get past their filters and become part of their curated stream?

The goal here is influence and impact. Once you are filtered in, you can help Gen Z grow and become the best version of themselves. While they have the ability to be free range and grow by themselves, growth is always more significant when you have external input to bring balance and perspective. This will also impact the bottom line of your business.

Z

TRUTH #9
Gen Z Needs a GPS

If Gen Z can access everything they need online, do they need us? Can we compete with the internet? Are those of us from previous generations simply dinosaurs?

Tim Elmore calls the current state of some members of the younger generations artificial maturity. Even though Gen Z has access to all information, they often lack the maturity to know how to process this information.[1] In other words, they have access to all knowledge that has ever existed, but they don't always know how to apply that knowledge in the physical world. This is what I mean when I say Gen Z is growing up both fast and slow at the same time; it's essentially the same thing that Elmore calls "artificial maturity."

So we have this generation that is growing up very fast—much more quickly than previous generations. However, at the same time, Gen Z is growing up very slow—even slower than previous generations. They have all this knowledge, all this information, but they aren't always mature enough to know what to do with it. They may think they don't need adults, but they actually do need someone who will come alongside them and help them make sense of how everything they know actually plays out in the real world. They don't need a sage on stage (an SOS); they need a guide positioned by their side—a GPS to help them navigate this new world.

However, you don't automatically get to be the guide by their side just because you're a parent, teacher, or member of an older generation. In fact, Gen Z is one of the first generations that can receive mentorship on a myriad of topics from their peers via the internet. However, much of this tends to come in the form of adding more knowledge to the knowledge they already have, and another member of their same cohort—who shares their same challenges and struggles—probably won't be able to help much when it comes to developing the social and soft skills they desperately need. Whether or not they realize it, they need the older generations (not just their peers) to serve as guides by their side.

Legacy Knowledge

I was taking a walk the other day with my friend Dean Minuto.* Like it does on many occasions, our conversation shifted to Gen Z, and Dean stated that they know more than we do, but we are smarter than them. They possess raw knowledge, but we possess legacy knowledge—principles that have withstood the test of time and work in real life, not just in theory.

Legacy knowledge used to be handed down from one generation to the next. Today, this has changed and is no longer our default. The perfect storm has created the world that Gen Z has grown up in, a world where everything is at your fingertips; all the knowledge that has ever existed is just a click away—or if your hands are full, you can simply ask Siri. We are also more connected than ever before through social media, allowing Gen Z the opportunity to be mentored by their peers around the world. This has created a unique scenario that has never existed before, where Gen Z doesn't need the generations that have gone before them to teach them what they need to know. Their default posture toward older generations is that they are not relevant to their daily lives until they prove that they are.

This doesn't mean that these generations have nothing of value to offer; it simply means that they no longer automatically hold the place they once held in mentoring the next generation. They can still function in this role, but it must be earned. And it is worth it to earn this place of influence in the lives of your children or those you lead, to be the GPS to help them navigate this new world.

---

* Dean is a brilliant thinker with more than twenty-five years of sales experience as well as influence and persuasion research. He has coached tens of thousands of CEOs and developed business tools that apply brain science to engagement. He won the Vistage Speaker of the Year award in 2015 and created the YESCALATE® system, which I highly recommend.

I know it sounds crazy that parents must earn the right to be heard in the lives of their children, but it is absolutely true. If parents want to have any influence on their children, they must get into their curated streams. Sure, they will listen to you on some level because you're their parent, but it isn't the same as being in their stream. Just because you are talking doesn't mean your message is truly being heard and received. Just because you provide a roof over their heads, three meals a day, and pay for their college tuition doesn't mean you'll have lasting influence.

> Gen Z's default posture toward older generations is that they are not relevant to their daily lives until they prove that they are.

On one end of the spectrum, you have parents who are functionally absent from the lives of their children, and on the other end, you have overbearing parents who are trying to force their values and ways of doing life on their children. In the first case, Gen Z is forced to figure life out on their own, and in the second case, they are driven away from their parents as they turn to their peers for advice they can digest at their own pace without the pressure. In both cases, Gen Z will be mentored almost exclusively by their peers, and we are seeing this trend even with those who have wonderful parents because their kids also like to hear from multiple voices and explore different ways of doing things.

So even if you are a great parent, involved but not overbearing, and have a solid relationship with your kids, this does not necessarily mean you are a part of their curated stream and influence their lives. Not being overbearing is a wonderful place to start, but there's more to it than that. You have to be intentional yet subtle. You have to be willing to meet them where they are and come alongside them to help them move forward. You can no longer dispense wisdom in a sage-like manner and expect results; you have to become a guide positioned by their side who has become a part of their curated stream and been filtered into their circle of influence.

You can't just say, "Hey, I can help you make sense of everything you've learned on the internet." You have to make yourself relevant to them. You have to move them toward the goal without stating it. (We will discuss what it means to develop an invisible curriculum later in this chapter.) You have to become the guide they turn to, and you don't end up in that position by showing up and announcing that you're the guide. This is what we call the "sage on stage" mentality when one positions themselves as the expert but doesn't actually make a real connection. The information is great, and this approach used to work, but now information is so easily accessible that what this generation is really looking for is someone to help guide them through life. Sharing information is transactional and just a temporary interaction, but it can become transformational when a relationship is present.

> Gen Z doesn't need a sage on stage; they need a guide positioned by their side.

Often, Gen Z might not be able to articulate what they are looking for or even be consciously aware that they are looking for a guide. However, they feel it intuitively, and once they recognize that you are fit for this role, they will allow you into their curated stream and give you access to their life. In other words, you will gain influence.

Here's the good news: You don't have to be smarter than the keynote speaker or cooler than the influencers your kids follow. You don't need to become a variation of those or try to compete with those who are already influencing your kids, which slides many parents into "sage on stage" territory. You can't say, "I'm your guide. I'm here to be a positive influence in your life."

They already intrinsically feel the need and will recognize it when they see it and feel as if they are choosing to be influenced by you rather than you forcing your influence on them.

A great first step to entering their world is to find out what they are interested in and look for ways to meet them there. As Tim Elmore says, "Adults must use what is cultural to teach what is timeless."[2] If you have more than one kid, all your kids may be interested in certain things, and those things can become family activities. That is wonderful, but look for something specific that each individual loves so you can really dive deep and make a connection.

I was talking with a father once who was looking for ways to become more involved in the lives of his kids. I suggested that he start with something they're interested in, even if it made him uncomfortable. He ended up challenging his kids and their friends to a Nerf gun war. Everyone was running around the basement, shooting each other with Nerf guns and having an absolute blast. But he took it even a step further and stepped out of his comfort zone to enter their world: He filmed the whole thing on his phone. When they were finished, he got his laptop out and began downloading the footage. He's not a videographer by any means, but he used iMovie to edit the footage together into a video that highlighted the epic battle that had just taken place, which they then uploaded to YouTube so his kids could share it with their friends. Not only was Dad bonding with his kids in a shared experience, he entered their world of tech by filming it and putting it online. He's now the coolest dad of all time in the eyes of his kids and their friends, and it really wasn't that difficult to curate himself into their current interests: not so much Nerf guns, but technology and social media.

The point is this: Instead of sitting your kid down to talk about the meaning of life, do something that they enjoy. The conversation and relationship won't feel so forced and will instead develop naturally. Once you become part of their curated stream and begin sharing legacy knowledge with the next generation, you will often find that you can learn a lot from them as well (and not just how to work technology). If you are open to it, reverse mentoring can begin to take place, as knowledge is not just passed down but passed up as well. Mentoring becomes a two-way street when the mentor recognizes that the mentee has something valuable to share with them as well. Just because someone is younger and less experienced does not mean they cannot mentor you as well. They may not share information or life experience but a positive attitude, drive, or perspective that you can learn from.

I experienced this first-hand with a young man named Jack, who was twenty-three when he approached me and asked if I would mentor him. He had an online business that was particularly active in the real estate space, automating lead generation from social media marketing efforts. We communicated regularly, and I was there to guide him when he needed advice or feedback. Talking with Jack gave me ideas about ways I wanted to shift my own company's marketing, and as I would unpack new ideas and concepts with him and challenge him, I realized certain things about myself as well. I admired his energy and entrepreneurial spirit, his youthful "I'm going after this and not letting it go" determination to reach his goals. He wasn't the first person I had seen this in, but seeing Jack's passion helped reignite my own.

> Many people say they want open and honest feedback but get their feelings hurt and pull away when you give it to them.

I also appreciated Jack's vulnerability and openness. He had an attitude of "Whatever you have to say to me, I'm ready to hear and receive it." Many people say they want open and honest feedback but get their feelings hurt and pull away when you give it to them.

GPS versus SOS

Behavior patterns through history often follow similar trends and sequences: People use a tried-and-true system that works, but at some point, a better way begins to emerge, although it is usually rejected at first. People think, *The old way works just fine. If it ain't broke, don't fix it. Don't challenge the status quo. Change is uncomfortable. It's too costly. We'll wait until someone else tries it first.* We make a myriad of excuses when presented with a new way of doing things, even if the new way is objectively better. We continue to use the system that works—until one day, when it doesn't.

We've all heard the stories and probably had our own moments when we held on to the status quo, only to realize how much wasted time and energy it cost us. We think, *Why didn't anyone tell me sooner?* Well, they probably did. You were just stuck in the old way.

I recently found myself intrigued with the details surrounding the call for help that the ship the *Titanic* made back in 1912 before it sank, claiming the lives of more than fifteen hundred passengers and crew members. We can draw a perfect parallel between their team's use of old communication technology in a time of crisis and understanding the way Gen Z communicates can change the way we lead, parent, teach, and mentor this generation.

The *Titanic* was equipped with the latest wireless communication system, the Marconi Telegraph. Since 1904, the Marconi Wireless company required all its operators to use the signal CQD for a ship that was in distress or required urgent assistance. Guglielmo Marconi was awarded the 1909 Nobel Prize in physics for telecommunications as a result of this discovery. While it was reliable for relaying messages, both internally and to receivers ashore, the system had its flaws. It was susceptible to interface, and its long radio wavelengths didn't travel very far either. The telegraph was never designed or intended for use as an emergency device, but doing so was standard practice at the time.

On April 15, 1912, the RMS *Titanic* senior and junior radio operators, Jack Phillips and Harold Bride, were overwhelmed by a high volume of telegram messages, and the Marconi system was limited to only sending or receiving one message at a time. As a result, when telegrams came in about ice threats in the surrounding waters, they were buried in the piles of messages to and from onboard guests. When the SS *California* sent a telegraph to alert the *Titanic* that she was surrounded by ice, Jack Phillips apparently brushed them off, exclaiming how busy he was. While the *California* ended up stopping for the night, the *Titanic* continued on through the icy waters at their normal speed.

In that era, different organizations and countries had their own in-house distress signals. Even when using International Morse Code, they had to overcome a language barrier with would-be rescuers in international waters. Due to this and other issues, several countries came together to discuss the idea of creating international regulations for radiotelegraph communications. In 1906, a group met in Berlin to establish an international distress call. Two years later, another group determined that moving forward, SOS would become the new official distress call. This series of dots and dashes was simple to tap out in Morse Code and easy for anyone to understand. The first recorded use of SOS came a year later, in August 1909, when the wireless operators of the SS *Arapahoe* sent the signal after their ship became disabled off the coast of North Carolina by a broken propeller.

Not everyone was as eager to get on board with the new system, including the Marconi Company, which was particularly reluctant to give up on

CQD. Four years had passed since SOS was first made official, and the Marconi telegraph operators had dragged their feet in adopting the new distress signal. As a result, when the *Titanic* first struck the iceberg, Jack Phillips only sent out the CQD signal. Harold Bride then suggested they try SOS, and half-jokingly said this might be his last chance to use the new code. Phillips then began to alternate between the two codes. The line was flooded with incoming messages and a barrage of questions from outside operators (perhaps because they were sending out two different signals), and everyone struggled to understand one another. Bride survived that night, but Philips perished when the *Titanic* sank.

Could the *Titanic* have been saved if they had sent out the proper distress call earlier? Instead, they sent out a signal no one outside their organization could understand, and by the time they thought to use the universal signal, it was too late. Of worth noting, after the *California* dropped anchor for the night, their radio operator turned off the system and went to bed. While they were the closest ship to *Titanic* on that fateful night, they had no idea the ship had struck an iceberg and was in need of rescue. The next closest ship was at least four hours away, and it only took two and a half hours for the *Titanic* to sink from the time they struck the iceberg.

Needless to say, the tragedy of the *Titanic* sped up the process of adapting SOS as the international distress signal. The United States Congress passed the Radio Act of 1912, which strengthened previous legislation from 1910 and required wireless communications at sea to operate twenty-four hours a day and that at least two operators be working at all times. They also called for the regulation of the American radio industry, the restriction of longwave frequencies, and the official adoption of SOS as the standard maritime distress call. The use of SOS remained in place until 1999, when it gave way to modern advancements like the satellite-based Global Maritime Distress and Safety System.

Perhaps when you see the letter SOS or hear the dots and dashes, you know that someone is issuing an immediate call for help. This system was developed during the second Industrial Revolution, and it worked then. We currently find ourselves in the fourth Industrial Revolution, but even today, we have laggards who are slow to adapt. Just as was the case with the *Titanic*, holding onto old mindsets for too long can prove fatal to an organization. Yet we find ourselves at an alarming SOS moment in business and at home when it comes to Gen Z. Is it possible that we are not getting through because we are using the wrong signal? Are we relying on an outdated system that a new generation does not understand rather than adapting to the world's current methods and trends?

I also cannot help but notice the parallels between the *California* and *Titanic* with different styles of leadership we see today. The *California* noticed the waters were treacherous and decided to stop for the night, knowing it would be easier to navigate around the ice in the light of day. The *Titanic*, on the other hand, not only ignored the warnings of icebergs but charged ahead just shy of top speed. We look at this behavior today that appears totally reckless, but it was standard maritime practice at the time. In the same way, many leaders are charging into this new era at full speed without taking a moment to pause and reflect on how the world has changed and how a new generation requires new tactics. They are often aware that this change is necessary, but like the *Titanic*, they tend to ignore the warnings.

I recently read a report from Lumen Technologies that I'd like to share an excerpt from:

Most C-suite leaders and IT decision-makers at large and medium-sized organizations around the world agree that the 4th Industrial Revolution will have a substantial impact on both society and the future of business. The 4th Industrial Revolution presents an opportunity for sustainable competitive advantage. Businesses can take advantage of new opportunities through next-generation applications such as predictive analytics, smart factories, telemedicine, retail customer self-service and more. These applications need a platform that delivers and computes across multiple cloud environments, the metro edge and on-premises. Together, next-generation applications, adaptive network connectivity and connected security enable businesses to acquire, analyze and act on data to differentiate themselves with better products and services.[3]

A World Economic Forum article on the fourth Industrial Revolution also addressed the human element, which is the piece I really want to focus on:

> In the end, it all comes down to people and values. We need to shape a future that works for all of us by putting people first and empowering them. In its most pessimistic, dehumanized form, the Fourth Industrial Revolution may indeed have the potential to "robotize" humanity and thus to deprive us of our heart and soul. But as a complement to the best parts of human nature—creativity, empathy, stewardship—it can also lift humanity into a new collective and moral consciousness based on a shared sense of destiny. It is incumbent on us all to make sure the latter prevails.[4]

When it comes to leading people in this new, direct-to-customer world, strategies and processes that always worked are now being dismantled and recreated. The sage-on-stage style of leading (my definition of SOS) is not producing the same fruit and outcomes with Gen Z as the GPS approach, the guide positioned by their side. Like the GPS in your smartphone, a guide positioned by the side is always at Gen Z's disposal (but isn't on all the time), it's tailored to their needs, and it gives them the information they seek in the manner, methods, and amount that they want to receive it. When you type in an end point, the GPS guides you to that destination in a customized, step-by-step fashion. You can take the fastest route, avoid highways, avoid tolls, zoom out and see the larger picture, or zoom in to focus on the current and next step. The GPS can do all the guidance for you, or you can take control and orient yourself on the map and follow the suggested route or create your own. Depending on the terrain, weather, and surroundings, the driver can choose to either follow the suggested route or make adjustments. The GPS then adjusts, recalculates, and offers new options.

The fourth Industrial Revolution will have a substantial impact on both society and the future of business.

You must also have the proper vehicle to traverse your landscape of choice; you don't drive on the beach with tires inflated for paved roads. Your engine must be serviced, and you must be fueled up. You also need to have a set of tools in the trunk, as you never know when you will need them.

Now comes the parallel. Parents and leaders must have the right leadership training and tools to journey alongside Gen Z, otherwise they will become an SOS instead of a GPS—and not the universally understood SOS but the old school way the Titanic initially used before they realized they needed to update their strategy based on their coordinates and audience.

With an understanding of Gen Z comes an awareness that this generation has grown up differently than all who came before them. Forty-two percent of the world population is under the age of twenty-five,[5] and they are the only new generation entering the workforce until 2030. At this time, they make up 30 percent of the global workforce.[6] They also represent 40 percent of consumers.[7] They are determining *what* will be bought and *how* it will be bought. They are also redefining what work will look like in the future (i.e., right now) and what leadership will need to look like. Leaders must leave everything behind and only pull from their archive of legacy knowledge, wisdom, and experience—components that are required to be a GPS to each individual. They must only offer what is needed in the GPS relationship to move the employee forward. They already have access to all knowledge, and they do not need our version of an SOS or mixed signals (as the *Titanic's* radio operators created by alternating between the old and the new). They need help understanding and implementing the information they already possess. This future-proof leadership is all about using every opportunity to upskill and grow employees as they learn how to apply their knowledge in a company or industry-specific setting.

The SOS style of leadership is easily identified in many businesses and even in some education models. During the third Industrial Revolution, they needed to produce graduates that fit a very specific mold who could work, learn, and behave in a predictable manner. Our landscape today is dramatically different and unpredictable; we live in a world where we do not know what tomorrow will look like, but we can take steps today to future-proof ourselves even when the future is uncertain.

A process like this must begin with one small step, and that is to change your perspective. A new perspective always precedes a change in behavior. Thus, a shift will only become visible in your bottom line when there is truly a change in perspective so that your behaviors will produce lasting change rather than short-term results. Moving from SOS to GPS will certainly require a change in behavior, but if you do not first shift your perspective and change the lens through which you see this generation, the results will not last.

While this may sound like an option or a choice, it will become abundantly clear that the only corporate ships (both large and small) still sailing the waters have avoided the icebergs. They have adapted their DNA and are sincerely leading their people using a GPS model. It will soon become the only way to attract, develop, and retain employees.

The *Titanic* was unsinkable until it sank. In the same way, Blockbuster and Kodak also felt invincible at some point. Like the *Titanic*, they refused to adapt, and as a result, their businesses collapsed.

Mutual Uncommon Ground

Something that can help on your quest to become a GPS is to look for what I call *mutual uncommon ground* (MUG). This means you find something you both know nothing about and learn it together. (If you're not already in someone's curated stream, this can help you get there.) It can be a topic you research online, something you figure out how to build, or just a simple activity that you can do together where everyone is a beginner, which makes it easier to avoid becoming the wise but disconnected sage. Instead, you are learning alongside them as you share the experience together and connect on MUG. In this new world, we are often all beginners. There are no experts; the playing field is level, and we're figuring things out and learning together.

If you recall the axe-throwing story we discussed toward the beginning of "Truth #7," I'd like to point out how it is *not* an example of mutual uncommon ground. The biggest reason is because MUG is specific to each individual. So rather than hyping up that you have a big surprise for everyone, which they may or may not actually want to do, find out what they want to do. This may very well be axe-throwing. But at least this way, you'll make it about them, especially if it's something you're doing to show them that you appreciate them. It's not about what you want to do or even what you think they want to do.

Of course, it's not possible (especially in a large company) to find something that everyone wants to do. However, I have found that when you put in a little extra effort, you can find groups of people who want to do certain activities. You can customize what you do with that group and then set up different activities for different groups for the employee appreciation day.

You also need this mindset in the day-to-day, not just on the one day a year when you gather everyone together for a company picnic. Find small groups of people and target their interests in order to connect with them. This may mean starting a fantasy sports league with six of your team members or learning to code with two others. Once, an entire organization I helped lead came together and did Whole30 in order to pursue healthier lifestyles. If you're familiar with this plan, it involves eating very specific foods and avoiding other foods for 30 days, so it can be a bit challenging to plan meals. However, since we were all doing it together, different people took turns cooking and bringing in lunch for the team. Because we were all beginners and learning together, we had a lot of fun—much more fun than if we had a "Whole30 expert" in the office lecturing us on what we should and should not eat without actually doing the diet with us.

MUG involves small steps that amount to big changes. The actions themselves may even seem trivial or insignificant, and you may find yourself doing things that don't make sense to the traditional-minded leader. The "what" does not matter so much because what is left when you finish the journey is a foundation of relationship that you can build on. This creates a far better work environment than a group of people who have to work with one another toward goals but who have no other relational foundation. It also breaks down generational barriers. How often

> Mutual uncommon ground involves small steps that amount to big changes. When you finish the journey, you will have the foundations of a relationship that you can build on.

does the CEO of a company learn coding alongside a Gen Z new hire? These kinds of activities don't just happen, but they certainly break down walls and preconceived notions that many young people today have about upper management. It levels the playing field but in a professional manner that maintains the necessary elements of a hierarchy in the workspace. What I mean by that is, younger employees should see you as the boss and respect your position, but that doesn't mean you have to be stuffy. It's kind of like parenting: There is a fine line between being a friend and laying down the law when needed, and you never want to slide into either extreme.

I once took a learning journey with someone in my office where we studied for hours together to become Microsoft certified. I wasn't really interested in this certification, but I saw it as a great way to connect with him on MUG and grow in our relationship. As it turned out, neither of us ended up utilizing the certification, but the process itself was a key building block for our professional relationship. This is a great example of pursuing MUG with one specific person. You won't be able to get this specific with everyone—just be sure you include everyone.

Make each person on your team feel valued as individuals. You're showing them that you value them as people and care enough about them to find the best way to show your appreciation. It is amazing what happens to an employee when they feel like the boss sees them and cares about them, and it will ultimately positively affect your bottom line as well because engaged employees produce more in less time with less likelihood of turnover. So if you want to really show your team you appreciate them, skip the generic team activities you do once or twice a year and seek to build mutual uncommon ground on a daily, weekly, or monthly basis.

MUG in the workspace is not about the magnitude of your actions; it's about being deliberate, and it's actually incredibly simple. This is not your home, your family, your kids, or your close friends. It's not about having breakthrough moments where your team credits you with changing the trajectory of their life. That can certainly happen in a mentoring relationship at work, but you won't have that level of relationship with your entire team, if for no other reason than the fact that there are not enough hours in the day. My point is, MUG will look different at work than it

174

does at home, but many leaders don't take intentional steps. They just let the work flow happen (or not) without implementing an intentional strategy outside the annual big event. A leader thinks, *Oh, we need to show the team we appreciate them*, or *Well, I guess it's that time of year again*. Sure, it's nice, and I don't think you should stop doing it, but it really doesn't drive employee engagement as much as one might think, especially when it comes to Gen Z.

> Finding mutual uncommon ground is not about the magnitude of your actions; it's about being deliberate.

Of course, you can still do a big event at the end of the year as well. The key is taking time to learn what your team wants and not getting caught up in doing the same thing year in and year out because "you've always done it that way," which could very easily lead to an Abilene paradox moment. Even if everyone liked the event ten years ago, they may not like it now. (For a refresh on this phenomenon, see the beginning of "Truth #7").

I did not actually come up with the phrase "mutual uncommon ground." I was unpacking the concept while speaking in the Netherlands when a friend approached me afterward. His name was Jaco Smit, and he holds a doctorate of cultural anthropology and works at a university. We began to discuss this concept, which I called something else, and he told me, "It's like mutual uncommon ground." I absolutely loved this name and it stuck.

This concept of mutual uncommon ground is so powerful because when one person is an expert and the other is not, the relational connection is limited. Often, the individual with the knowledge doesn't want to take the time to teach the beginner, or they are ready and willing to share their expertise, but the beginner would rather learn from someone else. (This could be because the person who views themselves as an expert isn't really an expert—or they truly are an expert in their field but don't have the best teaching style.)

While speaking on this in the Netherlands, I told the audience, "If you want to connect with your kids, don't ask them to teach you how to use Snapchat because they will be the expert, and you will be the noob with no experience. And don't you go trying to teach them how to drive a stick shift, because they will become frustrated by your teaching style and go learn themselves on YouTube."

This actually happened with me and my son, Jeremy. I was trying to teach him how to drive a stick shift, but he was just getting frustrated and stressed out. We ended up stopping the lesson, and he learned by watching YouTube videos and never looked back.

Even if you are truly an expert in a certain arena, you can still find mutual uncommon ground as you guide someone else by not positioning yourself as the expert or by allowing someone to learn from someone else and helping guide them from a distance as they learn. Even if you know the answer, you don't have to be the one with all the answers. It all comes down to attitude. As a guide positioned by the side, you want to lead them to discover things for themselves. This is what I call implementing an invisible curriculum, which we will discuss later in this chapter.

> **As a parent, you want to lead your kids to discover things for themselves, and I believe this concept can be adapted for the workspace as well.**

Becoming a Guide

Most of us can relate to having someone older try to teach us something but either become frustrated by our lack of expertise or become so fascinated by their own expertise that they take the opportunity to show off how much they know rather than actually teaching us how to do it. A classic example is when a father and son do something together, and the father just ends up doing the whole thing himself. The son is disappointed because even though the project was done, he really wanted the opportunity to learn how to do it himself. This kind of person is a great person to hire to perform a task, but they can be a difficult person to learn from because they are more of a sage than a guide, and the beginner might even feel demoralized by their expertise.

This is especially true in a parent/child scenario, and now that mentorship can be found online. Gen Z isn't in the same position as someone from my generation was where we had few options outside of relying on older folks to teach us what to do even if their mindsets and methods were not the most helpful. Gen Z does not want or need a sage, as they already have access to any knowledge they need. They are, however, much more receptive to a guide who can help bring wisdom and context to their knowledge—especially if that guide seeks to find mutual uncommon ground and is vulnerable enough to show that they don't have everything figured out and are learning too. This is what should happen naturally between parents and their adult children as the kids grow up and the role of the parents changes. We certainly see how detrimental it is when parents don't make this shift and still treat their adult children like little kids, which almost always leads to their children pulling away and going to others for advice.

> Guides help bring wisdom to the knowledge the younger generations already possess.

I once heard Paul Scanlon say, "A coach tells you what to do; a mentor helps you discover who you are."

I also like the way Paul unpacks the difference between a coach and a mentor. He defines coaching as more about performance and accomplishing certain tasks and achieving metrics, whereas mentorship is more about personal development and is more relational in nature; it's about who you are rather than what you do.[8]

Paul also brings up a great point that our coaches are usually chosen for us, but we get to choose those who mentor us.[9] Coaches are parents, teachers, a boss, or perhaps a literal sports coach or instructor who is trying to help us accomplish a task within a specific arena. This coaching is often done in an SOS manner. Mentors or guides take it a step further and dive below the surface. They are the ones who help us figure out life and what we are passionate about not just those who teach us to interview well and land a good job.

A coach can become a guide, which is exactly what I'm talking about. Perhaps you've had that teacher who was more than a teacher, a boss who was more than a boss. Parents can also make the shift—even before their kids become adults—to becoming a GPS who doesn't just enforce rules and discipline (which is necessary) but helps their kids navigate a new world.

The SOS is out in front; they have already arrived at a place and are urging you to get there yourself. A GPS actually enters the journey, enters the process with you as if to say, "Let's learn together." Of course, parents are in a unique place where they have to be both; at times, they have to function more as a coach, and at times, they will get the best response by playing the role of a guide.

We see this principle play out in so many movies when two characters go on a journey together. One may be slightly more advanced or have a competitive edge over the other, but circumstances arise that level the playing field. The person you least expect saves the day. These stories often involve a hero and heroine—who nearly always end up falling in love. If one of them is stuck up and thinks they know everything at the beginning, a shift can soon take place, and their attitude or approach changes. These movies follow the same formula over and over, and it works because people can relate. Even though it's predictable, we love these movies because they show us a deeper truth about our own lives. We wouldn't be nearly as interested in a movie if an expert in something helps someone else become an expert. That's too boring. We want to see a conflict, a journey, a shared experience—and in the shared experience, relationships (not just romantic ones) and connections are formed. Aside from movies about a hero and heroine who ultimately fall in love, another common trope is often about a person who is experiencing conflict that is holding them back and how a guide comes along and helps them move beyond it and into their fullest potential. These two storylines are found in nearly every movie (the good ones, at least), and we find them in our own lives as well.

We often face tension between being a coach and a guide.

This all sounds wonderful, but in parenting or the workspace, we often face tension between being a coach and a guide because our role will change based on the circumstances.

Last year, my son began to show an interest in chess. I am actually a strong chess player (by my own account, of course), but I had not played in quite some time. So when my son found a place where he could play online, I knew this scenario called for me to be his GPS, not his coach.

Jeremy began playing online and found a coach, but he still came to me for guidance because he knew I was great at chess.[*] He showed me what his opponents were doing, and we'd discuss tactics. When he finished a game, we reviewed the moves and analyzed everything, which gave us the opportunity to discover what he had missed during the game.

As Jeremy became a better and better chess player, I connected him with our family friend, Craig, who he already knew from his childhood. Back in South Africa, Craig and I used to play tennis and chess together. He beat me at chess, and I beat him in tennis. Craig eventually became a very competitive chess player, but he had not played in a while. Because we are now in the United States and Craig is in Canada, Jeremy and Craig began playing chess together online. This was mutual uncommon ground for both of them but in different ways. Jeremy was new to chess, and Craig was new to playing chess online, so they learned from each other. Craig mentored Jeremy in chess, and Jeremy mentored Craig in online gaming.

As Jeremy took lessons and played chess with Craig, he asked me for advice as he played. "Hey, Dad, Craig just made this move. What should I do?" I didn't sit him down and teach him the fundamentals of chess; I wasn't teaching, coaching, or training—he was seeking advice from me, and really, we were learning together. He was discovering the game for the first time, and I was rediscovering it after not playing for several years. We didn't play against each other, but I answered his questions and helped guide him as he kept improving. After some time, he asked me to play a game with him. Of course, I still beat him, but I was rather surprised by how much better he had become in such a short time. He has since surpassed me, but I refuse to rematch him so the record stands at 1-0, me. (It's quite genius, if I do say so myself.) Jeremy continues to play chess today, and his goal is to eventually beat Craig.

Guiding Jeremy through the world of chess brought us closer together, even though I wasn't his coach and someone else was functioning in that role. By serving as a guide and going through a shared experience together,

[*] Jeremy's first instinct was not, "My dad is good at chess. I'll see what he can teach me." Instead, he started playing online (mentored by his peers), and because I positioned myself in the role of a guide rather than in the role of a sage or coach, I could share some influence with him and even learn in the process as well. Even though this was not truly mutual uncommon ground, we both benefitted greatly from the process.

our relationship was deepened in ways that a student/teacher relationship cannot accomplish.

This is an example of a parent knowing when to function as a guide rather than a coach, even if it is not truly uncommon ground. The workspace will provide similar opportunities as well—both for leaders with their teams and for colleagues with each other.

If you're a leader, you are responsible for setting metrics and goals, helping your team move toward those goals through coaching, holding them accountable when they come up short, and making sure they are growing in their skills as they go. At the same time, you have the opportunity to help guide those that you lead into becoming the best versions of themselves. This will start not with you telling them "I'm here to help you become the best version of yourself" but by finding common ground to build upon.

Invisible Curriculum

Gen Z is in particularly short supply and practice when it comes to problem-solving, communication, perseverance, and gratitude. This is a result of the perfect storm we discussed at the onset of this book. As a guide positioned by the side, you can help them develop these skills both at home and in the workplace. Quite literally, you can be their GPS to help them navigate this new world.

In the workspace, I call this strategy an *invisible curriculum*. At home, I call it *deliberate parenting,* and it could also be called *intentional* or *connected parenting*. Invisible curriculum and deliberate parenting are, in essence, the same thing; the strategy will just vary slightly if you implement it with your children as opposed to with your employees. Both invisible curriculum and deliberate parenting help guide Gen Z in four key areas: communication, problem-solving, perseverance, and gratitude.

In the past, two primary parenting styles (and also management styles) were helicopter parenting and uninvolved parenting. Neither is helpful to Gen Z at home or in the workspace. They don't need a parent or boss constantly hovering over their shoulder (and they won't stay in jobs where the boss does this; they will quit and use an app to make money on their schedule), but they also don't need to be left completely alone to figure everything out themselves.

Because Gen Z and now Gen Alpha have and are growing up in a world that is siloed where everything is available on-demand and can be fully customized, parenting and leadership strategies must be customized and tweaked to fit each individual. A one-size-fits-all approach will no longer be effective.

Successful parenting and leadership in this new world is much more subtle than in times past. The parent or leader seeks to become the guide positioned by the side, working invisible lessons into everyday life and the workspace to teach younger generations how to effectively use all the information they have access to in a manner that benefits their overall development.

Let's take a look at the four key areas where this approach can help guide Gen Z:

Communication: Gen Z is great at communication via electronics, phones, and the like. They are used to informal written and even nonverbal communication. They have grown up texting, sending messages over social media and using emojis and abbreviations like LOL, SMH, and IDK to communicate their feelings.

But when it comes to in-person communication, they become anxious and stressed. Since they have communicated so much online, they struggle with interacting in person. They aren't sure how to find the words to express their feelings about a certain situation when they are used to selecting an emoji.

Problem-Solving: Gen Z struggles with problem-solving in some respects. They can easily focus on the problem instead of finding creative solutions. The answers to so many things are at their fingertips, thanks to their smartphones. They can ask Siri any question or find a video that shows them how to do something on YouTube. These easy answers are convenient but have robbed them of the critical thinking that is developed when by taking the time to consider how to navigate a challenge. This ties in with the next element.

Perseverance: Since Gen Z sometimes struggles with problem-solving, they also seem to quit more easily than previous generations did. While previous generations had to be more agile and seek out the solutions to problems, younger generations just seem to give up when they face challenge situations at school, in the workspace, and even in marriages rather than pressing in to solve the problem. Like the eight-second filter, they sometimes spend just moments attempting to solve a problem, only to conclude that the solution doesn't work.

Gratitude: We live in an instant society where you can order almost anything you want online and get it within hours if not minutes. The other day, a friend of mine was told his car needed a new engine, so he used an app to purchase a new car that would be delivered to his house. The only problem was, this would take a week. Yes, an entire week—never mind the fact that he bought a car on an app in half an hour (in sweatpants from his living room) rather than going to a car dealership and spending several hours with a salesperson. So my friend used another app to rent a car until his new car arrived. The rental was delivered to his driveway twelve hours later (which was the time he selected; he probably could have gotten it in an hour or two), and he scheduled it for pickup the following week an hour before his new car was slated to arrive.

My friend was dumbfounded by how much the world of car buying had changed. This was new to him, but this is not new to Gen Z. As such, they have high expectations when it comes to getting things instantly. This can lead to a sense of entitlement as well: They feel that they are owed by others and by life in general. The perfect storm has shaped them, so they need to be shown the bigger picture so they can develop a deeper sense of gratitude even and especially when life does not turn out how they expect.

I once asked one of my Gen Z employees to create a spreadsheet and track a significant amount of data. I walked him through the process and asked if he understood the assignment. He said he did, so I left him to it and came back three hours later to find that it was all wrong.

I learned an important lesson from this and saw it as an opportunity for me to help this employee upskill in the area of communication. The next time, I asked him to repeat back to me what he heard. He understood, which was fine, but I asked him to do a couple of data entries and then bring it back to me so we could ensure we were on the same page. When he did this, I asked him if he thought there was a better way to present the information. He said yes and explained his perspective. I sent him off to implement the items he had brought up and again asked him to show me his work after a few entries.

When he brought it back to me the third time, I asked some clarifying questions about the practicality of how the information on the spreadsheet was presented. We then reviewed the purpose of the project. He figured out that it did not meet all our desired needs and proposed a few tweaks (now we were moving into sharpening his problem-solving and perseverance skills). We agreed on one of his suggestions, and he went off again to work on the project. This time, it was perfect, and what was interesting was it was not what I originally had in mind, yet it checked every box of what I needed it to do.

This may sound like a lot of unnecessary work, but it only took us an extra thirty minutes, and we saved three hours over the previous time. Even that time was not wasted, as it was all part of the learning process, and he was strengthening his muscles with each project.

— — —

Another friend and I were discussing our kids one day, and he was telling me that his son loved to build and tinker with things. I told him this was worth celebrating, but my friend explained to me that he was frustrated because his son used his tools but never put anything back in its proper place after he finished working on a project.

I quickly recognized a deficiency in the area of gratitude and began devising an upskill plan with this dad that would help strengthen these muscles. This wasn't just about a parent's frustration but about preparing a young man for life.

One day, the son came home with a small set of drawers he had found. He planned to rebuild and paint them and sell them for a profit. As the two discussed the project, Dad knew this was the perfect opportunity to put his plan into action. He went to the garage and quietly put several tools in the wrong places. The son began working on the project and soon began asking where the missing tools were. Dad answered twice and then intentionally made himself unavailable.

The son was flustered when his dad returned two hours later and asked why the project was progressing so slowly. His son told him he had had trouble finding the right tools. When he was spray-painting the drawers, he noticed that some dust from where he had sanded had gotten onto the paint, and it needed to be redone.

To make a long story short, the dad ended up getting involved and told his son, "Let's do this right." They spent the first half hour organizing all the tools. That way, once the project was underway, they would not have to stop and search for what they needed. He did not take over and do everything for his son. Instead, he worked with him. He gave his son buy-in to the process, asking him where they should put each tool for easy accessibility while they were working.

Dad then pointed out all the dust, and they came up with a plan to remove it so it wouldn't blow onto the wet paint or get tracked into the house. A little extra effort with this finer detail of clean-up ensured that the drawers would not need to be repainted. The son soon completed his project and was pleased with the final result. When it was time to clean everything up, the dad left his son unattended to see if he would put everything back where it belonged.

The next day, dad went into the garage and found that all but one of the tools were where they belonged. The son was in the middle of playing an online game, and even though Dad did not actually need any of the tools at that moment, he asked his son to stop playing and come into the garage so they could find the missing tool. When they found it, he thanked his son and told him he would make sure the tool was returned to the agreed-upon place so he wouldn't have to waste his son's time in the future.

This seemingly ordinary story about basic expectations most parents have for their children shows how the dad looked for the right opportunity to strengthen his son's muscles rather than getting upset with him that the tools weren't where they belonged. Getting upset may have served the purpose of modifying his son's behavior to get the desired result, but it wouldn't have given him influence to speak into his son's life. Similarly, the dad never took advantage of an "I told you so" moment. He told his son he didn't want to waste his time—which was the exact lesson the father wanted to teach the son; it just wasn't presented as "you need to put the tools back where they belong because you're wasting my time." Instead, this dad let his son experience the frustration of being interrupted and wasting time because something wasn't done properly in the first place.

This was an opportunity for both the dad and the son to grow. The son learned an important lesson, and his dad learned a new way to coach his son to connect better than parenting styles of the past.

Perhaps the best example that comes to mind to describe how the invisible curriculum works is from the movie *The Karate Kid*. In the film, Daniel wants to learn karate but Mr. Miyagi instead has him perform seemingly unrelated and mundane tasks, such as painting a fence, panting the house, and waxing the car. Later, Mr. Miyagi unveils the "why" behind his instructions; he was actually teaching Daniel karate moves all along, and rather than simply showing him the moves, he was teaching him deeper life lessons and developing character and mental toughness.

It's the same way with the invisible curriculum. Leaders introduce bite-size projects and tasks in the run of a typical day that build and strengthen weak muscles, including the areas we have discussed earlier: in-person communication, problem-solving, perseverance, and gratitude. Gen Z has not had as much opportunity to exercise these muscles as previous generations have had, so they need some assistance and direction to develop these areas. This requires a Miyagi-esque figure (a leader, manager, parent, teacher, etc.) who is aware of the myriad of daily opportunities that present themselves as chances to strengthen these muscles. We must develop these muscles (soft skills) in order to future-proof Gen Z for the world of tomorrow.

Rather than telling Gen Z they are not grateful enough, teach them the value and importance of gratitude. If you pounce on the first exhibition of impatience and tell them, "You need to be more grateful," they will very likely filter you out, and you will lose the opportunity to influence them. It's the "OK Boomer" phenomenon, regardless of the generations involved.

Instead, use the opportunity to teach them a practical lesson with a deeper meaning. You do this invisibly, behind the scenes, and they don't even realize it. This is exactly what happened with Daniel, who was frustrated with Mr. Miyagi until he understood the greater purpose and preparation his teacher was instilling in him. It wasn't the way he wanted to learn, but it was what he needed to learn.

However, I must challenge you with a crucial reminder of the times we live in. *The Karate Kid* was released in the early 1980s. In just a few years, it will be fifty years old. The world has changed since then. Daniel got frustrated when he felt like he was being used as a personal errand boy instead of learning karate, but Gen Z will become frustrated much faster. They will not paint the fence, paint the house, and wax the car. If you do not give them glimpses of the greater purpose in the process, they will grow disillusioned much more quickly. So even though it is an invisible curriculum, with this generation, you must let them see behind the curtain more quickly. This doesn't mean you have to reveal your entire game plan. Instead, you can help them see how living in an instant society has affected them, help them recognize that some things in life can only be achieved slowly over time, and help them learn that cultivating gratitude will actually benefit them in the long run. Instead of making it about what you want them to do, you have to let them see that what you are doing is not about you at all; it's actually for them and designed to positively impact their life. Once you do this, they will see the value you can offer and let you past their filters and into their curated stream. When you execute this well, you will find that both you and those you lead will learn in the process.

Takeaway

Most workplaces today are cross-generational. Some have as many as four generations working together. A focus on Gen Z is not meant to exclude previous generations. Rather, they are well positioned to impart legacy knowledge to this generation, providing context and real-world experience to Gen Z's knowledge of what they have learned online or from their peers.

Gen Z needs a GPS (a guide positioned by the side) not an SOS (sage on stage). Even though SOS became the standard distress call after the sinking of the *Titanic*, it too had a shelf life and was largely retired by 1999. The same is true with leadership strategies.

There is a fine line between being a business leader and serving as a GPS to guide your Gen Z employees. The key is intentionality. It doesn't just happen.

One strategy leaders and parents can employ is finding MUG (mutual uncommon ground). In this strategy, the leader or parent seeks out something both they and the younger person have little if any experience in. This provides the opportunity for both parties to discover something together and learn as they go. This is also one of the easiest ways to be invited into Gen Z's curated stream. MUG is a great place to form quick connections because both individuals are beginners. If one person is already an expert, the other party will face barriers entering into the journey. For example, your teens may be active on Snapchat but have a difficult time explaining to you how it works. Rather than asking them to teach you how to use Snapchat, which could come across as the parent trying to force their way into the teen's world, find an area of mutual uncommon ground instead.

Despite the fact that Gen Zers are contagious creators, they especially struggle in the practice of communication, problem-solving, perseverance, and gratitude. This manifests both at home and in the workspace.

Parents must implement what I call *deliberate parenting*, which is a necessary strategy for raising the next generation(s). The solution to underparenting is not overparenting but deliberate, intentional parenting. The world today is siloed, which means everything is available on-demand and can be fully customized to fit a user's preferences. So parents will need to come alongside each of their children and customize the way they engage and communicate with them on an individual basis; a "one-size-fits-all" approach to each child will no longer be effective.

At work, the strategy is essentially the same, but I use the term *invisible curriculum*. Like deliberate parenting, the goal is to become a GPS that coaches Gen Z and leverages opportunities to upskill them in the areas of communication, problem-solving, perseverance, and gratitude. Many of these opportunities will be small and, in some cases, seemingly insignificant, but they are in fact bite-size moments to help Gen Z develop these critical soft skills that will future-proof them for the road ahead.

TRUTH #10
Gen Z Is Always Becoming

We have discussed the numerous ways our world is changing and, in fact, already has changed. These changes have produced a disconnected generation that is very different from those who have gone before them. But perhaps what is most groundbreaking about this generation is the tenth surprising truth: Gen Z is always becoming.

We are right in the middle of the transition into a new era. However, this new era is not an end destination. It's not 70 percent, 80 percent, 90 percent loaded; okay, we are now 100 percent of the way there. We won't arrive at this place in another ten years and say, "Okay, we're here!" and wait another hundred years for the world to change again. In fact, as we get deeper into this new era, our world will continue to change rapidly at ever-increasing speeds. We don't just have one car for several decades; we drive it for a few years and then buy (or lease) a new one. We don't just use the TV for watching a few channels; we've loaded it with apps, connected it to the web, and are only beginning to see what it can do. What we thought only had one purpose now has seventeen purposes. This won't end anytime soon. This itself is part of the new era. We are now in a place of *always becoming.*

I first learned of this phrase—*always becoming*—while reading Kevin Kelly's fantastic book, *The Inevitable.* I was struck by the concept and began to dive deeper. This principle perfectly illustrated what I had seen in Gen Z. The world they have grown up in had changed rapidly, and they have had to change with it. Embracing this change is like second nature to them, more than with previous generations who were used to significant changes

189

every few decades or, for certain things, once in a lifetime. But some items commonly go from cutting-edge to totally obsolete within a few years.

Even the movie *District 9*, which I paid $3.99 to rent on Amazon Prime to re-watch as I wrote the concept of *Aliens Among Us*, was free to stream on the same service a few weeks later. If you have an iPhone, go to the app store. When I did this, I had twelve new updates to download—and I do regular updates. Our world is always becoming. The rules that applied yesterday may no longer apply tomorrow. It's true with technology, and it's true with management styles.

Through a conversation with Dean Minuto, I also discovered the concept of "becoming" is actually ancient. This theory originated in ancient Greece in the sixth century BC with the philosopher Heraclitus of Ephesus, who believed that nothing in this world is constant except change and becoming.[1] This helps us understand and relate to different generations and ways of thinking. We don't live in the same world our grandparents did, so we don't think the same way or do the same thing. As Heraclitus put it, "No man steps in the same river twice."[2] The river is always new as it is being fed with fresh water from somewhere else, and our world is the same way. This is not good or bad—it just is. We have gotten so distracted with arguments about which way is better—the old way or the new way—to the point that many of us have been left behind as the old way gives way to the new way. We argue that electric cars will never replace gas cars, going back and forth about the pros and cons of each model—then the car manufacturers solve the dilemma for us by announcing that in a few years we will only have one option. The decisions are ultimately made for us as the world moves in a certain direction. Thus, we miss our opportunity to shape the future and influence the next generation.

> The only thing that I am certain will happen consistently is that everything will change.

To be clear, I am not saying that a person may not hold to timeless and unchanging principles or values. Our core values may very well remain the same, but the methods we use to obtain them will certainly shift and change every few years—or at least they should.

We are living in a world that has never existed before, and this world itself will someday become obsolete. We're in transition, and we will *stay* in transition. We are always becoming, and the only thing that I am certain will happen consistently is that everything will change.

Always becoming has both a positive side and a negative side. The positive side is it keeps us in a place of humility. We are always learning, always growing. We will always have new opportunities to connect with others on mutual uncommon ground.

The negative side is a constant sense of unsettledness, that things are incomplete. It's that feeling you get when the sun sets on Sunday evening because you know Monday morning is coming and it's back to your routine. It's that feeling that you're never there, never finished, never have it all figured out. It can leave you with haunting questions: When will my life feel settled? When will my business feel more stable? When will we get there? When will we arrive?

We will certainly face false finish lines when it feels as if we have obtained these things. At times, we will feel settled, and life will seem stable. It will seem as if we have things figured out and as if everything is going smoothly—but just wait. Life never stays this way. Work never stays this way. We are always becoming. The sooner we recognize this, the sooner we will be able to embrace the little victories along the way without being thrown for a loop when life suddenly falls apart. It keeps us humble, it makes us more grateful, and it enables us to stop and enjoy the most important things in life—the moments we can never get back. We are now okay when life isn't totally perfect, and we can leave certain things incomplete or unresolved because the process itself is the main point. Every life and business has problems that can easily be solved, but other things will never be solved, and we must live in the tension—constantly trying new things and making adjustments. If we really think about it, things have always been this way; it's just far more obvious now as our world changes more rapidly before our eyes.

Your attitude and approach on this journey of leading, teaching, parenting (or whatever role you find yourself in) the next generation must also be one of "always becoming." This means you never reach the place where you find the A + B = C formula and think, *I know how to work with young people.* Rather, you are continually and intentionally asking, How do we continue this journey? How do we maintain our influence? You do this because you know what works today might not work tomorrow. Everything is for a season. It may be a few years, months, weeks, or even days before another tactic is needed, but the end goal is always the same.

Blockbuster was cool. MySpace was cool. But neither one exists today—not on the level they once did. If Blockbuster had known they needed to always be reinventing themselves, they might have become the next Netflix. Instead, Netflix is streaming the documentary that tells the story of what happened to Blockbuster.*

You don't need to rush out and change everything you're doing overnight, but you don't want to get too far behind the curve either. You cannot think, *Oh yeah, we really should do that. We just don't have the time.* Because you will come back to this again and again until it's too late, and you no longer have influence and can no longer connect or until your business no longer exists or doesn't have the influence it once did.

Netflix did not pop up out of nowhere and put Blockbuster out of business overnight. During a transition period, both models existed and overlapped. In fact, other video companies with business models like Blockbuster's went out of business first until Blockbuster was all that was left. But rather than seeing the writing on the wall, they kept doing what they'd been doing—they made some tweaks here and there but never disrupted the core model. They didn't "become" fast enough. Now only one store is left while Netflix has 203.7 million subscribers, with 37 million added in 2020 alone.[3]

> They didn't "become" fast enough. Now there's only one store left.

Let's take a closer look at the home entertainment space. Family Video was founded in 1978; Blockbuster and Movie Gallery, in 1985, and Hollywood Video, in 1988. Netflix didn't come along until a decade later in 1997 when these chains were in their prime. Blockbuster was, without a doubt,

---

* The 2020 documentary *The Last Blockbuster* showcases Blockbuster, LLC's last remaining store, located in Bend, Oregon.

the largest of all of them with a robust international presence and over nine thousand stores at its 2004 peak.[4]

Movie Gallery was the second largest chain and purchased competitor Hollywood Video in 2005, bringing their total number of stores to nearly forty-five hundred.[5] The company began to struggle in 2007 amidst the Great Recession, and by 2010, the company had declared bankruptcy, and every Movie Gallery and Hollywood Video location was closed.

Blockbuster didn't do much better. The company essentially went under in 2010 as well (though it held out on life support for a few years and technically still exists as a single independently owned store). After declaring bankruptcy, Dish Network won the bid for Blockbuster's remaining assets. By this time, the company only had seventeen hundred stores remaining—a large drop from the nine thousand stores just seven years prior.

In 2016, Hastings—a company that sold all sorts of products besides DVD rentals—ceased operations, leaving Family Video as the sole surviving video rental chain in the United States. They probably held out much longer because they focused on rural communities while Blockbuster and Hollywood Video focused on cities. Movie Gallery stores were often found in more rural communities, but they possibly went under more quickly because they tried to expand by buying a competitor when the market was dying. The future wasn't in brick-and-mortar stores at all; it was in streaming. Interestingly enough, another company that contributed to the downfall of Blockbuster—Hulu—was founded in 2007, the same year that physical stores began having major issues.

So it actually makes a lot of sense that Family Video lasted longer than Blockbuster because, by focusing on rural communities, they placed themselves in an environment where less of their customer base were early adopters. This demographic is much more likely to live in cities—or leave their hometowns to move to them—and they were Blockbuster and Hollywood Video's clientele. They didn't wait for these stores to close before looking for an alternative; they were already shifting in that direction before these stores met their fate.

Family Video operated nearly eight hundred stores at its peak and was actually doing quite well until the COVID-19 pandemic. They ended up closing 200 stores in the fall of 2020, and at the beginning of 2021, announced they would close their remaining locations.[6] If our world had not evolved so quickly in 2020, perhaps they would still exist. For those prone to nostalgia, remember, it was not just about a virus. These trends were already at play before 2020, and the pandemic simply sped up the process. People didn't think it "wasn't safe" to go to a video store the entire year; during the initial lockdowns, they turned to online, on-demand streaming and realized the way of the future was actually much more convenient.

> Blockbuster grew to more than nine thousand stores in 19 years, but shrunk down to one store over the next fourteen years because the world changed and they did not change with it.

The main force that caused Blockbuster and other video stores to go out of business was not so much new competitors but the fact that the world changed and they did not change with it. Yes, there was Netflix, Hulu, and Redbox, but those companies alone were not the only factors that caused Blockbuster's downfall. They survived Hollywood Video and Movie Gallery; why couldn't they survive a little new competition? Redbox came on the scene in 2002, but they are not that relevant to this conversation because they were just a more convenient Blockbuster—they were in places you already went anyway and didn't require a special trip or extra stop on the way home. They also innovated their approach and began offering streaming and on-demand services, and they had something Netflix and Hulu did not: exclusive rights to certain newly released blockbuster films (pun not intended). That is why we still see these little red boxes everywhere.

Hulu is also not relevant to Blockbuster's downfall because they didn't come on the scene until 2007 when streaming was on its initial ascent into popularity. The company that is particularly relevant is Netflix because when they launched, they were another business. They started out selling and renting DVDs and quickly shifted their focus to rentals. Streaming wouldn't come on the scene until 2007, the same year Hulu launched. In 2000, Netflix had three hundred thousand subscribers, relied on the US

Postal Service to deliver their DVDs to the homes of their subscribers, and they would go on to lose fifty-seven million dollars that year alone.[7] (In fact, Netflix is just now breaking even in 2021.)

The founders, Reed and Marc, hounded the CEO of Blockbuster for months until he agreed to meet with them. One day, they walked into a meeting room of a skyscraper in Dallas and asked the six billion dollar company to buy their small outfit for fifty million dollars.[8] It may have seemed like a ridiculous move since the company lost more than that each year, but they weren't just pitching a company but an idea. The founders of this DVD-by-mail startup asked Blockbuster's CEO to buy Netflix and rebrand it as Blockbuster.com—an online video rental service.[9] It was truly the best of both worlds; the companies would work together harmoniously. And for a six-billion-dollar company, fifty million dollars was a drop in the bucket. However, while Blockbuster's CEO was a tough negotiator, he failed to see where the home video industry was heading; he didn't realize they were in the process of "becoming." Blockbuster would have made the deal in a heartbeat if they had recognized it was the way of the future. But they didn't—much like how older generations look at younger ones and only see the present reality rather than the tremendous potential.

Reed and Marc did not walk out of this meeting and become an over-night success. In fact, they struggled. The dot com bubble burst and 9/11 attacks of 2001 forced Netflix to lay off one third of their 120 employees.[10] However, the tide would quickly turn by Christmas as the average price of DVD players fell from $299 to $199, making them much more accessible.[11] In less than a year, Netflix was mailing 190,000 DVDs per day to their 670,000 subscribers—more than double the amount they had less than two years before.[12]

The growth was exponential from there. But what made Netflix a household name was their decision to innovate. In fact, they were born out of innovation when Reed racked up a forty-dollar late fee on *Apollo 13* at Blockbuster and thought, *There must be a better way to rent movies.*[13] The company was born out of a desire to improve the video rental industry, to "become" the next thing. Thus, the founders knew it was necessary for their company to be "always becoming." They were not the same company in

2001 that they are in 2021. Back then, they were a DVD-by-mail company. Today, they are primarily a streaming company—though you can still get DVDs mailed to you through a service you sign up for separately. I also love how the story of their company overlaps with the story of the generations we have discussed in this book. At one time, both options existed side-by-side. You could choose one or the other—or both. You could get DVDs by mail, and you could also have a streaming plan. At first, the streaming plans were limited to a couple hours a month, but these limits were quickly removed, and users could stream as much content as they liked. The catch, however, was that the streaming library was limited. If you wanted the latest and greatest movies or all the classics, you still had to get the DVDs. The streaming allowed you to watch something instantly while you were mailing your disc back and waiting for the next one to arrive, but you had to wait for the good stuff. Now, if it's not available to stream, it's basically not available.

Today, Netflix has plenty of competitors and certainly does not have a monopoly on the streaming space, though they are the largest streaming service. They are what they are today because they are a company that is always innovating, always becoming. They are never content with the status quo; they are always changing, evolving, and looking for the next big thing. Which is why, even after losing hit TV shows like *The Office*, *Friends*, and *Parks and Recreation*, they are still so popular—and the streaming networks that hold the exclusive rights to these shows aren't as popular. The big thing in streaming is now original content. Netflix spent a fortune buying rights to the best TV shows and movies, and they've now spent a fortune to make their own—taking them from a DVD rental service to a streaming service to a film production company. Amazon, Hulu, and Disney Plus have all followed suit, offering original content that can only be streamed on their platform. These companies can compete with one another because they have each embraced the mindset of always becoming.

Fascinating enough, Blockbuster was once an innovative company. When they first opened in the 1980s, they quickly put smaller video stores out of business by offering better selections and extended hours. They also developed computer databases to track who rented what movies while most video stores were still writing out this information by hand.[14] But they did not continue on this path of innovation. Meanwhile, Movie Gallery thought buying the competition would make them relevant; they quickly became irrelevant because they didn't do anything new. They simply got in the boat with another dying company that was offering a dying trend. Blockbuster made efforts to change, they just didn't make the right changes, and they didn't make them fast enough.

Blockbuster actually attempted to create a streaming service as early as 2000 through a partnership with Enron (yes, that Enron), which owned fiber optic lines that would allow users to download movies on demand to their computers, a step in the direction of streaming.[15] This was right before Netflix approached them, looking for a buyout, which was perhaps part of the reason Blockbuster blew off the startup founders. They already had a plan in place for making their mark in the digital space. As it would turn out, the deal between Blockbuster and Enron fell apart after just eight months.[16]

In 2004, Blockbuster launched Blockbuster Online, a subscription service that cost $19.99 and allowed subscribers to have three movies at a time, which were sent in the mail.[17] This strategy might have worked, though it overlooked Blockbuster's greatest asset—their retail locations. At its peak, more than 90 percent of Americans lived close to a Blockbuster. However, franchise owners were very resistant to the new online offering and did not jump on board.[18] In 2007, Blockbuster knew they needed to make a major move in order to future-proof their business against online competitors, so they launched a billion-dollar campaign for their online business called Total Access. This strategy to compete with Netflix allowed customers to rent movies online and receive them in the mail—with the newly added option of returning them to Blockbuster stores and picking out a new movie for free. This was a huge hit with consumers; the only problem was those "free" movies cost Blockbuster two dollars each.[19]

Total Access must have scared Netflix, because this quickly led to Reed approaching Blockbuster once again in an attempt to negotiate a truce. This time, he wanted Blockbuster to sell its online business to Netflix, and the two companies would create a system where people could return the movies they rented online and received in the mail to Blockbuster stores. This deal nearly went through but, in the end, fell apart due to infighting within Blockbuster. The CEO was then ousted as investors wanted to take the company in a direction that involved spending less money on digital options.[20]

In 2010, Blockbuster watched as their primary competitor (Movie Gallery, which had purchased Hollywood Video) was eliminated, but they still ended up being delisted from the New York Stock Exchange just a few weeks later. In less than a year, the U.S. Department of Justice revealed that Blockbuster did not have the necessary funds to continue restructuring and advised that 3,300-store chain liquidate. They were purchased by Dish Network in 2011, which struggled to negotiate with landlords to keep 600 stores open. However, at the same time, they realized the future would not lie in those stores alone, which is why that fall, they announced their answer to Netflix—Blockbuster Movie Pass—a ten-dollar-per-month service with streaming and DVDs by mail.[21] This actually wasn't Blockbuster's or Dish's first attempt at offering on-demand content, but it was the first real competitor to Netflix's offering.

Except it actually wasn't.

I believe Blockbuster and Dish made a fatal flaw.

That is, their new service was only available to Dish customers. So you had to have a Dish satellite subscription in order to purchase the ten-dollar-per-month Blockbuster Movie Pass.

Here's why this was such an issue: The idea itself was innovative. But they used the innovative idea to try to shore up the necessity of the dying technology—traditional network television. Of course, cable and satellite are still not dead a decade later in 2021, but streaming is clearly the way of the future. And who wants to have to purchase the old, outdated thing for over one-hundred dollars a month just to get the ten-dollar-a-month thing they actually want?

At one time, Netflix actually didn't have a great reputation. They had 25.6 million customers, but expected to lose 2 million in the third quarter of 2011 alone.[22] Dish had an incredible opportunity to innovate—and they didn't even need to create a new thing; they just needed to replicate the existing new thing. However, in the end, that is not what they did. They created a new thing but required you to commit to the old thing to get it so the new thing wouldn't make the old thing obsolete. This isn't embracing the way of the future; it isn't what always becoming is all about.

One commentator put this very bluntly in an article entitled "Blockbuster Movie Pass is No Netflix Killer," which opened with the line "Talk about a serious letdown."[23] The article went on to say, "Anticipation was high that Dish Network would unveil a streaming video service through Blockbuster that would compete—and even possibly undercut—Netflix, which isn't exactly feeling the love right now. Instead, Dish announces a bundle of streaming videos; DVDs and games by mail; and access to premium movie channels—but only to Dish customers."[24]

A comparison might be if a group of Boomers announced they had created a product designed for Millennials, but Millennials would have to use the product under the supervision of their Boomer parents. What Millennial would want that?

Just a year after Dish announced Blockbuster would compete with Netflix, they made a new announcement in October 2012 that they were giving up on trying to reinvent the company.[25]

In November 2013, it was announced that the three hundred remaining corporate-owned Blockbuster stores and Blockbuster Movie Pass would cease operations.[26] In 2014, fifty-one franchised Blockbuster stores were remaining in twelve states.[27] With no corporate entity to support them, they would be short-lived. Within a few years, Blockbuster only had a presence in Alaska and Oregon's high desert. In the summer of 2018, Alaska's last two Blockbusters shuttered,[28] leaving a lone Blockbuster in the United States—in Bend, Oregon, population 76,693. And that is how Blockbuster went from a six-billion-dollar company to a single store that their competitor wanted to become part of to a single holdout in a remote locale out West. And now, that competitor is streaming the documentary that details their demise.

Poor leadership is often blamed for Blockbuster's failure. Franchisee Ken Tisher, who owns the last Blockbuster and who used to own three locations in Bend before closing the other two, was quoted in 2015: "Blockbuster, if it isn't already, is going to go into *The Harvard Business Review* for how not to run a business or how to run a business into the ground."[29]

A former Blockbuster marketing executive stated, "Blockbuster didn't lose its customers to Netflix or digital; they'd long ago stopped belonging to the company in anything other than name. Membership meant nothing or nothing good."[30]

Embracing the concept of always becoming will keep you relevant in an evolving world.

This is what we mean when we say you must get in Gen Z's curated stream if you want to be relevant to them. Otherwise, you will be filtered out. Embracing the concept of always becoming will keep you relevant in an evolving world.

When you're relevant, you can always build relationship and influence people, regardless of the generation or background they are from. It's not about dressing a certain way or saying the right things but about knowing what others want, what they value, the ability to speak their language and find common ground (or, of course, mutual uncommon ground).

Netflix did this when they began making original content. They knew their customers would like *House of Cards* long before the series aired in 2013 because they pulled data from their algorithms. They can see so much more than what people are watching; they can see when users pause, fast forward, rewind, and lose interest in a show without finishing it. Their algorithms told them people liked Kevin Spacey and watched films directed by David Fincher all the way through, and the British version of *House of Cards* had also performed well.[31]

We now see streaming services evolving before our eyes as they fight for the rights to exclusively air popular movies and TV shows, and most streaming services are creating their own original content. This is less of a risk than it was in the past because algorithms help predict what their customers will like before it's made, and the streaming service owns the content forever. They don't have to worry about relicensing at a higher rate from the copyright owners if the show becomes more popular in the future.

The same Blockbuster executive I mentioned a few paragraphs ago was also quoted as saying, "Digital would have changed Blockbuster's business, for sure, but it wasn't its killer. That credit belongs to Blockbuster itself."[32]

In other words, digital streaming alone did not kill Blockbuster. In fact,

Blockbuster died some time before because they were too slow to adapt because they didn't "become" fast enough. By the time they realized that the future didn't involve physical stores, it was too late. Netflix, on the other hand, is always becoming. They started out sending DVDs in the mail, but now they are into streaming and production. You don't need the DVDs mailed to you. They still offer this service, but it's essentially dead. They had the foresight to make the main thing the secondary thing before it died off. At some point, they will likely stop mailing DVDs entirely, but it may not even register as news. Less and less people will use it as it slowly tapers off into nothing, and then it will just stop existing at some point, but it won't be the dramatic death dealt to Blockbuster.

Keith Hoogland, owner of Family Video and son of its founder, attributed poor decisions from leadership as the primary reason why Blockbuster did not survive. His company, which owns all their own stores and the real estate that houses them, had 759 locations in 2017, $400 million in revenue, and was still opening new stores—more than six years after the other chains had gone under. "I'm 57 years old," he told Forbes, "and this is the most exciting time I've ever had in my life."[33]

Hoogland didn't view his company as much different from its competitors. "Everybody thought the reason they went away was because of digital. But in reality, that wasn't the case. They weren't very well-run businesses. They had a lot of debt and leases that were poorly negotiated, and they also were sharing revenue with studios quite a bit."[34] In other words, when Blockbuster rented a movie, the studio that made that movie got a share of the rental fee. Family Video, on the other hand, bought the rights to their movies outright—allowing them to keep all the proceeds from rentals. And by owning their real estate, they made money when it appreciated in value to a collective total of $750 million in 2017, Hoogland estimated.

When the video industry began to decline, they shrunk the footprint of their stores, putting up drywall to create new spaces to lease out to other businesses. He also used his commercial properties to open eleven fitness centers, an electronics repair chain, and 149 Marco's Pizza franchises, which made him the company's largest franchisee. Family Video still accounted for 90 percent of his annual revenue, but he was always becoming. He didn't just see his properties as video stores but as fitness centers, repair shops for electronics, and pizza parlors. He even began selling CBD products in stores to attract the younger crowd.

Today, Family Video still exists as an online business that sells movies, games, entertainment memorabilia, and CBD products. They may have closed the last of their physical video stores in the last two years, but they are far from finished—and since they still own the buildings that housed 450 video stores until last year, we will have to wait and see what their next venture will be.

⸻ ⸻ ⸻

The best companies realize they may become something completely different five years from now; they may have to make radical changes to remain in business. Some of these changes will be small tweaks—like Family Video selling CBD products—but some of them may be more groundbreaking, more along the lines of Netflix reinventing their service from mail to streaming to actually making the movies themselves. It doesn't matter what these changes are; what matters is that companies recognize they must future-proof (Netflix) or become a relic of the past (Blockbuster).

Additionally, many companies are primarily tech companies, and what they do is secondary. I'm not talking about companies like Family Video shifting from brick-and-mortar retail to online. I'm talking about companies like Uber, AirBnB, and even Amazon. Think about it: Uber (and Lyft) do not actually own any vehicles—yet they are giving taxi services a run for their money, especially in places like New York City. Then there is AirBnB, one of the heavy hitters in the lodging space, which doesn't own any properties; they have simply created a tech platform where people can list their properties. And there is Amazon, which does more than ship everything to your door. At their heart, they are a data collection company. They know your buying habits and what you like to watch (through their streaming service), and they are in your homes, interacting with you through Alexa—not just delivering packages to your door but actually inside your home. If you think Amazon is just about free two-day shipping, you are wrong. They are really about analyzing data to create powerful algorithms that will predict what their customers want to buy next. It's no different than how social networks use algorithms to show different products and services to different users. They want you to spend more time engaged with their app, so they show you more of what you like and filter out what you don't. Just like Gen Z.

Some of these changes will happen rapidly—like COVID-19 moving Family Video to go all online. Other things will take time to develop as the tipping point tips. Until then, we find ourselves in a transition space. The next generation will experience things quite differently. Netflix may still be around when I have grandchildren, but they will be shocked to learn that they used to mail me a disk that contained a movie I told them I wanted to see—or one the algorithm chose for me. My grandchildren will also be shocked when they find that in addition to waiting for movies to arrive in the mail, I only had access to one or two at a time. I had a lot of choices in regards to what was sent to me, but when I sat down on the couch with my popcorn on Friday night, I didn't have too many options. Still, the service seemed revolutionary to me—and it was at the time. But for one who grew up with instant access to stream any movie, it seems painfully outdated. Twenty years from now, streaming will possibly be a thing of the past entirely. At this point, we might be further along in our journey of "always becoming," where one technology goes through a transition phase, eventually giving way to another.

— — —

One of the few things we can count on in life is change. Just when we get comfortable with one thing, it seems like it is replaced with a new thing. Some changes are quick and abrupt while we can see others coming. A lot of changes are for the better. At one time, I couldn't imagine a world without video stores, but streaming is better. I may get nostalgic for the old way at times, but I cannot argue that the new way is objectively better. Gen Z has even seen movies change in the short time that they have been adults. During COVID, when movie theaters were closed, many studios just decided to release their latest movies directly to streaming for a premium price. Even as theaters open back up, this has become another entertainment avenue that is probably here to stay. In fact, the other day, I saw a Netflix movie that was free to stream on Netflix while it was also in theaters. This would have been unheard of just a few years ago. A movie studio would have never allowed their movie to stream for free while they were asking people to pay to see it in theaters, but in today's world, the varied options approach actually works.

Not all changes will be for the better. Many of them will be neutral, and we will be indifferent to them—if we even notice them happening at all. Other changes will be negative, and of course, we will resist some at first because we view them as negative, only to find out down the road they were not as bad as they initially seemed and are perhaps even positive changes.

The world is always becoming, our kids are always becoming, and we are always becoming ourselves. We are all changing as the world changes. Even if you resist the latest technologies or methods, you're still slowly changing. It's inevitable.

This means we must constantly update our lens, our perspective, our processes, and the tactics we use in our businesses, with our employees, with our families, and with life in general. We constantly need new ways of seeing so we can lean into a world that is always becoming and ride the wave of change to our advantage. This will make us more effective, efficient, and productive as we tap into the positive benefits in nearly every change, despite the sense of uncertainty the change itself may bring.

We must become aware that these changes are not just phases but a new normal and position ourselves with a perspective that is always looking forward while not forsaking lessons we have learned in the past. This is not business as usual, and we will probably never get back to a place where change is minimal and things stay the same for an extended period of time. We must always be willing to challenge what we did yesterday to see if it will stand up to what tomorrow will bring. We must be flexible enough to adapt to new changes and recognize we are now in a state of always becoming and change is here to stay.

Mindset and attitude are the two most powerful attributes to bring to this conversation. We don't know what the next phase of becoming will be, but by recognizing that it is coming and by having a positive attitude as change unfolds, we can see it through a new lens, even if it doesn't seem positive at first. This will allow us to see the world differently—more clearly—and take the steps we need to future-proof our lives and business.

＊＊＊

As we close out this final chapter of this book, I want to contrast two stories for you: Major League Baseball (MLB) and the Indian Premier League (IPL), which is a cricket league based in India.

Major League Baseball officially started in the United States in 1903, though the Cincinnati Red Stockings were first established in 1869. During an MLB season, a resounding 2,430 games are played over a six-month period. As of 2021, the average age of an MLB fan is fifty-seven years old, which has increased from fifty-two in 2000.[35] To contrast, the average age of an NFL fan is fifty while the average NBA fan is just forty-two.[36]

Currently, the NFL is the most profitable league in the world, followed by the MLB, the NBA, and the IPL.[37]

MOST PROFITABLE SPORTS LEAGUES	FOUNDED	AGE
1. National Football League (NFL) — $13 Billion	1920	102
2. Major League Baseball (MLB) — $10 Billion	1903	119
3. National Basketball Association (NBA) — $7.4 Billion	1946	76
4. Indian Premier League (Cricket) — $6.3 Billion	2008	14
5. English Premier League — $5.3 Billion	1992	30
6. National Hockey League (NHL) — $4.43 Billion	1917	105
7. Australian Rules Football — $2.5 Billion	1896	126
8. La Liga (Spanish Football League) — $2.2 Billion	1929	93
9. Serie A (Italian Football League) — $1.9 Billion	1929	93
10. Ligue 1 (France/Monaco Football League) — $1.5 Billion	1932	90
11. Nippon Professional Baseball (Japanese Baseball league) — $1.1 Billion	1950	72

*Source: Adapted from an article by Dusan Randjelovic June 3, 2020, in Athletic Panda

What is fascinating about this chart is that the first three leagues are nearly or more than a hundred years old while the fourth-most-profitable league on the chart was founded just fourteen years ago. We'll come back to this a bit later.

Here is the larger issue: the average age of an MLB viewer has been steadily climbing in recent years, but the MLB has not found ways to market to younger audiences. The pace of the sport itself is much slower than its competitors, and the season is significantly longer. The bottom line is the MLB, like Blockbuster, is losing its audience, and something must be done or it will become completely irrelevant.

On the other hand, only 17 percent of IPL fans are over the age of fifty-one, and the highest number of viewers is young adults in their twenties.[38] When the IPL first started in 2008, their eight-week season consisted of fifty-six matches. People were losing interest, so they made a dramatic change. They shortened their matches, which originally lasted weeks, to days and, finally, to mere hours. They reinvented themselves and are now much more easily accessible to younger audiences who filter much more quickly than older generations.

In a very short time, the IPL has managed to do what the MLB has not done in decades: attract a more youthful audience. They realized that change was not optional, and when they adjusted their strategy, they became one of the most successful leagues in the world, both in terms of profitability and longevity.

Gen Z is literally our future, and anyone with a ten-billion-dollar company where the average client is fifty-seven years old should be concerned. Surely, they are aware of this data. So why don't they seem to be doing anything about it?

This isn't about just putting Wi-Fi in the stadium or creating an app to follow one's favorite team. Blockbuster did not fail because of another video store with a wider selection of movies and candy; they failed because a competitor allowed its clients to receive movies in the mail at home. To make matters even more interesting, the model that put Blockbuster out of business then put itself out of business by shifting from DVDs in the mail to streaming. In other words, Netflix wasn't afraid to both reinvent the status quo and reinvent itself.

Baseball is certainly nostalgic and one might argue, timeless. But with an average age of fifty-seven, perhaps it is a not-so-timeless sport? Eventually, if they don't attract a younger audience, they will become the next Blockbuster. They will cease to exist—regardless of the fact that they've been around for more than a hundred years.

If MLB wants to survive, they must not be afraid to reinvent the core product. The average MLB team plays more than one hundred games each season. The sport simply does not cater to a generation with an eight-second filter. An NFL team, by comparison, plays around sixteen games in a regular season, and collegiate football teams play even less. You will also note that more fans come to each individual game. Less is truly more, which has been the case in football for some time if we are comparing it to baseball. But with Gen Z, less is more when it comes to nearly everything if you want to hold their attention.

In the same way, when we look at the leadership space, some traditional methods that seem to have withstood the test of time are quietly not bearing the same amount of fruit as they did in times past. If businesses and parents can take anything away from this comparison, it will be that making some changes in your perspective and approach could be a game-changer when it comes to your role as a leader or parent.

The IPL learned to pivot while MLB did not. We know we need to change, but we don't always change when we need to. Instead of looking at change in a negative light, we need to see it from a positive perspective. The world is always becoming, and we are always becoming.

A CEO once told me, "While I believe everything about leading Gen Z is different, we have so much going on that I don't know where to begin. That dilemma will be up to the next CEO to navigate. I hope they last until then!"

As these words sunk in, my first thought was what a loss this is: not only for this organization but for the CEO who is ready to throw in the towel before the game has begun. They are missing out on a fantastic opportunity to play a key role in shaping the future. It would be like all the MLB owners getting together and deciding they should just let one of the oldest games in the world fade away into the history books rather than putting in the work to reinvent the sport for the next generation. Even if this were to happen, wouldn't you rather have it known that you at least tried to save the sport? I know I would.

So what does the IPL moment look like for businesses? One can begin by considering just three of the things we have learned about Gen Z:

1. This is the first generation that knows "everything." Due to internet access, they view the need for leadership differently.
2. They are now used to being CEOs of their own lives. Everything is customized and available on-demand, which can make it difficult for Gen Z to adapt to being an employee in a corporate setting where they are expected to listen to the sage on stage (SOS) and submit to "do as I say" leadership styles.
3. Despite the fact that they are incredibly contagious creators and eager to work hard, they often lack practice in the areas of problem-solving and perseverance.

These three factors alone reveal the need for a customized leadership strategy that is tailored to each individual or small groups of individuals in a large organization. Leadership will need to focus on bite-size projects that upskill employees every step of the way. Not only will this help them reach their full potential, it will activate the unintended consequence of future-proofing your business.

In a large organization, one cannot possibly have this level of interaction with every employee. Therefore, once you have put on your new set of lenses and see Gen Z differently, you must impart this knowledge to the middle managers in your organization. Even though these leaders will probably be Millennials, they grew up in a world that was very different from the world Gen Z has grown up in, so they will also need to see through a new lens in order to effectively lead this generation and the generations to come.

Takeaway

Every business today has a difficult yet incredible opportunity to future-proof themselves. This process begins by recognizing that Gen Z is fundamentally different from other generations. Furthermore, we must acknowledge that Gen Zers are our future employees and customers. Either way, they are a key to the future success of your business.

Coined by Kevin Kelly, the phrase *always becoming* refers to the state of the world that is currently evolving rapidly with technology (the fourth Industrial Revolution) at the heart of this evolution. We find ourselves in a state of continual change as we are bombarded with updates and upgrades. Many of us sense a restlessness within us due to this "always becoming" as the goal posts always seem to be moving. No, not all these changes are for the better, but if we shift our perspective, we will find that many of these changes are indeed better and some of them are not good or bad—they just are what they are. We must put our feelings about these changes aside and learn to pivot if we desire to impact the next generation and future-proof our businesses and influence.

Defining moments and cultural shifts for Gen Z include the rapid advancement of technology, social media as part of our daily lives, the constant threat of global terrorism, climate change, the Great Recession, and COVID-19.

As a result, this generation has grown up so differently than previous generations, which is why I refer to them as aliens. While we have one more chapter of this book that covers the next generation to come, I'd like to leave you with a list of eleven unique qualities that apply to Gen Z:

1. They are the first generation to know "everything" due to on-demand internet access. Unlike Millennials, they have a device in their pocket that is with them virtually all the time. They don't need to wait until they get home or go to the library to use a computer. This is both positive and negative.
2. While Gen Z is connected globally, they might have a large network of friends that they only connect with online, which can

make in-person social interactions and workplace relationships more difficult, even though they desire these connections.

3. They have a very different perspective of leaders as they sometimes think they can bypass the character-building it takes to be a leader and instantly do as well in management positions with little to no experience.

4. They tend to be fiscally conservative and are willing to work a monotonous job that offers financial security. As such, they tend to want stability instead of relying on working gigs. In addition, they look for personal and relational security. They want to learn wise spending habits and how to invest. This means they are also savvy consumers.

5. They want to learn how to be in business for themselves. They watched their parents and others lose a lot during the Great Recession, so their natural instinct is to safeguard against that. At the same time, this has also made them more risk-averse, so it can be difficult for them to take the leap necessary to start a business.

6. They are competitive and want to be the very best. They desire recognition for their accomplishments.

7. They look for instant gratification in this microwave society.

8. They want independence and a focus on autonomy, not teamwork. This relates to their competitive drive.

9. Both personally and professionally, they speak their minds and expect to be taken seriously. Topics that were socially taboo to previous generations are not to Gen Z.

10. They are effective multitaskers, again, due in part to their mobile devices. This can help or hinder them at work, depending on the nature of their jobs.

11. They face numerous mental health challenges. This is due in part to all the time they spend online. In addition, global turbulence has affected their mental state of mind as well. The instant access to news and problems has resulted in increased stress.

Z

GEN ALPHA AND FUTURE GENERATIONS

Just as we began to figure out Millennials, a new generation emerged on the scene. As I have been working on this book over the last few years, discussions about Gen Z have become much more mainstream. However, just when we get to the place where we think we have them figured out, there will be another shift. This shift has actually already happened. You see, kids being born today are not part of Gen Z. Neither are your young children. A new generation is here—Generation Alpha. (Yes, now that we finished out the alphabet with *Z*, we are starting all over again.)

The first members of Generation Alpha were born around 2010, and the last members will be born in 2025. They are the children of Millennials, and about nine thousand of these generation Alpha babies are born every day in the United States.[1] Mark McCrindle, an Australian researcher, is credited with naming Generation Alpha after conducting an online survey in 2008 to find the best name for this age group.[2]

This generation has already been heavily marketed to, even more so than previous generations. Both the fast-food industry and K–12 educational technology (edtech) industry have already spent upward of twelve billion dollars *every year* to reach this generation, even though the oldest members have not even reached their teenage years yet. The educational app for kids, ABCmouse, has more than one million subscribers and is valued at more than a billion dollars.[3]

Like Gen Z, they are also growing up fast and slow. Some of them are already making their mark as social influencers in the fashion space, as reviewers of toys on YouTube, and as baking experts. More than 80 percent of parents of Gen Alpha children say that their kids either play games on devices or watch videos every day.[4] (Frankly, I am surprised the number is not higher.) However, because they are still so young, it's difficult to conduct polls on how they feel about issues.

Members of Gen Alpha are highly likely to be an only child.[5] As such, they might seek instant gratification and be selfish, the latter of which is more akin to their Millennial parents than Gen Z.

Gen Alpha will be the best-educated generation ever, in part due to technology and immediately accessible information. This will change the future of higher education institutions and likely disrupt traditional learning models. They prefer to communicate via images (think emojis and GIFs) or speech-to-text as opposed to straight texting or typing.

With better education about money and the advent of digital money transfers and purchases, Gen Alpha will also be the wealthiest generation. Additionally, they will be the most technologically advanced. Technology encompasses all aspects of their lives. They will never know life apart from technology, virtual reality, and the internet. They will also bring us all into the AI space, and AI will impact how we view the world. The internet itself may even change as we shift from Web 2.0 where big power players such as Google, Meta, and Amazon call the shots to Web3, which will be much more decentralized and localized.[6]

Businesses and marketing teams will begin working feverishly to build algorithms to track and understand Alpha, having already learned (with Gen Z) that the up-and-coming generation holds the keys to tomorrow. They really make the decisions about which direction our world will go, and when they put their voice and buying power toward something, the market is powerless to resist. I hope that leaders will have learned these lessons with Gen Z so that they are not blindsided when Alpha takes center stage.

As the concept of family changes, Gen Alpha will spend at least part if not all their childhood without both biological parents.[7] Like Gen Z and their parents (to a lesser extent), racial diversity is a huge part of their lives.

As the United States becomes even more of a melting pot than ever before, Gen Alpha will have friends and classmates from varying backgrounds and with many different viewpoints. These are just the friends they make in person and doesn't factor in everyone they connect with online.

Lest you think Alpha is still way off in the future, the oldest members of this generation will begin to get their driver's licenses in 2026 and will enter the workforce a short time later (in 2030 if we assume they pursue a four-year degree). At this point, few Boomers will be left in the workforce, as most will be retired. This will mean that Millennials, Gen Z, and Alpha together will form the largest generation bloc that will overwhelm Gen X in the workspace and push them out of their role of influence. This is why future-proofing is essential if Gen Xers like me (and even Millennials) want to remain relevant. Even though Millennials, Gen Z, and Alpha will probably have more in common with each other than they do with Gen X, Millennials will get a taste of what it feels like to be the old generation in the workspace, and they too will have to future-proof themselves if they are not doing so already.

> Future-proofing is not a one-time activity but a continual process.

Generations might soon begin to shift even more rapidly. Gen Alpha was born over a fifteen-year span as was Gen Z. However, the world will begin changing at an even greater speed than it already has been, which will make it a necessity to break up different generations into shorter spans of time. The coming changes will probably make children who are born just eight or ten years apart radically different.

If it's true that Gen Alpha started in 2010, we were really slow to talk about Gen Z. It took almost a full decade for the term to become commonplace; previously, anyone under thirty was a Millennial by default to most people.

By the time we have begun to identify what makes Gen Z unique, we are almost through with Gen Alpha—and we have even less data on this generation. By 2030, when this generation begins to come of age, we will have more data on them than we do now, but Gen Z may possibly be the last generation for which we have access to a large amount of data in real time.

Eventually, if the generations begin changing more quickly than every fifteen years, we will soon reach the point where we do not have data on a new generation in time to shift how we lead them. That is part of why this strategy is not a one-size-fits-all approach. It's more about learning what a generation values and how to best connect with them rather than expecting them to adapt to your world and the way things have worked in the past.

— — —

Several decades ago, my friend Julian's dad was asked by a friend to give a man a ride from Pittsburgh to Philadelphia, as he was already traveling in that direction. As they approached the city, the man told Julian's dad, "You can just drop me anywhere."

Julian's dad shook his head. "No, I'll take you to your house."

"You don't have to do that," the man replied. "You've already taken me so far."

"Exactly. I've come all this way with you. I'm going to take you to your door."

In the same way, if you're going to embark on this journey of impacting the next generation, you might as well fully commit to them. Why would you travel three hundred miles with someone and then make them take an Uber the last two miles?

My hope is that this book has given you a new lens through which to view this generation. That has been my goal rather than providing a few tips and techniques. Gen Z is so unique that your approach cannot be one-size-fits-all, and this will not be the case with Gen Alpha either. Rather, when you shift your perspective, a shift in your behavior will follow, which will increase your chances of success when it comes to connecting with and impacting younger generations.

Now that you have a new lens, you cannot lead or parent the way you did before and achieve the results you desire. Now that you see differently, behave differently.

By 2030, we will reach the point where what seems to be temporary, what feels like just teenagers going through a phase, will become permanent. We will see that this phase was not really a phase at all but the early stages of a new way of working, communicating, buying and selling, and expressing care. Even the family unit as we know it will probably be disrupted, and a new normal will emerge. This may seem terrifying, but it is also a time that is ripe with opportunity and potential.

In closing, I want to leave you with one final thought that a colleague shared with me recently. While teaching a class for General Stanley McChrystal at Yale, Diane Sawyer was quoted as saying: "People will forgive you for not being the leader you want to be, but never for not being the leader you claim to be."[8]

What a powerful sentiment. Remember, when leading the next generation, you do not have to be perfect, but you absolutely must be authentic.

NOTES

Aliens Among Us

1 *District 9*, directed by Neill Blomkamp (Sony, 2009).
2 Ibid.
3 Ibid.

A New Lens

1 Crystal Kadakia, "72 Percent of HS Students Are Entrepreneurial and Corporate America Just Doesn't Get it," *Huffpost*, August 3, 2015, http://www.huffpost.com/entry/72-of-hs-students-are-ent_b_7922384/.
2 Tweet from Pete King (@RepPeteKing), March 17, 2020, 6:03pm; edited for grammar.
3 Tweet from Nicole (@ItsNicNow) replying to @RepPeteKing.
4 Tweet from Kristine (@kaydeearie) replying to @RepPeteKing.
5 Tweet from John Tuddy (@jTUDI44) replying to @RepPeteKing, edited for grammar.
6 Partial tweet from Alyssa Sweetman (@Alykkat) replying to @RepPeteKing, edited for grammar.
7 Tweet from Allison Murray (@allie_murray) replying to @RepPeteKing, edited for grammar.
8 My paraphrase.
9 Hillary Hoffower, "'It's Gen Z You Want': Millennials are Defending Themselves from Accusations That They're Out Partying and Ignoring Warnings Amid the Coronavirus Pandemic," *Business Insider*, March 23, 2020, http://www.businessinsider.com/coronavirus-millennials-say-its-gen-z-partying-ignoring-warnings-2020-3/.
10 Elyse Wanshel, "Millennials Want to Make It Clear That They're Not the Ones On Spring Break," *HuffPost*, March 24, 2020, http://www.huffpost.com/entry/spring-break-millennials-gen-z-coronavirus-social-distancing_n_5e7a63fdc5b620022ab2800b/.

Truth #1

1   Apple Music, accessed March 3, 2020, http://www.apple.com/apple-music/.
2   "The Fourth Industrial Revolution, by Klaus Schwab," *World Economic Forum*, accessed March 3, 2020, http://www.weforum.org/about/the-fourth-industrial -revolution-by-klaus-schwab/.
3   Ibid.
4   Jon Porter, "Google Confirms 'Quantum Supremacy' Breakthrough," *The Verge*, October 23, 2019, http://www.theverge.com/2019/10/23/20928294/google -quantum-supremacy-sycamore-computer-qubit-milestone/.
5   Ibid.
6   Cade Metz, "Google Claims a Quantum Breakthrough That Could Change Computing," *New York Times*, October 23, 2019, http://www.nytimes.com/2019/10/23 /technology/quantum-computing-google.html/.
7   Grace Dickens, "Computer Scientist Weighs in on Quantum Supremacy," *The University of Texas at Austin: College of Natural Sciences*, October 24, 2019, http://cns .utexas.edu/news/ut-austin-professor-weighs-in-on-quantum-supremacy/.
8   Ibid.
9   Tesla Support, accessed March 3, 2020, http://www.tesla.com/supportsoftware -updates/.
10 Jessica Mathews, "Tesla joins elite club as its market cap passes $1 trillion for the first time," *Fortune*, October 25, 2021, http://fortune.com/2021/10/25/tesla-market-cap -passes-1-trillion-first-time-apple-microsoft-facebook-amazon-alphabet/.
11 Phil Wahba, "Tesla Shares Jump More Than 12% on Report That Hertz is Ordering 100,000 Teslas to Overhaul its Rental Business," *Fortune*, October 25, 2021, http:// fortune.com/2021/10/25/tesla-stock-hertz-100000-electric-vehicles/.
12 Roberto Baldwin, "GM Announces Goal to Eliminate Gas and Diesel Vehicles by 2035," *Car and Driver*, January 28, 2021, http://www.caranddriver.com/news /a35352321/gm-eliminate-gas-vehicles-2035/.
13 Neal E. Boudette and Jack Ewing, "Ford Says it Will Phase Out Gasoline-powered Vehicles in Europe, *New York Times*, February 17, 2021, http://www.nytimes.com /2021/02/17/business/ford-says-it-will-phase-out-gasoline-powered-vehicles-in -europe.html/.
14 Jack Ewing, The Age of Electric Cars is Dawning Ahead of Schedule," *New York Times*, September 20, 2020, http://www.nytimes.com/2020/09/20/business/electric-cars -batteries-tesla-elon-musk.html/.
15 Louise Story, "Anywhere the Eye Can See, It's Likely to See an Ad," *New York Times*, January 15, 2007, http://www.nytimes.com/2007/01/15/business/media/15every where.html
16 Ibid.
17 Inno Evergreen, "Dunkin' Donuts Sprays the Smell of Coffee onto Buses to Increase Sales," *Bostinno*, July 24, 2012, http://www.bizjournals.com/boston/inno/stories/news /2012/07/24/dunkin-donuts-sprays-the-smell-of-coffee-onto.html/.

18 Story, "Likely to See an Ad."

19 Ibid.

20 Ibid.

21 Ibid.

22 "General Prevalence of ADHD," *CHADD*, accessed March 3, 2021, http://chadd.org /about-adhd/general-prevalence/.

23 Challenging Media, "The Mean World Syndrome – Desensitization & Acceleration (Extra Feature)." YouTube video, 8:49. February 18, 2010.

24 "Cultural Indicators Project," *Britannica*, accessed April 21, 2022, http://www.britannica .com/topic/Cultural-Indicators-Project

25 Max Roser, "The Short History of Global Living Conditions and Why It Matters That We Know It," *Our World in Data*, accessed March 3, 2021, http://ourworldindata.org /a-history-of-global-living-conditions-in-5-charts/.

26 Ibid.

27 Ibid.

28 Bruce Tulgan, "The Under-Management Epidemic," *Society for Human Resource Management*, October 1, 2004, http://www.shrm.org/hr-today/news/hr-magazine/pages /1004hrtools.aspxBruce/.

Truth #2

1 "The Racist Origins of 'Tipping Point,'" *Merriam-Webster*, accessed March 3, 2021, http://www.merriam-webster.com/words-at-play/origin-of-the-phrase-tipping-point/.

2 "Minority Rules: Scientists Discover Tipping Point for the Spread of Ideas," *Rensselaer News*, July 25, 2011, http://news.rpi.edu/luwakkey/2902/.

3 Bryan Farrell, "You Only Need 10 Percent: The Science Behind Tipping Points and Their Impact on Cultural Activism," *Waging Nonviolence*, January 2, 2012, http:// wagingnonviolence.org/2012/01/you-only-need-10-percent-the-science-behind -tipping-points/.

4 Kia Kokalitcheva, "Humans Cause Most Self-driving Car Accidents," *Axios*, August 3, 2017, http://www.axios.com/humans-cause-most-self-driving-car-accidents-151330 4490-02cdaf3d-551f-46e6-ad98-637e6ef2c0b9.html/.

5 Ibid.

6 Ibid.

7 "How Many Car Accidents Are There in the USA Per Day?", *The Brannon Law Firm*, September 18, 2017, http://branlawfirm.com/many-car-accidents-usa-per-day/.

8 "Protect Yourself and Loved Ones by Addressing Roadway Risks," *National Safety Council*, accessed March 3, 2021, http://www.nsc.org/road-safety/safety-topics/fatality -estimates/.

9 Brannon, "How Many Car Accidents?"

10 National Highway Traffic Safety Administration, "2017 Summary of Motor Vehicle Crashes," DOT HS 812 794, September 2019.

11 National Highway Traffic Safety Administration, "Overview of Motor Vehicle Crashes in 2019," DOT HS 813 060, December 2020.

12 Taylor Swift, "For Taylor Swift the Future of Music is a Love Story," *The Wall Street Journal*, July 7, 2014, http://www.wsj.com/articles/for-taylor-swift-the-future-of -music-is-a-love-story-1404763219/.

13 Kaitlyn Tiffany, "A History of Taylor Swift's Odd, Conflicting Stances on Streaming Services," *The Verge*, June 9, 2017, http://www.theverge.com/2017/6/9/15767986 /taylor-swift-apple-music-spotify-statements-timeline/.

14 Chris Willman, "Exclusive: Taylor Swift on Being Pop's Instantly Platinum Wonder … And Why She's Paddling Against the Streams," *Yahoo! Entertainment*, November 6, 2014, http://www.yahoo.com/entertainment/blogs/music-news/exclusive--taylor -swift-on-being-pop-s-instantly-platinum-wonder----and-why-she-s-paddling-against -the-streams-085041907.html/.

15 Tiffany, "A history of Taylor Swift's stances."

16 Taylor Lorenz, "'OK Boomer' Marks the End of Friendly Generational Relations," *New York Times*, October 29, 2019, http://www.nytimes.com/2019/10/29/style/ok -boomer.html/.

17 World Economic Forum released a study in 2016 that stated 65 percent of children entering first grade will end up working in jobs that do not currently exist. (http:// reports.weforum.org/future-of-jobs-2016/chapter-1-the-future-of-jobs-and-skills). If we adjust the date to 2021, that would have this population entering the sixth grade.

Truth #3

1 Ron Marshall, "How Many Ads Do You See in One Day?", *Red Crow Marketing*, September 10, 2015, http://www.redcrowmarketing.com/2015/09/10/many-ads-see -one-day/.

2 Sam Nichols, "Your Phone Is Listening and it's Not Paranoia," *Vice*, June 4, 2018, http:// www.vice.com/en_au/article/wjbzzy/your-phone-is-listening-and-its-not-paranoia/.

3 Timothy B. Lee, "Spanish Soccer League's App Caught Eavesdropping on Users in Anti-piracy Push," *Ars Technica*, June 12, 2019, http://arstechnica.com/tech-policy /2019/06/spanish-soccer-leagues-app-caught-eavesdropping-on-users-in-anti-piracy -push/.

4 Kevin Kelly, *The Inevitable* (New York: Viking, 2016), 10-11.

Truth #4

1 Erik Samdahl, "93% of Gen Z Says Societal Impact Affects Where They Work," *I4CP*, December 16, 2015, http://www.i4cp.com/productivity-blog/2015/12/16 /new-i4cp-research-93-of-gen-z-says-societal-impact-affects-where-they-work/.

2 Richard Fry, "For First Time in Modern Era, Living With Parents Edges Out Other Living Arrangements for 18- to 34-Year-Olds," *Pew Research Center*, May 24, 2016, http://www.pewresearch.org/social-trends/2016/05/24/for-first-time-in-modern-era -living-with-parents-edges-out-other-living-arrangements-for-18-to-34-year-olds/.

3 Crystal Kadakia, "72 Percent of HS Students Are Entrepreneurial and Corporate America Just Doesn't Get It," *HuffPost Contributor*, August 3, 2015, http://www .huffpost.com/entry/72-of-hs-students-are-ent_b_7922384/.

NOTES

4 Pallabi Munsi, "Working As Teens? Not Gen Z," *OZY*, September 7, 2020, http:// www.ozy.com/the-new-and-the-next/working-as-teens-not-gen-z/374274/.

Truth #5

1 David Russell Schilling, "Knowledge Doubling Every 12 Months, Soon to be Every 12 Hours," *Industry Tap*, April 19, 2013, http://www.industrytap.com/knowledge -doubling-every-12-months-soon-to-be-every-12-hours/3950/.

2 Ibid.

3 Ibid.

4 "Gen Z: The Future of the Internet and Social Platforms," *Cognizant*, June 6, 2019, http://www.cognizant.com/us/en/latest-thinking/perspectives/gen-z-the-future-of-the -internet-and-social-platforms/.

5 Jean Twenge, "Teens Have Less Face Time with Their Friends—and are Lonelier Than Ever," *TheConversation.com*, March 20, 2019, http://theconversation.com /teens-have-less-face-time-with-their-friends-and-are-lonelier-than-ever-113240.

6 Andy Kiersz and Allana Akhtar, "Suicide is Gen Z's Second-Leading Cause of Death, and it's a Worse Epidemic than Anything Millennials Faced at That Age," *Business Insider*, October 17, 2019, http://www.businessinsider.com/cdc-teenage-gen-z-american -suicide-epidemic/.

7 Cigna, "2018 Cigna U.S. Loneliness Index," May 2018, http://www.multivu.com/ players/English/8294451-cigna-us-loneliness-survey/docs/IndexReport_152406937 1598-173525450.pdf/.

8 Anna Gunther, "Younger Generations Are Lonelier and Social Media Doesn't Help, Survey Finds," *CBS News*, January 23, 2020, http://www.cbsnews.com./news/younger -generations-are-lonelier-and-social-media-doesnt-help-survey-finds-2020-01-23/.

9 "Gen Z and Millennials Now More Likely to Communicate With Each Other Digitally Than in Person," *LivePerson*, October 17, 2017, http://www.prnewswire.com /news-releases/gen-z-and-millennials-now-more-likely-to-communicate-with-each -other-digitally-than-in-person-300537770.html/.

10 Social Capital Project Report No. 1-17, "What We Do Together: The State of Associational Life in America," May 2017, http://www.lee.senate.gov/services/files/b5f224 ce-98f7-40f6-a814-8602696714d8/.

11 Pallabi Munsi, "Working As Teens? Not Gen Z," *OZY*, September 7, 2020, http:// www.ozy.com/the-new-and-the-next/working-as-teens-not-gen-z/374274/.

12 Shane McFeely and Ryan Pendell, "What Workplace Leaders Can Learn from the Real Gig Economy," *Gallup*, August 16, 2018, http://www.gallup.com/workplace/240929 /workplace-leaders-learn-real-gig-economy.aspx/.

13 Ibid.

14 Diane Mulcahy, *The Gig Economy* (New York: AMACOM, 2017), 187.

Truth #6

1 Tweet from Brian Kiley (@kileynoodles), May 24, 2018, 6:37am.

2 Kevin Kelly, *The Inevitable* (New York: Viking, 2016), 109.

3   Tom Goodwin, "The Battle is for the Customer Interface," *TechCrunch*, March 3, 2015, http://techcrunch.com/2015/03/03/in-the-age-of-disintermediation-the-battle-is-all-for-the-customer-interface/.
4   Kelly, *The Inevitable*, 115.
5   Car Sharing, accessed February 14, 2021, https://www.zipcar.com/carsharing/.
6   Kate Conger, "Facebook Starts Planning for Permanent Remote Workers," *New York Times*, May 21, 2020, http://www.nytimes.com/2020/05/21/technology/facebook-remote-work-coronavirus.html/.
7   Ibid.
8   Ibid.
9   Ibid.
10 Ibid.
11 Ibid.

Truth #7

1   Jerry B. Harvey, "The Abilene Paradox: The Management of Agreement," *Organizational Dynamics* Volume 3, Issue 1 (Summer 1974): 63-80.
2   Miyo McGinn, "'OK, Boomer': The Perfect Response to a Generation That Failed on Climate," *Grist*, November 6, 2019, http://grist.org/article/ok-boomer-the-perfect-response-to-a-generation-that-failed-on-climate/.
3   Madeleine Carlisle, "Welcome to 2020: The Phrase 'OK Boomer' Was Said for the First Time in the Supreme Court," *Time*, January 16, 2020, http://time.com/5766438/john-roberts-ok-boomer-scotus/.
4   Taylor Lorenz, "'OK Boomer' Marks the End of Friendly Generational Relations," *New York Times*, October 29, 2019, http://www.nytimes.com/2019/10/29/style/ok-boomer.html/.
5   Ibid.
6   Ibid.
7   Margaret Grayson, "A Champlain Student's 'OK Boomer' Song Went Viral on TikTok. Can He Turn It into a Career?", *Seven Days*, November 18, 2019, http://www.sevendaysvt.com/LiveCulture/archives/2019/11/18/a-champlain-students-ok-boomer-song-went-viral-on-tiktok-can-he-turn-it-into-a-career/.
8   "What is Sonic Art?", Soundproof Cow, April 5, 2018, http://www.soundproofcow.com/what-is-sonic-art/.
9   Grayson, "Champlain Student's 'OK Boomer' Song."
10 Ibid.
11 Ibid.
12 TJ McCue, "E Learning Climbing to $325 Billion By 2025 UF Canvas Absorb Schoology Moodle," *Forbes*, July 31, 2018, http://www.forbes.com/sites/jmccue/2018/07/31/e-learning-climbing-to-325-billion-by-2025-uf-canvas-absorb-schoology-moodle/?sh=83b95c93b395/.
13 Ibid.

14 Kim Parker and Ruth Igielnik, "On the Cusp of Adulthood and Facing an Uncertain Future: What We Know About Gen Z So Far," *Pew Research Center*, May 14, 2020, http://www.pewresearch.org/social-trends/2020/05/14/on-the-cusp-of-adulthood -and-facing-an-uncertain-future-what-we-know-about-gen-z-so-far-2/.

Truth #8

1 Till Alexander Leopold, et all., "The Future of Jobs: Chapter 1," World Economic Forum, 2016, http://reports.weforum.org/future-of-jobs-2016/chapter-1-the-future -of-jobs-and-skills/.

2 Daily Mail Reporter, "Forget Being a Nurse or Doctor, Three Quarters of Today's Children Would Rather be YouTubers and vloggers," *Daily Mail UK*, May 22, 2017, http://www.dailymail.co.uk/news/article-4532266/75-cent-children-want-YouTubers -vloggers.html/.

3 @majutrindade had 5.6 million Instagram followers as of December 19, 2021.

4 "Influencer Marketing Agency," *Dapper Goat Social Media*, accessed December 19, 2021, https://dappergoat.com/influencer-marketing-agency/.

5 @gracespuppies had 15,100+ Instagram followers as of December 19, 2021.

6 As of December 19, 2021.

7 Paige Leskin, et all, "Meet the 22-year-old YouTube Star Mr. Beast, Who's Famous for Giving Away Millions of Dollars to Strangers," *Business Insider*, May 5, 2021, http:// www.businessinsider.com/mrbeast-youtube-jimmy-donaldson-net-worth-life-career -challenges-teamtrees-2019-11/.

8 Lucas Shaw and Mark Bergen, "The North Carolina Kid Who Cracked YouTube's Secret Code," *Bloomberg*, December 22, 2020, http://www.bloomberg.com/news /articles/2020-12-22/who-is-mrbeast-meet-youtube-s-top-creator-of-2020/.

9 Leskin, et all, "22-year-old YouTube Star Mr. Beast."

10 Trilby Beresford, "YouTuber MrBeast Launches Multiplayer Endurance Game 'Finger on the App,'" *Hollywood Reporter*, June 30, 2020, http://www.hollywoodreporter .com/news/general-news/youtuber-mrbeast-launches-multiplayer-endurance-game -finger-app-1300746/.

11 Geoff Weiss, "MrBeast Crowns $100,000 'Finger on the App' Winner After 50-Hour Contest," *TubeFilter*, March 23, 2021, http://www.tubefilter.com/2021/03/23/ mrbeast-crowns-finger-on-the-app-winner-50-hours/.

12 Tweet from MrBeast (@MrBeast), March 22, 2021, 9:07pm.

13 James Hale, "MrBeast Opens His Own Food Bank, Shares Details On 'Beast Philan-thropy,'" *TubeFilter*, March 26, 2021, http://www.tubefilter.com/2021/03/26/mrbeast -philanthropy-food-pantry-youtube-donations/.

14 Amie Watson, "The Untold Truth Of MrBeast Burger," *Mashed*, April 21, 2022, http://www.mashed.com/308763/the-untold-truth-of-mrbeast-burger/.

15 Express Web Desk, "Burgers With a Side of iPads? YouTuber Opens Fast-Food Chain, Gives Away Money, Gadgets," *The Indian Express*, December 22, 2020,

http://indianexpress.com/article/trending/trending-globally/mrbeast-youtube-burger -ipad-gifts-7112546/.

16 Geoff Weiss, "MrBeast's Latest Video Stunt Spawns Nationwide, Delivery-Only Burger Chain," *TubeFilter*, December 21, 2020, http://www.tubefilter.com/2020 /12/21/mrbeast-video-stunt-spawns-burger-chain/.

17 Alicia Kelso, "How the Pandemic Accelerated the US Ghost Kitchen Market '5 Years in 3 Months,'" *Restaurant Dive*, October 5, 2020, http://www.restaurantdive.com/news /how-the-pandemic-accelerated-the-us-ghost-kitchen-market-5-years-in-3-mont /585604/.

18 Jennifer Marston, "MrBeast Burgers' Overnight Success Actually Holds Some Lessons for Aspiring Virtual Restaurants," *The Spoon*, December 22, 2020, http://thespoontech /mrbeast-burgers-overnight-success-actually-holds-some-lessons-for-aspiring-virtual -restaurants/.

19 Marissa Conrad, "You've Heard of Ghost Kitchens. Meet the Ghost Franchises.," *New York Times*, February 25, 2021, http://www.nytimes.com/2021/02/25/dining/ghost -kitchen-mrbeast-burger.html/.

20 Felix Behr, "This YouTube Star Just Started His Own Burger Chain," *Mashed*, December 28, 2020, http://www.mashed.com/303180/this-youtube-star-just-started -his-own-burger-chain/.

21 Anna Caplan, "YouTuber MrBeast Brings Delivery-Only Burger Chain to Dallas Area, and Business Has Already Been 'Crazy,'" *Dallas Morning News*, December 21, 2020, http://www.dallasnews.com/food/restaurant-news/2020/12/21/youtuber-mrbeast -brings-delivery-only-burger-chain-to-north-texas-and-business-has-been-crazy/.

22 Conrad, "Meet the Ghost Franchises."

Truth #9

1 Tim Elmore, founder and CEO of *Growing Leaders*, published a book entitled *Artificial Maturity* in 2012.

2 Tweet from Tim Elmore (@TimElmore), March 23, 2021, 7:45pm.

3 "Global Trend Report: How the 4th Industrial Revolution is Changing IT, Business and the World," *Lumen*, July 2020, http://assets.lumen.com/is/content/Lumen/global -trend-report-4th-industrial-revolution-4IR?Creativeid=d3d10187-3a60-4195-b0bf -d1d0528631c3/.

4 Klaus Schwab, "The Fourth Industrial Revolution: What It Means and How to Respond," *World Economic Forum*, January 14, 2016, http://www.weforum.org/agenda /2016/01/the-fourth-industrial-revolution-what-it-means-and-how-to-respond/.

5 Tariq Khokhar, "Chart: How is the World's Youth Population Changing?," *World Bank*, April 17, 2017, http://blogs.worldbank.org/opendata/chart-how-worlds -youth-population-changing/.

6 Deyan Georgiev, "Gen Z Statistics—What We Know About the New Generation," *Review42*, January 19, 2022, http://review42.com/resources/gen-z-statistics/.

7 Ibid.

8   Adapted from Paul Scanlon, "Five Keys to a Great Mentoring Relationship,"
    PaulScanlon.com August 11, 2020, http://www.paulscanlon.com/blog/mentoring
    -relationship/.
9   Ibid.

Truth #10

1   Johanna Seibt, "Process Philosophy," *The Stanford Encyclopedia of Philosophy* (Sum-
    mer 2022 Edition), Edward N. Zalta (ed.), http://plato.stanford.edu/archives/
    sum2022
    /entries/process-philosophy/.
2   Bob Desautels, "No Man Ever Steps in the Same River Twice," *BobDesautels.com*
    (August 16, 2018, http://www.bobdesautels.com/blog/2018/8/6/no-man-ever-steps-in
    -the-same-river-twice-for-its-not-the-same-river-and-hes-not-the-same-man-heraclitus
3   Gregory Lawrence, "Netflix Passes a Subscriber Benchmark So Big It'll Mess with Your
    Brain's Buffering," *Collider*, January 19, 2021, http://collider.com/netflix-number-of
    -subscribers-2020/.
4   Christopher Harress, "The Sad End of Blockbuster Video: The Onetime $5 Billion
    Company is Being Liquidated as Competition from Online Giants Netflix and
    Hulu Prove All Too Much for the Iconic Brand," *International Business Times*,
    December 5, 2013, http://www.ibtimes.com/sad-end-blockbuster-video-onetime
    -5-billion-company-being-liquidated-competition-1496962/.
5   "Troubled Movie Gallery is Closing 520 Stores," *Portland Business Journal*, September
    25, 2007, http://www.bizjournals.com/portland/stories/2007/09/24/daily10.html/.
6   Joey Morona, "Family Video, the Last Video Store Chain in the U.S., is Closing All
    250 Stores," *Clevelannd.com*, https://www.cleveland.com/entertainment/2021/01
    /family-video-the-last-video-store-chain-in-the-us-is-closing-all-250-stores.html/.
7   Reed Hastings, "CEO Reed Hastings On How Netflix Beat Blockbuster, Marketplace
    .org, http://www.marketplace.org/2020/09/08/ceo-reed-hastings-on-how-netflix
    -beat-blockbuster/.
8   Ibid.
9   Ibid.
10 Patty McCord, "How Netflix Reinvented HR," *Harvard Business Review*, January-
    February 2014, https://hbr.org/2014/01/how-netflix-reinvented-hr/.
11 DVD Sales See Hot Growth Projections," *CNET*, January 2, 2002, http://www.cnet
    .com/news/dvd-sales-see-hot-growth-projections/.
12 Peter Wayner, "New Economy; DVD's Have Found an Unexpected Route to a Wide
    Public: Snail Mail," *New York Times*, September 23, 2002, http://www.nytimes.com
    /2002/09/23/business/new-economy-dvd-s-have-found-an-unexpected-route-to-a
    -wide-public-snail-mail.html/.
13 Aaron Sankin, "How Blockbuster Almost Beat Netflix," *The Motley Fool*, November
    14, 2013, http://www.fool.com/investing/general/2013/11/14/how-blockbuster
    -almost-beat-netfilx.aspx/.

14 *The Last Blockbuster*, directed by Taylor Morden (1091 Pictures, 2020).

15 "Enron, Blockbuster Partner for Movie Mania," *Forbes*, July 20, 2000, https://www .forbes.com/2000/07/20/mu4.html?sh=315cdae73541/.

16 "Blockbuster's Broadband-Video Deal Collapses, *Los Angeles Times*, March 11, 2001, http://www.latimes.com/archives/la-xpm-2001-mar-11-mn-36306-story.html/.

17 "Blockbuster Launches New Online DVD Rental Service," *The Wayback Machine*, taken from *Blockbuster.com*, http://web.archive.org/web/20081201174655/https:// blockbuster.mediaroom.com/index.php?s=press_releases&item=563/.

18 Sankin, "Blockbuster Almost Beat Netflix."

19 Ibid.

20 Ibid.

21 Matt Burns, "Blockbuster Movie Pass: Dish Network's $10/Month Answer to Netflix," *TechCrunch+*, September 23, 2011, http://techcrunch.com/2011/09/23/blockbuster -movie-pass-dish-networks-answer-to-netflix-and-qwikster/.

22 Roger Cheng, "Blockbuster Movie Pass No Netflix Killer," *CNET*, September 23, 2011, http://www.cnet.com/news/blockbuster-movie-pass-no-netflix-killer/.

23 Ibid.

24 Ibid.

25 Alex Sherman, "Blockbuster Hits Rewind on Plan to Return as Netflix Killer," *Bloomberg*, October 5, 2012, http://www.bloomberg.com/news/articles/2012-10-04 /dish-s-ergen-scraps-blockbuster-plans-after-wireless-delays/.

26 Lance Whitney, "Blockbuster Throws in the Towel," *CNET*, November 6, 2013, http://www.cnet.com/news/blockbuster-throws-in-the-towel/.

27 Blockbuster.com Franchise List, http://www.blockbuster.com/franchise.html, accessed May 6, 2021.

28 Abigail Abrams, "There Will Only Be 1 Blockbuster in America Soon," *Time*, July 12, 2018, http://time.com/5337725/last-blockbuster-america-oregon/.

29 Stephen Hamway, "Bend Blockbusters Among Last in the Country," *The Bend Bulletin*, April 24, 2015, http://www.bendbulletin.com/business/bend-blockbusters-among -last-in-country/article_37029bc6-3583-5a7e-89ef-8bcfe2b2c45e.html/.

30 Jonathan Salem Baskin, "The Internet Didn't Kill Blockbuster, The Company Did It to Itself," *Forbes*, November 8, 2013, http://www.forbes.com/sites/jonathansalem baskin/2013/11/08/the-internet-didnt-kill-blockbuster-the-company-did-it-to-itself /?sh=65f3f64c6488/.

31 David Carr, "Giving Viewers What They Want," *New York Times*, February 24, 2013, http://www.nytimes.com/2013/02/25/business/media/for-house-of-cards-using-big -data-to-guarantee-its-popularity.html/

32 Baskin, "The Internet Didn't Kill Blockbuster."

33 Noah Kirsch, "The Last Video Chain: The Inside Story of Family Video and Its $400 Million Owner," *Forbes*, February 21, 2017, http://www.forbes.com/sites/noahkirsch /2017/02/21/the-last-video-chain-the-inside-story-of-family-video-and-its-400-million -owner/?sh=654fb3a8da60/.

34 Ibid.

35 Matt Johnson, "MLB Ratings: 2021 World Series Television Ratings Improve, Still Long-Term Concerns for Baseball," *Sportsnaut*, November 9, 2021, http://sportsnaut. com/mlb-ratings-tv-viewership-numbers/.

36 Ibid.

37 Dusan Randjelovic, "11 Most Profitable Sports Leagues: Their Value Will Surprise You," *Athletic Panda*, June 3, 2020, http://apsportseditors.org/others/most-profitable -sports-leagues/.

38 Sandhya Keelery, "Share of Viewership of the Indian Premier League (IPL) Across India in 2018, by Age Group," *Statista*, November 2, 2021, http://www.statista.com /statistics/943943/india-viewership-share-of-ipl-by-age-group/.

Gen Alpha and Future Generations

1 Christine Michel Carter, "The Complete Guide to Generation Alpha, the Children of Millennials," *Forbes*, December 21, 2016, http://www.forbes.com/sites/christinecarter /2016/12/21/the-complete-guide-to-generation-alpha-the-children-of-millennials/.

2 Ibid.

3 Ibid.

4 Ibid.

5 Ibid.

6 Bobby Allyn, "People Are Talking About Web3. Is It the Internet of the Future or Just a Buzzword?," *NPR*, November 21, 2021, http://www.npr.org/2021/11/21/1056988346 /web3-internet-jargon-or-future-vision

7 Ibid.

8 Michelle Russell, "Gen. Stanley McChrystal on Empowering Leadership," *PCMA*, January 17, 2018, http://www.pcma.org/gen-stanley-mcchrystal-empowering -leadership/.

ACKNOWLEDGEMENTS

Colleen, Jeremy, and Sarah Robertson—No words can adequately express how your love and encouragement inspires me to be the best me every day. And Coll, a special thank you for your commitment to proofing and refining this work and for being a part of every crazy journey we have been on together.

Jared Stump—What a wild ride you agreed to join me on! Through it all, I think what I cherish the most is that you now speak in a South African accent and use my colloquialisms so naturally. Thank you for your commitment, your dedication to this work, and your friendship.

Julian Krinsky and Adrian Castelli—My family and I are who we are and where we are today because of the roles you played in our lives. You were there every step of the way, cheering us on, and gave without reservation. What you taught me could fill another book. A few of the pearls of wisdom you deposited in me are the importance of relationships, building and maintaining bridges, and what authentic leadership looks like.

Duncan Irvine, John Thole, Roger Pearce, and Ashley Dymond—My friends from as far back as I can remember. You have always provided unconditional counsel, love, and support that has been unfettered by distance or time zones.

Nick Hackett, Alan Kirkpatrick and Tim McDonald—Your deep friendship, endless support, and genuine care for me has been transformative.

Dean Minuto—I have only met a few people who are as selfless, caring, and giving as you are. Thank you for your friendship and sharing your wisdom with me during this process.

ACKNOWLEDGEMENTS

I have been fortunate to have met so many incredible people in my life. Each one of you mentioned here have influenced and impacted my life in such meaningful ways.

Arvind Aravindhan, Steven Bernstein, Felippe Borges, Adam Bower, Keri Branch, David Cambridge, Joshua Epstein, Joshua Finley, Jamie Galloway, Jeff Gibbard, Pam Hackett, Will Hart, Teofilo Hayashi, Jack Jensz, Bryan March, Eric Peoples, Troy Podell, Sarah Ohanesian, Colleen Robertson, Joshua Schneider, Jaco Smit, Lefteris Soulas, Mark Spann.

You all have encouraged, supported, taught, and laughed with me. Every one of you have played a role in this work coming to its completion and I appreciate you. Thank you for standing alongside me in the ways that you did.

Z

ABOUT THE AUTHOR

Steven Robertson
Author. Speaker. Business Leader.

Having been in the summer programming industry for almost 25 years in the northeastern United States, Steve has had a unique vantage point to observe Gen Z as they have grown up. His two children, both Millenials, but on the cusp of Gen Z, have also given him a glimpse into these distinctly different generations. This has positioned him to speak with authority on what makes Gen Z unique and how it pertains to the work space, homefront, and the sphere of education. Steve's passion for leading and guiding the next generation well is evident in his writing, keynote speaking, and corporate training.

Steve and his wife, Colleen, are natives of South Africa and currently live and work near Philadelphia, Pennsylvania. Connect with him online at www. stevenjrobertson.com.

Notes & Observations

Notes & Observations

Notes & Observations

Notes & Observations

Notes & Observations

Notes & Observations

Notes & Observations

Made in the USA
Middletown, DE
14 December 2022

18530551R10144